T H E
LIVING HEART
C O O K B O O K

Gourmet Low-Fat Recipes from Chez Eddy
Previously published as *The Chez Eddy Living Heart Cookbook*
Antonio M. Gotto, Jr., M.D., D.Phil.; Helen Roe, M.S., R.D./L.D.;
and the Staff of the Chez Eddy Restaurant

Foreword by Michael E. DeBakey, M.D.,
co-author of *The Living Heart Diet*
Edited by Babette Fraser

A Fireside Book
Published by Simon & Schuster
New York   London   Toronto   Sydney   Tokyo   Singapore

FIRESIDE
Rockefeller Center
1230 Avenue of the Americas
New York, New York 10020

First Fireside Edition 1994

FIRESIDE and colophon are registered trademarks
of Simon & Schuster Inc.

Designed by Crowded House
Manufactured in the United States of America

10   9   8   7   6   5   4   3
10   9   8   7   6   5   4   3   2   1   (PBK)

ISBN: 0-671-76721-6
ISBN: 0-671-88388-7 (PBK)

ACKNOWLEDGMENTS

....

THE OPERATION OF A FINE restaurant and the development of a cookbook are labors of love that require an enormous amount of hard work. For creating an organizational climate that allows Chez Eddy Restaurant to pursue its educational mission successfully, we thank Mr. Larry L. Mathis, president and chief executive officer of the Methodist Hospital System, and the senior executives in our corporate structure. To Mr. Ted Bowen, former president and chief executive officer, we express our gratitude for enabling Dr. Gotto's vision to become a reality, with the opening of the restaurant in 1981.

Our cookbook is the result of an intensive cooperative effort by many people. Thanks to Millie Hast, assistant vice-president, TMH Enterprises, Inc., who coordinated the development of this book. Helen Roe, M.S., R.D., manager of Chez Eddy, who developed and tested recipes with the able assistance of Chef Dennis Dorsch, assistant manager, and Chef Enrico Gaggioni, former assistant manager. She also performed the nutritional analysis, with the help of Karen Brantley Angevine, R.D., and Babette Fraser, who wrote and edited the manuscript. We also appreciate the assistance of Lynne W. Scott, M.A., R.D., who reviewed medical and nutritional information; Graden Edward Butler, Jr., who provided word processing and manuscript preparation; and Norma Olivarez, who assisted in manuscript preparation. To Toula Polygalaktos, our editor at Prentice Hall Press, Chez Eddy is deeply grateful for her tireless dedication to this cookbook that was equaled only by her patience and expertise. And thanks to the editor of the paperback edition, Sydny Miner, executive editor of trade paperbacks at Simon & Schuster.

Thanks also to the employees of Chez Eddy Restaurant, each of whom contributed to its success: Otis Johnson, Jr., Cheng-Jen Hsu, Annie Fisher, Bridgette Hopkins, Samuel Fadipe, Eghosa Edebor, Don J. Selkridge, Daniel E. Conrad, Gerardo Zamarripa, Ahmad Sadrialaei, Antonio Bravo, Jaime Montero, Ismael Montero, Adan Lopez, and Zaynale Agha.

Special thanks to the past employees of Chez Eddy Restaurant for laying the groundwork that made this book possible.

To the family of the late Eddy Scurlock, whose name Chez Eddy bears, we express our sincere appreciation and gratitude for his dedication and support of the Methodist Hospital. He was a humble man, loved by all who knew him. He was a man of many legacies, the greatest of which is his family.

We are grateful to Chez Eddy chef Thomas Palmer, who developed the new recipes for this edition. With his culinary expertise, the food at Chez Eddy has exceeded all expectations.

Thanks to the Methodist Hospital Public Relations Department, Sallie Rawlings, vice-president. Special thanks to Blythe Schaffer for her energetic support of Chez Eddy.

Heartfelt gratitude to the many loyal patrons of Chez Eddy, especially Mayde Wydelle Butler, who serves as an inspiration to all.

Finally, our deepest gratitude and love to Marilyn Abraham, vice president and editor-in-chief of Touchstone and Fireside, for her belief in the prevention of heart disease and her undying support of Drs. DeBakey and Gotto over the years, beginning with *The Living Heart Diet*.

CONTENTS

....

FOREWORD

....

I HAVE BEEN AN ADVOCATE of a heart-healthy diet since scientists first noted a relationship between diet and heart disease some years ago—having written *The Living Heart Diet* with Drs. Antonio M. Gotto and John Foreyt, and Mrs. Lynne Scott.

But promoting a heart-healthy diet has not been easy. The phrase *heart-healthy diet* always elicits a predictable response: a grimace, sighs of resignation, and visions of bland vegetables and tasteless meats. This response is certainly understandable. In the past, heart-healthy foods seemed restrictive, devoid of flavor and inventiveness—unpalatable even with hot pepper sauce, a favorite seasoning of mine.

For the past three decades, I have performed open-heart surgery on tens of thousands of patients suffering from heart disease, people I would have preferred meeting under more favorable circumstances. I have told them countless times that a more healthful, lower-fat diet might have helped prevent their needing surgical treatment.

But even when the physician's recommendations may mean the difference between life and death, convincing people to make lifestyle changes is always a challenge. And there is a special challenge because people with atherosclerotic heart disease often feel immunity until they actually experience a heart attack. I am continually thinking of new ways to motivate people to alter their diets. After years of searching, I found the answer in my own "backyard."

Chez Eddy is a restaurant I have patronized since its opening in 1981. It was conceived by my colleague and friend Tony Gotto, one of the world's leading researchers in cardiovascular disease. As he listened to dieting patients, he, too, was struck by their sense of deprivation—an attitude that often prevented the kind of compliance necessary to manage their illness.

Chez Eddy cuisine is a manifestation of Tony's belief that heart-healthy dining need not be restrictive or bland. Through the years, these talented chefs have devised methods of adapting gourmet cuisine—with its subtle sauces and flavorful stocks—to the needs of people who follow a heart-healthy eating plan. The fare that characterizes Chez Eddy today has evolved along with the public's changing and more sophisticated tastes. Its delightful mix of American, ethnic, and southwestern components will satisfy the most discriminating palates. And every dish meets the guidelines set by the American Heart Association for fat, cholesterol, and sodium, while being low in calories as well. So you not only get delicious gourmet fare, you get it heart-healthy as a bonus.

This cookbook offers the innovative recipes that have brought the restaurant national recognition. Each dish—from Crab Royal to fajitas, blackened fish, and Creole-inspired recipes—reinforces the idea that in taking care of yourself, you don't have to compromise taste.

The foundation of Chez Eddy cuisine is taking natural foods—the freshest vegetables, fruits, and meats—and enhancing their flavor with special herbs and sauces, the key to Chez Eddy's success.

You won't find foods masked with seasoned breading or heavy condiments, but you will be pleased with the variety. And the message is that any cuisine can be healthful if you know how to adjust recipes.

Inside this book, you will find a gamut of recipes, from appetizers to desserts, including dishes for special occasions, entertaining, and holiday dinners. The menus are modern, simple to prepare, and satisfying. You will find explicit information on the facts and myths regarding cholesterol, as well as the most current data on lipid research and heart disease. You will learn how to adapt recipes at home, keeping heart-healthy guidelines in mind. An easy-to-read nutritional breakdown follows each recipe. There is even a "basics" section that includes items to keep on hand for easier preparation. But most important, you will be able to enjoy a delicious, low-calorie, full-course meal.

These recipes have been savored by some of the best-known food connoisseurs and by those who, like me, simply want healthful food that tastes good. I take my guests to Chez Eddy, and I have tasted almost every item they serve—of course, I have my favorites. The meals may be simple to prepare, but the difference they will make in your diet will assuredly make you a convert.

Dr. Michael E. DeBakey

INTRODUCTION

....

THE HEALTH HABITS OF AMERICANS have changed a great deal over the past twenty-five years. In general, we are exercising more, smoking less, and eating a leaner, more healthful diet. It is not surprising, then, that our cardiovascular health has improved during this period. In fact, deaths from cardiovascular disease have decreased by almost 50 percent since the 1960s. Also as a result of dietary changes, serum (blood) cholesterol levels have declined significantly.

Although research concerning the healthful effect of these changes in our lifestyle remains ongoing, a consensus exists regarding their importance. It is a consensus so broad that it includes under its umbrella such varied entities as the American Heart Association, the National Institutes of Health, the Surgeon General's office, the National Research Council, and the American Cancer Society.

Accordingly, a tremendous national effort has been undertaken under the auspices of the National Cholesterol Education Program (NCEP) to educate both the medical profession and the American public about the importance of diagnosing and treating elevated blood cholesterol. In 1987, the National Institutes of Health (NIH) published guidelines—as part of the NCEP—recommending that all Americans over the age of twenty have their cholesterol levels checked. For those whose levels exceeded 200, special attention was advised. See the table below for further information.

Classification Recommendations

Total Cholesterol		LDL Cholesterol
<200	Desirable	<130
200–239	Borderline High*	130–159
≥240	High	≥160

Source: Summary of the 1987 National Cholesterol Education Program (NCEP) adult treatment guidelines.

* Treat as high if coronary heart disease (CHD) or two risk factors are present.

As a result of the interest created by this educational effort, research studies concerning diet, cholesterol, and heart disease have received wide media attention. Every week, it seems, the public is bombarded with reports that describe new findings. It is the nature of the scientific process, of course, for information to emerge this way, in increments that gradually accumulate into a solid body of knowledge. Similarly, it isn't surprising that some of these research reports appear to contradict one another, or, indeed, to challenge present guidelines in some respects. Medical controversy of this kind often exists among experts as they work their way toward a consensus, but it can seem bewildering to individuals trying to make sense out of what they hear.

Given those circumstances, a backlash of some sort was probably inevitable. And, in fact, several critics emerged in 1989. In general, they questioned details of recommended diagnostic and treatment methods as well as the core issue of any debate in this area, namely, the general importance of blood cholesterol as a factor in cardiovascular health.

Many of their questions centered on issues that, so far, remain unresolved. But in their approach to the core issue, their criticisms have contributed to some degree of public confusion. What is important to know is that **areas of agreement concerning how blood cholesterol levels affect heart disease far outweigh areas of disagreement or uncertainty.**

WHAT WE AGREE ON

In the first place, we firmly believe that lowering high levels of blood cholesterol decreases the likelihood of developing cardiovascular disease. Strong evidence to this effect came from three primary prevention trials: the Coronary Primary Prevention Trial, the Helsinki Heart Study, and the Oslo Heart Study.

Second, we believe that diet remains the first line of defense as far as treatment and prevention of heart disease are concerned. Not only is the Step One American Heart Association Diet recommended as initial therapy for individuals with elevated cholesterol levels, but it is also the diet recommended for the entire American population over the age of two (see table below).

Step One American Heart Association Diet

Key Features

1. Reduction of total fat consumption to no more than 30% of total calories.
2. Decreased consumption of saturated fat to comprise no more than 10% of total calories.
3. Consumption of monounsaturated fats to comprise 10–15% of total calories.
4. Consumption of polyunsaturated fats to comprise 10% of total calories.
5. Total cholesterol intake of less than 300 mg per day.
6. Total calories adjusted to achieve or maintain ideal body weight.
7. Calories from carbohydrates should comprise 50–60% of the total consumed per day, with a recommendation to emphasize complex carbohydrates.
8. Protein should constitute 10–20% of the total number of calories consumed per day.

Source: Summary of the 1987 National Cholesterol Education Program (NCEP) adult treatment guidelines.

That is because extensive research focusing on the connection between diet and cardiovascular health has established that a diet high in saturated fatty acids and cholesterol will promote a higher level of the harmful form of cholesterol in the blood, leading to early heart disease.

The nature of cholesterol is probably worth reviewing briefly at this point. It is, of course, a substance essential for life, required by all human tissues and cells. We do not, however, have any need for dietary cholesterol because, in actuality, approximately 60 to 80 percent of the cholesterol in the blood is manufactured by the body, mainly in the liver and intestines.

All cholesterol and fatty substances in the blood are carried by lipoproteins, a complex of lipid (fat) combined with protein. Fat would be insoluble in the blood were it not for these detergentlike proteins and phospholipids such as lecithin.

There are several major fractions, or varieties, of lipoproteins. The low-density lipoprotein (LDL) is called the "bad" cholesterol fraction because high levels are associated with early heart attacks. In contrast, the high-density lipoprotein family (HDL) is termed "good" because it appears, in some way, to protect against heart disease. Other families of lipoproteins include the chylomicrons, which carry dietary cholesterol and triglycerides; and the very low-density lipoproteins (VLDL), which are made in the liver and carry cholesterol and triglycerides from the liver to the tissues of the body.

Most of the LDL in the blood is removed by LDL receptors in the liver. As a result of research findings, we now believe that the activity of these LDL receptors is suppressed by a diet high in saturated fat and cholesterol. As a result, persons eating such a diet will have higher levels of LDL circulating in the blood, leading to early heart attacks.

Conversely, a diet low in saturated fat and cholesterol would have the opposite effect, namely to increase the activity of LDL receptors, which would decrease levels of LDL circulating in the blood, and thus protect against atherosclerosis and heart disease. Just as higher levels of circulating LDL and cholesterol increase the risk of heart attacks, a high concentration of HDL is associated with a lower risk of heart attacks in males as well as females.

FATS IN THE DIET

Saturated fats, which have such a negative effect upon cardiovascular health, are one of several forms of fatty acids that figure in the human diet. They are obtained primarily from animal sources and are solid at room temperature. The other forms of fatty acids are generally termed *unsaturated* and may be subdivided into monounsaturated and polyunsaturated varieties. Foods with the highest concentration of monounsaturated fatty acids include olive, canola, and peanut oil, among others; those with the highest concentration of polyunsaturated fatty acids include safflower, corn, sunflower, and soybean oil. Unsaturated fats tend to be liquid at room temperature and are believed to have the benefit of lowering LDL cholesterol, as compared with the effect of saturated fats.

ANGIOGRAPHIC STUDIES

The effect of diet on the development of cardiovascular disease continues to receive concentrated attention. Recently, in fact, we have learned that reducing the total amount of fat one eats is of major benefit in decreasing the formation of new atherosclerotic lesions, hence of coronary heart disease. In one study it was reported that reducing one's total fat intake can even cause existing lesions to regress or decrease.

Evidence to this effect comes from what we call regression studies, which use coronary angiography to measure whether the blockage of coronary arteries becomes worse (progression), improves (regression), or remains the same (stabilization). Although a number of these studies achieved stabilization/regression through aggressive drug therapy, in three of them a beneficial effect was gained through dietary changes alone.

The first of these was the Leiden Intervention Trial, which demonstrated that a high ratio of HDL in relation to total cholesterol was correlated with a decreased rate of progression.*

Another of these studies reported dramatic regressive effects that could be achieved by adhering to a diet extremely restricted in fat. This was the Lifestyle Heart Trial by Dean Ornish of the Preventive Medicine Research Institute in Sausalito, California, and associates in San Francisco and Houston (University of Texas Medical School). As reported in *The Lancet* (July 1990), its subjects experienced regression through adherence to a strict vegetarian diet containing no more than 10 percent fat, coupled with mild exercise and regular practice of stress-reduction techniques.

The third study was the University of Southern California's Cholesterol Lowering Atherosclerosis Study (CLAS), by David H. Blankenhorn and associates, which demonstrated that progression of lesions could be retarded by adhering to a modified but palatable diet. As such, it warrants a more detailed examination.

The CLAS was carried out on male patients with advanced cases of atherosclerosis who had undergone bypass surgery. In this study, two groups of patients were compared. One had been given a placebo together with dietary instructions. The other had received a diet plan along with very large doses of nicotenic acid and the resin colestipol. As was anticipated, the drug group experienced dramatic reductions of cholesterol, LDL, and triglycerides as well as increases in HDL. In addition, after four years of follow-up, the drug group showed significantly less progression of their coronary disease as well as some indication of regression.

Yet even in the placebo-plus-diet group, there were a number of patients who did not develop new lesions. These were the participants who had decreased their consumption of total fat and of all fat categories "by substituting low-fat meats and dairy products [such as

* A. C. Arntzenius et al., "Diet, Lipoproteins and the Progression of Coronary Atherosclerosis." *New England Journal Med.* 1985, 312: 805–811.

skim milk] for high-fat meats and dairy products.* In general, those individuals had consumed only 27 percent of total calories in fats, as compared with 32 percent in the group with new lesions. This contrasts with 37 percent of total calories in fat and 437 mg of dietary cholesterol, which are the average intakes in the United States. The study concluded that "when total saturated fat intakes are reduced to NCEP recommended levels, protein and carbohydrate are preferred substitutes for fat calories rather than monounsaturated or polyunsaturated fat.†

In other words, these subjects improved the health of their diseased arteries through a directed but self-administered eating plan. This study suggests, therefore, that lesion stabilization is possible without the patient's adherence to an extreme diet and, indeed, in some patients, without additional medication.

COMPLIANCE

A finding such as this is potentially valuable also because of its implications for what we term *compliance difficulties.* In general, programs such as the NCEP and those of the American Heart Association do not urge the adoption of extremely restrictive diets because of the belief that the majority of people will not find themselves able to comply. Indeed, in many cases, people are reluctant to make even the modest dietary changes necessary to enjoy better health. Such compliance difficulties demonstrate one of the challenges we still have to master in the area of public health education.

People resist a physician's suggested dietary changes for several reasons, I believe. One is the fear on some level that they will be giving up forever the pleasures of the table, which are so central a part of daily life. Even where they find a certain degree of moderation possible during meals at home, many discover they are not prepared to forgo their accustomed social and business life, which may have included a number of shared meals with friends and associates, often in fine restaurants.

But the reluctance may go even deeper. After all, the ability to choose what one prefers to eat is a central one in the development of individuality. This development may be exempli-

---

* D. H. Blankenhorn, R. L. Johnson, et al., "The Influence of Diet on the Appearance of New Lesions in Human Coronary Arteries." *JAMA* 1990, 263; 1646–1652.
† Ibid., p. 1651.

fied when a two-year-old child asserts itself by rejecting, vehemently and often graphically, a spoonful of a food he or she no longer desires. As that small person grows, a part of her or his identity comes to be symbolized by those choices. A man may pride himself on preferring meat and potatoes, demonstrating by his viewpoint certain qualities of reliability and certitude. In a corporate lunchroom, a woman executive may give some consideration to the message projected should she prefer salad when her male colleagues are eating steak. In other words, the matter of food choice is a complex and even loaded subject.

Nevertheless, as we have said, dietary modification has the potential for helping significantly in the prevention and treatment of heart disease, and, as such, remains our first recourse of intervention. In addition, the type of low-fat diet recommended by the American Heart Association is also valuable in the prevention and treatment of diabetes, hypertension, and obesity (obesity being, in fact, one predictor of who may develop diabetes mellitus), all of which increase the risk of heart disease. Also, diets low in fat and high in fiber may help prevent colon cancer, although the evidence for this is less firm.

AREAS OF DISAGREEMENT

In certain specific areas, however, research conclusions to date are vague enough to allow room for honest disagreement. For example, we are not yet certain about the necessity of treating with special therapy individuals possessing lower cholesterol levels who are otherwise healthy, asymptomatic, and without additional risk factors—for example, persons whose cholesterol is below 240 mg/dl (milligrams per deciliter). Disagreement also exists concerning the treatment of premenopausal women, the elderly, and children.

In the area of dietary modification, there has been no firm consensus as yet about the relative benefits of consuming foods high in monounsaturated instead of polyunsaturated fatty acids, although recently some research has suggested that foods higher in monounsaturates may be more beneficial in that they have less of a tendency to lower HDL, the "good" cholesterol. Indeed, the diet of people from the countries of the Mediterranean, which has as one of its staples monounsaturate-rich olive oil, has been associated with a long, healthy life and a low frequency of coronary heart disease. Findings regarding the beneficial effect of incorporating omega-3 fatty acids in the diet also remain inconclusive, although most physicians recommend eating fish rather than ingesting fish oil supplements.

TRIGLYCERIDES

The good and bad cholesterol fractions mentioned so far are familiar, in name at least, to anyone who has received a complete blood lipid profile. Such a profile, however, will also include a value for triglycerides, which may be somewhat less understood. Triglycerides are chemical substances consisting of a molecule of glycerol that is bonded with three fatty acids. They are manufactured in the body (primarily in the liver), but are also derived from diet, and are particularly sensitive to the amount of fat, alcohol, and calories one consumes.

Although some confusion exists about the independent contribution of triglycerides as a risk factor for coronary heart disease, our present thinking is that, ideally, the triglycerides should be kept under a level of 140–150 mg/dl. One should bear in mind, however, that a high level of HDL cholesterol may counteract the effect of triglycerides in excess of this number.

Several factors have contributed to this belief. First, it is important to understand that the higher the triglycerides, the lower the level of HDL, the "good" cholesterol fraction. Also, elevations of triglycerides are particularly significant for patients with diabetes, kidney disease, elevated cholesterol, low HDL, or with several significant but relatively uncommon lipid disorders. Finally, The Framingham Study showed that high triglycerides in women may be considered an independent risk factor for heart disease.

WILL I LIVE LONGER?

A great deal of controversy has emerged over whether or not following the recommendations of the National Cholesterol Education Program and the American Heart Association will increase a person's life expectancy. The primary prevention trials that showed a decline in the incidence of heart disease connected to a reduction in high levels of serum cholesterol had not been carried out over a sufficiently long period to establish their effect on overall mortality. We are now beginning to obtain information about mortality, however. After 102 months of follow-up, for example, the Oslo Heart Study is experiencing fewer deaths than the control group (19 versus 13), and the difference is approaching statistical significance in the group treated with diet and smoking cessation.

Also, there has been a 10½-year follow-up of individuals in the Multirisk Factor Intervention Study, supported by the NIH, which was performed on persons considered at high risk because of elevated serum cholesterol, cigarette smoking, and high blood pressure. More than five years after the study concluded, the group of participants given special care had a 10 percent coronary mortality and a 7 percent decrease in overall mortality as compared to the group that had been referred to their physicians for usual care. The special-care group received intervention, focusing on diet, control of hypertension with medication (if needed), and advice to stop smoking.

Two drug treatment studies in heart attack patients have also shown a reduction in overall mortality. In the Coronary Drug Project, treatment for six years with niacin or nicotenic acid reduced heart attacks by 29 percent. At this time, when the drug was stopped, mortality was not decreased. Nine years later, or fifteen years after the trial began, the niacin group was found to have an 11 percent decrease in all-cause mortality. The Stockholm Ischemic Heart Disease Study, however, used two drugs, clofibrate (or Atromid S) and nicotinic acid, to achieve a dramatic reduction in overall mortality in five years, but the study was not a random, double-blinded one (meaning neither participant in an experiment or trial knows what's being tested on which group).

All of this leads us to conclude that most of the population will benefit from modifying risk factors—particularly from lowering cholesterol and LDL, and most likely by raising HDL. There is even emerging evidence that doing so will enable one to live a longer and healthier life. We do not know specifically which age groups will benefit from risk factor intervention. Lowering blood pressure, for example, appears to be beneficial to all age groups, while there is still debate about lowering cholesterol in the young and very old. At the present time, we recommend that adults and any high-risk individuals lower their cholesterol and LDL in accordance with NCEP guidelines.

However, continuing educational efforts, such as those of the American Heart Association and National Cholesterol Education Program, remain vital. We believe that most Americans do understand that it is important to decrease the risk of major diseases through dietary changes, but many of them do not have sufficient knowledge to make informed choices. The ramifications of that continued ignorance are overwhelming. Over 1 million Americans will die each year from cardiovascular disease, with annual costs of health care estimated to be more than $88 billion,* a figure that significantly underestimates the costs of lost economic

* *American Heart Journal* 1990, 119: 718.

production. In addition, more than 50 percent of middle-aged Americans have a total cholesterol level in excess of 200 mg/dl; and, based on the NCEP guidelines, 36 percent of Americans are at high risk of heart disease on the basis of both total blood cholesterol and LDL levels. Furthermore, it is estimated that 60 million of us suffer from elevated blood pressure.

We have already pointed out that dietary changes can have a beneficial effect on heart disease, and other chronic disease, including obesity, cancer, and hypertension. For example, reducing one's consumption of salt together with avoiding consumption of excess calories can also help to control high blood pressure in many individuals. Moreover, recent evidence suggests that diet combined with exercise can allow many people with high blood pressure to avoid the necessity of costly drug treatment.

WHO IS AT HIGH RISK?

We know that approximately 80 percent of the people who suffer disability or death from heart disease display one or more characteristics or behaviors categorized as major risk factors. This is particularly true with respect to elevated levels of total cholesterol, cigarette smoking, and hypertension. The summary of the National Cholesterol Education Program's adult treatment guidelines lists the following as Coronary Heart Disease (CHD) risk factors (see table below for details):

1987 National Cholesterol Education Program (NCEP)
Adult Treatment Guidelines: Summary

CHD Risk Factors

- Male Gender
- Family history of CHD before 55 years of age (parent or sibling)
- Cigarette smoking
- Hypertension
- Diabetes mellitus
- Definite cerebrovascular or peripheral vascular disease
- Obesity (≥30% overweight)
- Known low HDL-C (<35 mg/dl)

WHAT SHOULD I DO?

There are several things you can do to improve your health. The first, of course, is to stop smoking and, also, to make sure you get a reasonable amount of exercise. Beyond that, have your blood cholesterol and blood pressure checked regularly. It is also useful to know your lipoprotein profile, so that you can ascertain your level of HDL.

The initial test is the measurement of total serum cholesterol. It is best performed in your physician's office. You do not have to be in a fasting state to obtain an accurate reading of total cholesterol or HDL. For the measurement of triglycerides, however, it is necessary to fast overnight. Also bear in mind that, because biovariability can cause test results to differ, you should use an average of at least two or more tests to determine a more accurate cholesterol value. Measurement of total cholesterol, HDL cholesterol, and triglyceride levels allows one to calculate the LDL cholesterol from the following formula:

$$\text{LDL cholesterol} = \text{total cholesterol}$$
$$\text{minus HDL cholesterol and triglyceride}$$

Testing, however, only provides the basis for action. To decrease one's risk for premature death or disability, a person should implement a few simple but important changes in health habits. Of these, as we have said, diet, exercise, and the avoidance of tobacco remain the key points. The dietary principles are not onerous. They consist of the following:

1. Balancing calorie consumption and output to achieve and maintain your ideal body weight
2. Consuming a diet that is nutritionally adequate and that contains a wide variety of fresh foods
3. Avoiding an excessive consumption of salt and alcohol
4. Decreasing consumption of fat, particularly of saturated fats and cholesterol, according to the guidelines of the American Heart Association (see table for Step One Diet, page 13; persons wishing to restrict their fat intake further may refer to Step Two Diet on the next page).

Step Two American Heart Association Diet

Key Features

Same as Step One Diet, with two exceptions:

1. Consumption of saturated fat should be kept to less than 7% of total calories; and,
2. Total cholesterol intake should be kept to less than 200 mg per day.

Source: Summary of the 1987 National Cholesterol Education Program (NCEP) adult treatment guidelines.

Once these principles have been followed for a period of time, they become a way of life that offers many rewards. You will feel better, for one thing. And, in many cases, you will look better, too. Moreover, this beneficial change in lifestyle can be achieved without the sense of gastronomic deprivation that some may nervously anticipate at the outset.

CHEZ EDDY RESTAURANT

For many years, I have been convinced that gourmet dining should remain part of the lifestyle enjoyed by persons wishing to eat healthfully. And that is why, when we at the Methodist Hospital made the decision to develop an Institute for Preventive Medicine, we envisioned the establishment within it of a showcase restaurant that would dramatize that conviction. Chez Eddy is that restaurant.

At the time Chez Eddy opened in 1981, very little had been done to make healthful gourmet dining available to a discerning public. We started from scratch, investigating the fledgling nouvelle cuisine in France and the Pritikin approach in California. Neither seemed quite right for what we had in mind. So we hired a European chef and general manager and set them to work with our dietetic center staff. Together, they and their successors have devised methods of adapting gourmet cuisine, with its subtle sauces and flavorful stocks, to the needs of people who follow a heart-healthy eating plan.

ECLECTIC, INNOVATIVE

The development of Chez Eddy has been an evolutionary process, affected by national and international culinary trends. Eventually we arrived at the concept that characterizes Chez Eddy at this moment. In general, we present an eclectic cuisine blending classical with New American and New Southwestern components, but prepared according to the principles of the American Heart Association. The process continues daily, with innovations from the current staff, managed by Helen Roe, M.S., R.D.

As you will see from the recipes that follow, Chez Eddy's approach does not totally exclude any single food. That is because we hope that our recipes will be incorporated into an overall eating plan, such as the Help Your Heart Diet developed by Baylor College of Medicine, or one of the plans recommended by the American Heart Association. While there is beefsteak on the menu, we do not suggest consuming it every day. Nor do we suggest eating salmon at every meal. Enjoying a wide variety of low-fat foods, however, is strongly recommended.

FOOD AND DRINK

Although the philosophy and preparation of the food will be discussed at length further on, the most basic principle is that we use only fresh ingredients. The food is not calorie dense. Thus if one enjoys a three-course meal, composed of salad, an entrée with vegetables, and dessert, the number of calories consumed will total between 500 and 600. (The addition of bread, margarine, and wine, however, would provide additional calories.) Moreover, Chez Eddy's food is prepared without added salt, and there is no salt on the table, although it may be obtained on request.

In addition, at Chez Eddy one may enjoy a glass of wine, but hard liquor is not served. Research evidence suggests that moderate alcohol consumption can increase the level of HDL in the blood, but the clinical significance of this is not known. Also, other studies indicate that alcohol is processed in a slightly different way by women than by men, which may affect the amount they can consume without risk. We, therefore, agree with current opinion that alcohol consumption be kept at a moderate level, which should not exceed one to two drinks a day or their equivalent in wine or beer. (The table on the next page gives equivalencies among alcoholic beverages.)

Beverage Equivalencies*

Beverage	Serving	Ethanol (g)	Cal. (g)
Beer	12 fl oz	12.8	146
Wine, red or white	4 fl oz	11.0	82
Spirits (Gin, Rum, Vodka, Whiskey)			
80 proof	1½ fl oz	14.0	97
86 proof	1½ fl oz	15.1	105
90 proof	1½ fl oz	15.9	110
94 proof	1½ fl oz	16.7	116
100 proof	1½ fl oz	17.9	124

Source: Summary of the 1987 National Cholesterol Education Program (NCEP) adult treatment guidelines.
*1 jigger = 1½ fl oz.

AMBIENCE

Every aspect of Chez Eddy is intended to promote a gracious, relaxed dining experience. The clean, contemporary lines of the restaurant's architecture contribute to a quiet elegance. The lighting is soft and flattering. The ambience created is pleasant, but subdued. Eating in a fine restaurant should be an aesthetic experience, during which it is possible to concentrate fully on the food and conversation. Eating rapidly or under noisy or disturbed conditions does not satisfy the appetite or the soul. Noise and confusion, in fact, promote a distraction of focus and impaired control, thus increasing the probability of overconsumption. In contrast, a relaxing environment contributes to the sense of well-being and satisfaction that gourmet dining, at its best, creates. It is an atmosphere one should strive to create at home, too.

To sum up, it is the purpose of Chez Eddy to demonstrate that eating prudently, which has been proven beneficial from the point of view of preventive medicine, can be enjoyable. We at Chez Eddy and the Methodist Hospital hope to make a contribution toward your health and happiness through the material we provide in this book.

Have fun, and good eating!

THE BASICS OF HEART-HEALTHY CUISINE

....

CHEZ EDDY WAS THE FIRST restaurant in America to present heart-healthy gourmet cuisine prepared in accordance with the dietary guidelines of the American Heart Association. That means we restrict the amount of saturated fat and cholesterol in our food and we add no saturated fat during preparation. Also, we add no salt.

Like any restaurant, however, Chez Eddy is the embodiment of the ideas of a talented and creative staff that reacts to evolving attitudes, knowledge, and preferences about food, as well as to new ingredients that become available every year.

As a result, our culinary approach has evolved from its original emphasis on continental and French cuisine to a simpler, freer, more eclectic style that focuses on the natural characteristics and flavors of the ingredients. This has enabled us to be successful in our continuing efforts to decrease amounts of fat and cholesterol in our food. As you will see when you try our recipes, the dishes are such that most may be utilized even in diet plans that limit fat calories to levels substantially lower than the current AHA guidelines of 30 percent of total daily caloric intake. We have been able to be innovative in this fashion because we haven't changed at all in one crucial area—that is, with respect to the standards upon which we are based.

We at Chez Eddy believe that good food is most enjoyable when it appeals to all the senses. It must be full of flavor, fragrant, and beautiful to behold, thus nourishing to both body and soul.

Our customers have been delighted with the result. They express pleasure and surprise at how good Chez Eddy food tastes. "It can't possibly be low-fat!" they say. Many of our clients have asked us for our methods and recipes so they can try them at home with their families and when they entertain. Although we share individual recipes whenever we can, we decided that a more complete response would be to put our recipes in book form. Hence, this cookbook.

METHODS OF INTENSIFYING FLAVOR

We begin with the freshest seafood and seasonal produce as well as top-quality lean meats. Once we have obtained these fine ingredients, we focus on amplifying their clean, bright flavors. The palate likes to be kept busy. So, when we remove salt as a material that points up contrasts with a food's natural flavor, something else must be supplied to replace it. Fortunately, the process isn't difficult. After all, in addition to salty flavors, the palate perceives sour, sweet, and bitter tastes, as well as contrasts of temperature and texture.

Thus, we enhance a food's natural flavor by drawing on the stimulating characteristics of a variety of fresh herbs, peppers, and spices, as well as on flavorful acids, including infused vinegars and wine. Where appropriate, these are juxtaposed with sources of natural sweetness, such as honey and fruit juice. In addition, we employ sauces made from extreme reductions of fat-free stock to deepen the flavor of the accompanying meat and game.

In this fashion, the palate is kept so active that the diner forgets he or she isn't tasting salt. In fact, its absence turns out to be a culinary blessing, for instead of the overriding flavor of a single condiment, one can enjoy a palette of sparkling flavors achieved by evoking complementary alternative sensations.

Dealing with the absence of fats, however, is a little more complicated. That's because, in addition to contributing a modest degree of flavor (although far less than is commonly assumed), fats are the emulsifiers of traditional cuisine. In sauces, they give a tactile pleasure to the tongue, as well as evening out the tart or peppery effects of the ingredients they hold in suspension.

To deal with the challenge posed by their omission, we draw on a number of alternatives. One of the most important is our version of *sauce soubise,* a non-fat substitute for béchamel, or white sauce. This innovation, together with the use of other low-fat dairy products such as yogurt and buttermilk, allows us to achieve the mellow "roundness" in dishes that is conventionally evoked by the addition of cream. Thus we are able to create a variety of recipes that many versions of heart-healthy cooking cannot attempt.

Finally, by reducing our fat-free stocks to the demi-glace stage, we achieve the same thickening effect that traditional approaches rely on butter to accomplish. These reductions, which find their way into a large number of our dishes, contribute a welcome intensity of flavor as well.

BEFORE YOU COOK

Preparing Chez Eddy's heart-healthy cuisine at home doesn't require expert skill, but some cooking experience is necessary. You will note, nevertheless, that many of our recipes are quite simple. That's because we prepare our dishes in the restaurant *à la minute,* or to order. For that reason, a number of the recipes contain components such as the soubise or demi-glace that must be prepared in advance. For this reason, we recommend that you read a recipe thoroughly before beginning. That way you can also be certain of having all the necessary ingredients on hand.

NUTRITIONAL CONSIDERATIONS

The nutritional analysis at the bottom of each recipe details such important considerations as calorie content and amount of total and saturated fat, as well as overall nutritional information. This material should be used to integrate our dishes into your day's healthful eating plan. According to the Step One American Heart Association Diet (page 13), that plan should restrict fats to less than 30 percent of the total calorie intake, with less than 10 percent coming from saturated fat. In addition, cholesterol should be kept to less than 300 mg. a day. While this discussion focuses on fats, you should not forget that a daily eating plan should consist of a balanced diet, including foods from all four groups. It is particularly useful to include whole grains to round out calories and provide additional fiber in the diet.

There are several common misperceptions about the application of this 30 percent figure. It does not, for example, mean that every dish or even every meal you eat must contain less than 30 percent fat. Instead, it means that your fat intake should balance out to less than 30 percent per day. That way, if you eat something very high in fat, you must balance it with something much lower in fat so that the day's entire intake equals less than 30 percent of total calories.

A relatively simple method for calculating this figure is to count grams of fat. It requires only one piece of concrete information: how many calories a day you consume. Once you know that, the rest is easy. For example, if you consume 1500 calories per day, you would need to keep fat consumption below 50 grams. Here is how we calculate this figure: First, multiply 1500 by 30 percent, which equals 450. That means your total daily fat intake should amount to less than 450 calories. Because each gram of fat has 9 calories, divide 450 by 9, which equals 50 grams of fat.

Similarly, 30 percent of an intake of 2000 calories per day would equal 600 calories. Dividing this figure by 9 would result in approximately 67 grams of fat.

What does this mean in terms of real food? For purposes of illustration, let's look at a typical day's menu featuring foods from Chez Eddy. Since we don't serve breakfast, we have substituted the following common breakfast menu:

Food	Calories	Fat
Breakfast		
¾ cup bran flakes with ½ cup skim milk	138	0.7 gm.
1 six-oz. glass of orange juice	77	0.1 gm.
1 slice of wheat toast	58	0.7 gm.
tea or coffee without cream	0	0.0 gm.
Lunch		
Sliced Beef Salad with Five-Spice Dressing	193	10.0 gm.
French roll	90	0.0 gm.
Chez Eddy Cheesecake	211	8.2 gm.
Snack		
Frozen nonfat yogurt with fruit	100	0.2 gm.
1 Mrs. Fisher's chocolate brownie	161	4.2 gm.

Dinner

Spinach and Mushroom Salad with Zesty Buttermilk Dressing	40	1.0 gm.
Grilled Redfish with Black Bean Salsa	128	1.9 gm.
Corn Cakes	166	4.0 gm.
Blueberry Cobbler	212	6.2 gm.
with frozen yogurt	64	0.2 gm.

Total Calories = 1638
Total Fat Grams = 37.4

Of course, we have not included margarine in this menu. If, however, one wished to add 1 tablespoon of corn oil margarine to the above, it would increase the total by 100 calories and 11 grams of fat. At an overall intake of 1785 calories and 47.9 grams of fat, however, people eating such a menu would still have consumed significantly less than the recommended percentage [(1738 x .30) ÷ 9 = 58 gm].

Although this menu is given only for illustrative purposes, we believe it demonstrates how you can eat interesting, delicious foods—including many of your favorites—yet stay well within American Heart Association recommendations, using our recipes as part of a healthful eating plan. (For your specific requirements, we recommend you consult your physician or registered dietician.)

SHOPPING

Once you have read the recipe you have chosen, you will have to shop for ingredients. As we mentioned, we recommend that you choose the freshest meats, seafood, and produce you can find. Where canned vegetables must be substituted, select those that are prepared without added salt. Some of our recipes call for ingredients that contain salt (such as capers or canned tuna), but we have included methods for greatly reducing their sodium content.

When you rely on fresh ingredients, your pantry does not have to be stocked with a daunting array of prepared specialty items. When an unusual item such as Five-Spice is required for a particular recipe, it is listed prominently. Similarly, although our cuisine uses a lot of fresh herbs, they should be purchased on a recipe-by-recipe basis, and used as soon as possible after purchase. In general, however, the herbs we use most often include mint, tarragon, basil, thyme, dill weed, rosemary, oregano, cilantro, and parsley. Ingredients you will need on a regular basis include the following:

- SPICES: cumin, black peppercorns, green peppercorns, cinnamon, nutmeg, clove
- VINEGARS: balsamic, rice wine, sherry wine, champagne
- OILS: extra-virgin olive oil, canola oil
- DAIRY PRODUCTS: nonfat yogurt, skim milk, nonfat dry milk, nonfat vanilla yogurt (without gelatin), low-fat cottage cheese
- OTHER STAPLES: long-grain white and brown rice; wild rice; fresh or dried Italian pasta; dried black beans; dried lentils; barley; granulated sugar; honey; fructose; flour; corn meal; eggs and egg substitute; corn oil margarine; nonstick vegetable spray; canned tomatoes; tomato paste; and fresh garlic

When purchasing fresh foods, there are certain considerations to keep in mind. For example, it's best to purchase meats, poultry, and fish at the counter instead of selecting pre-packaged items. That way you can be sure the ingredient is selected, prepared, and trimmed to your specifications.

Also, make an effort to purchase poultry and fish with the skin on, removing it just before use. This maintains flavor and nutritional value. If either item is packaged in plastic, make sure you remove the plastic as soon as you get it home. By sealing out the air, plastic wrap creates an environment where bacteria can multiply rapidly.

It's also a good idea to use poultry and fish as soon as possible after purchase, although, if necessary, they may be kept in the refrigerator for a day or two. When storing such items, keep the food on a bed of ice to extend its freshness, but remember to drain any water that accumulates. Food should never sit in water.

FISH

Although until the last decade, most of America's heartland never saw a fresh salt-water fish, that is no longer the case, thanks to improved methods of air transport. Yet, even an allegedly "fresh" fish may have deteriorated by the time it is purchased. Here are a few hints on how to assure freshness.

A fresh fish will taste fresh, sweet, and briny. It will be a delight to smell as well as eat. (If it smells or tastes "fishy," that means it's old.) Smell the fish whenever possible before purchase. When that is not allowed, look for full bright eyes, healthy pink gills, a firm texture. In most of the recipes that follow, we specify skinless, boneless fillets, often cut from the fillets of larger fish, such as salmon and grouper. Ask your fishmonger to do this for you, instead of buying ready-cut fillets.

When dealing with these larger fish, or ones from which "steaks" are cut, such as tuna or swordfish, all you have to go on is the appearance of the flesh itself and the recommendation of your fishmonger. Again, the key is to know and trust the person you are dealing with. If you get the fish home and it isn't satisfactory, take it back.

SHELLFISH

At Chez Eddy, we do not serve uncooked shellfish. Accordingly, for these recipes you will buy oysters in bulk, lump crabmeat that has been cooked and picked and packed in containers, shrimp without the heads, scallops in bulk, live mussels, and live lobster.

Again, the key to quality is to know your fishmarket. That way you can believe it when the fishmonger tells you the oysters are good today. Regarding crabmeat, a few caveats: Sometimes lump crabmeat will be called "fresh" when it merely hasn't been vacuum packed. Make certain that your supplier understands that, to you, fresh also means that it has never been frozen. Never use frozen crabmeat in our dishes. Freezing crabmeat completely changes its texture. Also, don't attempt to substitute Alaskan king crab for blue crab, as the effect is quite different.

Shrimp, however, may be frozen without a significant loss of quality, although if you purchase shrimp that have been thawed, they must be used immediately. Again, either fresh or thawed shrimp should smell sweet and briny, not sulphuric. Their texture should be firm (although the texture of thawed shrimp will be less so). Shrimp that has been thawed for display will have released a noticeable amount of liquid into the display container.

When you arrive home with your shrimp, immediately place them on ice in the coldest part of the refrigerator, making sure they do not become submerged in water as the ice melts. If the shrimp is fresh, not thawed, it may be frozen without loss of quality. (Do not refreeze thawed shrimp.) In any event, the sooner it is used, the better.

KITCHEN EQUIPMENT

Although for the most part special cooking equipment is not needed to prepare Chez Eddy's recipes, the basic well-stocked kitchen is a necessity. In addition to the usual battery of implements, we strongly urge that you utilize nonstick cookware as much as possible. It allows much more efficient preparation of our recipes. Similarly, in recipes involving ingredients with a high acid content, we suggest the use of containers made from nonreactive materials, such as enameled cast iron, glass, or stainless steel.

A special word about sauté pans: Since so many of our recipes involve quick cooking, we recommend you use sauté pans with handles that are heat resistant so the pan may be transferred directly from the stove to a hot oven.

In addition, for many of our dishes you will need a good high-speed blender and food processor. You will also need an ice-cream maker for preparing frozen yogurt and sorbets. Because our recipes call for small amounts, we recommend you use one of the countertop varieties.

CHEZ EDDY COOKING TECHNIQUES

In preparing heart-healthy cuisine, you should use methods that require the least possible amount of added fat. Water-based techniques—for example, boiling and steaming—are excellent when you wish to render vegetables crisp, vivid, and nutritious. Better for meats and seafood, however, are approaches that conserve and concentrate flavor, such as braising, baking, grilling (or broiling), and pan roasting.

PAN ROASTING

Many of our meat and game recipes rely on this technique, which is really a low-fat variation of the conventional sauté. When we pan roast, we film a nonstick skillet with a trace of olive oil or clarified margarine and heat it over high heat until just below the smoking point. That's to keep the food from sticking. Then we pour out any oily residue and add the meat, searing it so juices and flavor do not escape. We finish the cooking process in the oven.

BRAISING

This technique begins in much the same way, by browning the meat at high heat to seal in flavor. Then it's simmered in a flavorful liquid infused with aromatic vegetables and herbs.

We avoid the greasy character of the traditional preparation by trimming meat carefully and by skinning meat such as chicken before browning. We also use meats that are naturally lean, such as rabbit, venison, and wild boar.

GRILLING

Grilling has been in vogue lately because it powerfully intensifies the character of the central ingredient. Not only does grilling over charcoal in particular add flavor during the cooking process, but the process in all its forms lends itself to the prior application of various marinades and spice rubs, which are effective flavor enhancers.

At the same time, however, there has been concern over carcinogens released into the smoke when fat falls into the coals or onto the heating element. Obviously, the leaner the meat or seafood you are grilling, the less fat there is to be rendered. Therefore, it stands to reason that you should choose lean ingredients when considering this process.

However, even the oilier varieties of fish, such as salmon, will release very little fat during the grilling process as compared with a T-bone steak. So, to a large degree, by selecting the leaner varieties of food we recommend, much of the concern about grilling may be minimized.

Nevertheless, if you are concerned about the potential carcinogenic effect of grilling fish and lean meat, you have several options. First, you may select another method of cooking. In each of our recipes that call for grilling, we offer other options. Second, you may partially precook the food in the oven, then finish it on the grill so it absorbs some of the grilled flavor. Or, you may grill according to the following indirect method. If you choose this latter route, be aware that it is a much slower process and therefore the cooking times called for in the recipe will need to be adjusted.

Lay your fire, as usual, in a conventional barbecue or charcoal grilling unit with a cover. First, cold-smoke the meat or fish by placing it on the side of the grill away from the coals and closing the cover. The objective here is to allow the flavor of the circulating smoke to penetrate. Then to finish grilling the meat or fish, spread the coals so they cover the bottom. Place a pan of water in the center of the coals, squarely under the part of the grilling rack where you will cook the meat or fish. That way, as you grill, most of the rendered fat will drip into the water, yet enough heat will still be generated to cook the meat or fish.

Otherwise, the key to charcoal grilling is the heat of the fire. It should be very hot for the preparation of fish and chicken fillets. Heat the coals until they are just filmed with a pale gray ash. Then grill your fillets on a rack two to four inches away from the heat. To gauge the heat, merely hold the palm of your hand over the fire. If you feel the urgent need to remove it in two seconds, then the fire is hot enough.

PRESENTATION

Attempting to stimulate the senses means that each dish must look delicious too. We want to ravish the eye without descending into the more precious regions of mannered composition. Food should resemble something wonderful to eat, so that eating does not destroy, but instead confirms, the work of art.

Although most of our recipes give specific suggestions regarding arranging and garnishing the food, they derive from a few basic principles. For example, when we arrange the food, we attempt to create a composition on the plate that is balanced in terms of color, form, and texture, yet simple and elegant. Chez Eddy food is placed on the plate cleanly, so that it does not appear "handled."

Another consideration is the size of the dinner plate. At Chez Eddy we use a plate large enough so that the food appears elegant and easy to eat, but not so large that the food looks marooned. You want to focus attention on the food's attractive qualities, not portion size.

Portion size, however, is very important. This is particularly so with respect to the protein segment of the meal, which often includes the most fat and cholesterol. You will note, for example, that our recipes limit cooked meat portions to three ounces. To make this seem more generous, you can slice roasted meats on the bias, so that the slices fall into ovals which increase the exposed surface area. This procedure also allows for a greater interplay between the surface of the meat and the sauce, which intensifies flavor. In other types of dishes—for example, main-course salads—you can mound a chiffonade of lettuce under the meat or seafood so its dimensions are increased. Specific details such as these are given in each recipe, where they are applicable.

We have used the 3-ounce portion size in our nutritional guidelines as well, because we feel it is satisfactory both with respect to the food's flavor and to considerations of controlling fat and calories. We do realize, of course, that an appropriate daily calorie intake varies among people. That's why in most cases we have analyzed the dressings and sauces separately. Persons needing more calories can have seconds, and so on. You can even double the portion size of meats and fish, as long as you remember to double the totals given in the nutritional analysis as well.

PREPARATION TIPS

The following are some special considerations encountered in cooking Chez Eddy cuisine. You can call them tricks, tips, or helpful hints, as you wish.

• Take care not to overcook fish. Fish is done when its flesh loses its translucence and becomes slightly resilient to the touch. If it flakes it has been cooked too long.
• In many of our sauce recipes, we call for reducing a liquid by half its volume. This is very easy to measure. Merely stand a wooden spoon in the pot or saucepan, allowing the liquid to mark it. Then simmer the liquid for a period of time and measure again, until the level in the pot, and on the spoon, is half what you began with. When preparing sauces where the level is too low to make this process viable, just reduce it until the liquid coats the back of a spoon. If you have cooked your demi-glace long enough, a sauce in which it is a component will thicken rapidly, when reduced.
• If the sauce doesn't thicken for one reason or another, you can rescue it with a little cornstarch stirred into an equal amount of wine and then slowly stirred into the hot sauce.
• Nonfat yogurt always means plain, unless otherwise specified.
• When straining stocks, do not stir or press down on the solids or you will cloud the liquid.
• How to strain stock for immediate use: Remove as much as possible with a spoon or wire skimmer; then skim the top again with a lettuce leaf, strips of dry paper towel, or coffee filters.
• We have made a valiant but ultimately unsuccessful effort to develop or locate an appropriate shortcut for making our beef, chicken, and veal stocks, and for our demi-glace. If you encounter an emergency need for one of these ingredients, we offer the following suggestion, although we emphasize that the result will be a pallid version of a sauce made with the real thing.

Take a commercial (fat-free, low-sodium) stock and simmer it with aromatic vegetables such as chopped onion, carrots, leeks, and celery until the vegetables are soft. Then strain, reduce it by half, and proceed with the recipe calling for stock. When attempting to substitute this for demi-glace, add the cornstarch and wine mixture referred to above.

• When reheating any frozen soup or sauce—or any that has been in the refrigerator for a couple of days—it's a good idea to refresh the herbs by adding more of the same, freshly chopped.

SUBSTITUTIONS

Although we discuss the issue of substitutions throughout, here is a basic list of ways to reduce the fat content of favorite recipes:

Use egg substitute or egg whites where whole eggs are called for.
Use plain cocoa instead of baker's chocolate.
Use skim milk instead of whole milk.
Use Chez Eddy demi-glace instead of roux-based gravies.
Use Chez Eddy soubise instead of traditional cream or white sauce.
Use nonfat plain yogurt instead of sour cream.
Use nonfat plain yogurt in a 2-to-1 ratio with reduced-calorie mayonnaise, instead of regular mayonnaise.

We hope you will enjoy the recipes which follow as much as we have enjoyed preparing them for your use.

BON APPÉTIT!

BASIC STOCKS
AND SAUCES

....

Beef Stock

Chicken Stock

Fish Stock

Lobster Bisque

Court Bouillon

Chez Eddy Demi-Glace

Chef Thomas Palmer's Quick and Easy Demi-Glace

Chez Eddy Soubise

Basic Tomato Sauce

Tomato Concassé

Fresh Tomato Coulis

Chez Eddy Fromage Blanc

Champagne Vinaigrette

Basic Fruit Salsa

Spice Blend

BEEF STOCK

1 bouquet garni consisting of:
  1 bay leaf
  ½ large yellow or white onion
  2 whole cloves
  10 parsley stems, no leaves
  1 clove garlic
  1 stalk celery
  1 whole carrot, peeled
  1 small leek, white part only, split lengthwise in half and
    rinsed carefully
16 cups cold water
5 pounds beef marrow bones or beef short ribs, all visible fat
  carefully trimmed

Prepare the bouquet garni as follows: Place the bay leaf on the flat surface of the onion half and secure both ends of the bay leaf to the onion by piercing with the whole cloves. Tie the parsley stems into a small bundle and tuck the garlic inside the celery crevice. With string, wrap all together, including the carrot and leek, so they make a tidy bundle. This makes it easier to remove the vegetables and herbs from the stock when it is ready.

In a large stockpot, bring about 4 cups of cold water to a rolling boil. Add the bones, making sure that the level of the water remains ½ inch above them, and let the water return to a rapid boil. Cook for one minute. Remove from the heat and drain. Add additional cold water to cover the bones and let stand for 5 minutes. Remove the bones, drain the water, and wipe residue from the stockpot. This blanching technique removes excess fat and impurities from the bones in order to impart better color and flavor to the stock.

Add the blanched bones, the bouquet garni, and 12 cups of cold water to the stockpot. Bring to a boil over high heat, skimming off the foam that rises to the surface. Reduce the heat and simmer gently for 3 to 4 hours, removing scum occasionally as it accumulates. At the end of this period, remove the pot from the heat. Discard the bouquet garni and strain the stock through a strainer or colander lined with several layers of dampened cheesecloth. If the stock is not to be used immediately, cool to room temperature, refrigerate, and remove the fat that will collect on the surface during refrigeration.

The stock may be kept in sealed jars in the refrigerator for about 5 days or may be frozen in serving-size containers for about 6 months.

N U T R I T I O N A L   N O T E   Because this stock is skimmed of fat and contains no added salt, its nutritional significance is minimal.

Y I E L D   *4 cups*

CHICKEN STOCK

1 bouquet garni consisting of:
  1 bay leaf
  ½ large yellow or white onion
  2 whole cloves
  10 parsley stems, no leaves
  1 clove garlic
  1 stalk celery
  1 whole carrot, peeled
  1 small leek, white part only, split lengthwise in half and
    rinsed carefully
2 whole chickens, skinned, all visible fat removed
16 cups cold water

Prepare the bouquet garni as directed on page 39.

Thoroughly wash the chickens by holding under running water. Remove any visible fat. Place the chickens in a stockpot, kettle, or other large pot and add the cold water. Bring to a boil quickly over high heat, then reduce the heat and simmer gently. Add the bouquet garni. Adjust the heat so that the surface of the liquid just breaks with bubbles, but does not boil. Skim off the foam that accumulates on the surface as the stock simmers. Cook uncovered for about 1½ to 2 hours. When done, the meat should fall from the bones, but the bones should remain intact.

Turn off the heat and remove the chicken and bouquet garni from the pot. Discard the bouquet garni and set aside the chicken until cool enough to handle. Strain the stock through a strainer or colander lined with several layers of dampened cheesecloth. If the stock is not to be used immediately, cool to lukewarm or room temperature, refrigerate, and remove the fat that collects on the surface during refrigeration. Separate the chicken meat from the bones and reserve for use in other recipes.

The stock may be kept in sealed jars in the refrigerator for approximately 3 to 5 days or may be frozen in serving-size containers for about 6 months.

NUTRITIONAL NOTE Because this stock is skimmed of fat and contains no added salt, its nutritional significance is minimal.

YIELD *8 cups*

Chicken stock has a multitude of uses beyond the obvious ones of soups and sauces. For example, poaching chicken in stock instead of water enhances the flavor of both meat and broth. Afterward, you may use that more intense stock for other purposes, such as poaching vegetables. Another way to arrive at a more richly flavored stock is to substitute chicken stock for the water in this recipe and proceed as directed.

FISH STOCK

For best results, we suggest that you use the bones and heads from mild fish, such as snapper, redfish, or halibut. More strongly flavored fish, such as tuna, swordfish, and mackerel, are not as suitable. To obtain a more concentrated fish fumet, simmer this very light stock so that it is reduced to half its volume.

1 bouquet garni consisting of:
  1 bay leaf
  ½ large yellow or white onion
  2 whole cloves
  10 parsley stems, no leaves
  1 clove garlic
  1 stalk celery
  1 whole carrot, peeled
  1 small leek, white part only, split lengthwise in half and
    rinsed carefully
20 cups cold water
2 lbs. fish heads and fish bones cut into pieces (ask fishmonger
  to remove gills)

Prepare the bouquet garni as directed on page 39.

   Place fish heads and bones in a bowl and let cold water run over them for 3 to 5 minutes. Add all the ingredients to a stockpot or large kettle. Bring to a boil quickly over high heat, then reduce the heat and simmer gently, uncovered, for approximately 1 hour, skimming occasionally to remove any foam that accumulates. When done, the flesh of the fish should fall away from the bones but the bones should not disintegrate when touched.

   Remove from the heat. Lift out and discard the bouquet garni, and strain the stock through a strainer or colander lined with several layers of dampened cheesecloth.

   If the stock is not be be used immediately, cool to lukewarm or room temperature, refrigerate, and remove any fat that may collect on the surface during refrigeration.

   The stock may be kept in sealed jars in the refrigerator for approximately 2 to 3 days or may be frozen in serving-size containers for 3 to 4 months.

   N U T R I T I O N A L   N O T E   Because this stock is skimmed of fat and contains no added salt, its nutritional significance is minimal.

Y I E L D   *14 cups*

LOBSTER BISQUE

4 cups lobster shells or shrimp shells
4 cups *mirepoix* (1 cup each of leeks, carrots, onions, and celery, finely diced)
1 cup dill weed, whole
3 tablespoons tomato paste
¼ cup white flour
¼ cup cognac
2 quarts water
1 bay leaf
½ teaspoon white pepper
1 teaspoon paprika

Preheat the oven to 350°F. Place the seafood shells in a shallow heavy-bottomed roasting pan. Stirring occasionally, cook until the shells are so dry they crumble when touched with a metal spoon (do not brown). Remove from the oven and add the *mirepoix* and dill weed, mixing thoroughly. Return to the oven and roast for 15 minutes. Stir in the tomato paste and cook for another 10 minutes, then remove from the oven.

Dust flour evenly over the shell mixture. Stir and return to the oven. Cook for 10 minutes. Remove from the oven and add the cognac, stirring carefully to avoid spattering. Add the water, the bay leaf, white pepper, and paprika, stirring to combine. Return to the oven and cook for 30 minutes. Strain the bisque through a fine meshed sieve or a colander lined with several layers of dampened cheesecloth. It should be light reddish brown in color and have a rich seafood aroma and taste. The bisque can be made ahead and refrigerated for 2 to 3 days before using for lobster sauce. It can also be frozen in serving-sized containers.

YIELD *2 quarts*

This bisque makes a richly flavored base for soups or other seafood sauces. The recipe works just as well when made with shrimp shells, which are easier to come by for most home cooks.

SERVING 2 OZ.

Calories 2.0
Total fat 0
Cholesterol 0
Saturated fat 0
Protein 0.1 gm.
Carbohydrate 0.5 gm.
Sodium 1 mg.

COURT BOUILLON

Court Bouillon is another variety of poaching liquid, suitable for simmering fish, meat, or vegetables. When a quick stock is needed for poaching fish or chicken à la minute, this is the liquid to use. It should be made fresh each day, and used the day it is made.

1 cup sliced yellow or white onion, separated into rings
1 cup peeled carrots, finely sliced
1 cup leeks, white part only, rinsed carefully and finely sliced
1 cup celery, finely sliced on bias
1 cup white wine
½ cup white-wine vinegar
2 quarts cold water
1 bay leaf
1 teaspoon black peppercorns

Combine all the ingredients except the peppercorns in a large saucepan or Dutch oven and bring to a boil over high heat. Reduce the heat and simmer for about 25 minutes. Add the peppercorns and simmer for another 10 minutes. Remove from the heat, cool slightly, and strain through a strainer or colander. The bouillon may be kept frozen for 1 to 3 months.

NUTRITIONAL NOTE Because this stock is skimmed of fat and contains no added salt, its nutritional significance is minimal.

YIELD *9 cups*

CHEZ EDDY DEMI-GLACE

10 pounds veal bones, split into pieces by the butcher
2 large onions, quartered
2 medium carrots, peeled and quartered
2 small leeks, white part only, split lengthwise in half and rinsed
  carefully
2 stalks celery, with leaves, cut into 2-inch pieces
6 medium tomatoes, whole
24 sprigs parsley, stems only
2 cloves garlic
2 teaspoons whole black peppercorns
1 teaspoon dried thyme
16 cups cold water
½ cup red wine
½ teaspoon tomato paste

Preheat the oven to 450°F. Roast the bones in a shallow roasting pan, turning occasionally with a slotted spoon, until they begin to brown, approximately 1 hour. Add the onions, carrots, leeks, and celery; roast until browned, about 45 minutes. The bones should be a dark golden color. (This stage is crucial for the full development of flavor. Do not rush it. Similarly, take care the ingredients do not scorch.)

Drain off the fat. With a slotted spoon, transfer the bones and the vegetables to a large stockpot. Deglaze the roasting pan by adding approximately 1 cup hot water to the pan and stirring to dissolve the coagulated cooking juices. Pour this liquid into the stockpot and add the tomatoes, parsley stems, garlic, peppercorns, thyme, and cold water.

Bring to a boil over high heat. Reduce the heat so that the liquid simmers gently. Skim off the foam as it collects on the surface. Cook uncovered, occasionally skimming off fat and foam, until the liquid is reduced to half its volume, approximately 4 to 6 hours.

Strain the stock through a fine sieve or colander lined with several layers of cheesecloth. Discard the solids, wipe out the pot, and return the liquid to the stockpot. Add the wine and tomato paste to the strained liquid. Return to a boil, then reduce the heat and simmer for approximately 3 to 4 hours, until reduced again to half its volume. Occasionally remove any scum that collects on the surface.

Cool to lukewarm or room temperature. Refrigerate until fat rises to

This is our basic brown sauce, the foundation for many of our most popular dishes. Unlike traditional preparations, our demi-glace contains no flour, starch, or arrowroot for thickening. Also, we use no butter, thus greatly reducing the calorie content of the sauce. Our demi-glace is thickened through the combined effect of long simmering and the natural gelatins contained in the bones. Therefore, the best bones to use for this sauce are veal knuckle bones with some meat attached but all visible fat removed. We roast the bones for enhanced color and flavor.

SERVING 2 TBS.

Calories 7.09

Total fat 0

Cholesterol 0

Saturated fat 0

Protein 1.3 gm.

Carbohydrates 0.5 gm.

Sodium 3.0 mg.

the surface and hardens. Skim off the solidified fat and discard. Place the completed demi-glace in serving-size containers and freeze for up to 6 months. Demi-glace will keep in the refrigerator for approximately 5 days.

N O T E Cooking times listed may need to be adjusted to allow the bones to achieve the necessary dark, caramelized color; similarly, reduction times may vary.

Y I E L D *8 cups*

GLACE DE VIANDE

At times you will want a more concentrated meat glaze to flavor sauces or intensify the flavor of a dish. That is the purpose of Glace de Viande. It is prepared simply by boiling demi-glace over a relatively high heat until it achieves the consistency of syrup. As the mixture cools, it will turn gelatinous. At that point it may be cut into cubes and frozen. Glace de Viande will keep in the refrigerator for about 5 days or frozen up to 6 months.

CHEF THOMAS PALMER'S QUICK AND EASY DEMI-GLACE

2 teaspoons olive oil
1 large onion, coarsely chopped
2 celery stalks, coarsely chopped
2 medium carrots, coarsely chopped
3 tablespoons tomato paste
½ cup red wine
2 bay leaves
½ teaspoon thyme, dried
½ teaspoon whole black peppercorns
2 tablespoons shallots, minced
3½ cups low-sodium beef broth

Heat the olive oil in a heavy skillet over high heat until just below the smoking point. Add the onion, celery, and carrots and caramelize by sautéing until evenly dark brown in color, being careful not to burn. Add the tomato paste, reduce the heat, and cook for 3 to 4 minutes, stirring frequently, being careful not to scorch. Add red wine, bay leaves, thyme, peppercorns, and shallots. Cook over low heat until reduced in volume by half.

Add beef broth, scraping the pan to incorporate all the juices. Cool over low heat until reduced to approximately 1 cup of liquid (approximately 10 to 15 minutes). Remove from heat, strain, and discard solids.

The demi-glace will keep refrigerated for 5 to 7 days or frozen for 3 months.

NUTRITIONAL NOTE Because this stock is skimmed of fat and contains no added salt, its nutritional significance is minimal.

YIELD *1 cup*

Chef Palmer has developed this quick and easy substitute for the classic brown sauce, the foundation for many of our dishes. It may be prepared in larger volume. If your finished sauce is not thick enough for your taste, you may add a little cornstarch to make it thicker.

CHEZ EDDY SOUBISE

Although a tra-ditional soubise utilizes onions, cooked rice, and crème fraîche, or whipping cream, together with a butter enrichment, our version omits all saturated fat, together with much of the cholesterol and calorie con-tent. In fact, since onions will cook in their own juices over low heat, no added fat is needed.

1 cup yellow onion, diced
1 bay leaf
1 tablespoon minced shallots
2 leeks, white part only, rinsed and diced
½ cup white long-grain rice
½ cup nonfat dry milk
1 quart chicken stock

Place the onion, bay leaf, shallot, and leeks in a heavy-bottomed saucepan or Dutch oven. Cook over low heat until translucent, stirring occasionally, about 5 to 7 minutes. Add the rice, dry milk, and stock, stirring to combine. Cook over low heat for 30 minutes until the rice and onions are tender. Remove the bay leaf, then transfer to a food processor or blender and process until smooth. Pour the mixture into a strainer or colander lined with several layers of dampened cheese-cloth. Using a rubber spatula, gently press the liquid through the strainer, discarding the solids left behind. The soubise should congeal when chilled. Although we do not recommend freezing soubise, it may be kept refrigerated for 3 to 4 days.

Y I E L D *4 cups*

SERVING 2 TBS.

Calories 18.0

Total fat 0

Cholesterol 0

Saturated fat 0.01 gm.

Protein 0.9 gm.

Carbohydrates 3.4 gm.

Sodium 10.0 mg.

BASIC TOMATO SAUCE

1 tablespoon olive oil
1 cup diced white onion
¼ cup carrots, peeled and finely chopped
¼ cup celery, finely chopped
2 garlic cloves, minced
3 cups ripe tomatoes, peeled, seeded, and chopped; packed
  firmly
1 tablespoon tomato paste
1 teaspoon fresh oregano, finely chopped
1 tablespoon fresh basil, finely chopped
½ teaspoon black pepper
1 cup red wine
1 tablespoon granulated sugar

In a heavy saucepan or skillet, heat the olive oil over medium heat. Add the onion and cook until translucent (3 to 5 minutes). Add the carrots, celery, and garlic and cook for 5 minutes, stirring occasionally. Add the tomatoes, tomato paste, seasonings, wine, and sugar, and cook over medium heat, stirring frequently, until the tomatoes are soft (approximately 10 to 15 minutes). Transfer to a blender or food processor and purée until smooth. This sauce may be refrigerated for 2 to 3 days or frozen in serving-size containers for approximately 3 months.

VARIATION Because this is a basic tomato sauce, the herbs used may be varied according to the taste you desire. Thus, you may substitute ¼ teaspoon of fresh thyme and ½ bay leaf instead of the basil. Or you may increase the oregano, either omitting the basil or not, as you prefer.

YIELD *4 cups*

This fundamental sauce has literally dozens of applications, depending on the herbs that are added to it. At Chez Eddy it is a component of other sauces, such as Horseradish-Gazpacho Sauce (page 70). And, of course, it forms the basis of many Italian dishes. For the richest flavor, use ripe tomatoes with a strong tomato aroma, and a top-quality tomato paste.

SERVING ½ C.

Calories 45.0
Total fat 1.9 gm.
Cholesterol 0
Saturated fat 0.26 gm.
Protein 1.0 gm.
Carbohydrates 6.9 gm.
Sodium 12.0 mg.

TOMATO CONCASSÉ

*M*any of our recipes call for tomato concassé, by which we mean ripe tomatoes, peeled, seeded, and chopped. The following is our method.

1 ripe tomato

Remove the stem of a tomato carefully so that you do not break into the seed pockets. Immerse the tomato in boiling water for 3 to 5 seconds; then immerse in ice bath. Remove peel. Cut the tomato in half horizontally. Taking one half of the tomato in your hand, gently squeeze the seeds into a bowl and discard. Repeat the process with the second half. Dice the seeded tomato pulp into ¼-inch pieces.

YIELD ¼ cup

SERVING 2 TBS.
Calories 9.0
Total fat 0.1 gm.
Cholesterol 0
Saturated fat 0.01 gm.
Protein 0.4 gm.
Carbohydrates 2.0 gm.
Sodium 4.0 mg.

FRESH TOMATO COULIS

1 cup tomato concassé (opposite page)
1 shallot, minced
1 teaspoon reduced-sodium soy sauce
1½ teaspoons fresh basil, finely chopped
1½ teaspoons fresh oregano, finely chopped
1½ teaspoons fresh tarragon, finely chopped
½ teaspoon fresh chervil, fincly chopped
½ teaspoon ground black pepper
⅛ teaspoon olive oil

Combine all the ingredients in a nonreactive bowl, cover tightly, and refrigerate. This will keep nicely in the refrigerator for 3 to 4 days.

YIELD *1 cup*

Some versions of tomato coulis call for cooking the ingredients. Ours, however, is more in the style of an uncooked tomato sauce.

SERVING 2 TBS.

Calories 7.0

Total fat 0.1 gm.

Cholesterol 0

Saturated fat 0.02 gm.

Protein 0.3 gm.

Carbohydrates 1.4 gm.

Sodium 19.0 mg.

CHEZ EDDY FROMAGE BLANC

This is a delight-ful substitute for sour cream on baked potatoes or in dips and dress-ings. Blended in equal parts with reduced-calorie mayonnaise, it makes a tasty low-fat sandwich spread.

½ cup low-fat cottage cheese
½ cup nonfat yogurt
1 teaspoon lime juice
1 teaspoon lemon juice
Pinch white pepper
2 teaspoons chopped chives
2 teaspoons chopped parsley
1 teaspoon scallions, green part only, finely chopped

Process the cottage cheese and yogurt in a blender at a medium speed, until smooth and creamy. Transfer to a small bowl and whisk in the lime and lemon juices. Fold in the pepper, herbs, and scallions. Cover and chill for at least 2 hours. Fromage blanc may be refrigerated for 5 days, but it is not suitable for freezing.

YIELD *1 cup*

SERVING 2 TBS.
Calories 21.0
Total fat 0.3 gm.
Cholesterol 1 mg.
Saturated fat 0.19 gm.
Protein 2.8 gm.
Carbohydrates 1.6 gm.
Sodium 68.0 mg.

CHAMPAGNE VINAIGRETTE

⅛ cup champagne vinegar
⅛ cup white wine
2 teaspoons Dijon mustard
1 tablespoon granulated sugar
⅛ cup corn or canola oil

Whisk together the vinegar, wine, mustard, and sugar in a small nonre-active bowl until the sugar is dissolved. Whisk in the oil to form a smooth emulsion. Store, tightly covered, in the refrigerator for up to 2 weeks. Whisk again, or blend, before using.

N O T E Sugar acts as a catalyst to blend the flavors of the ingredi-ents. The amount may be varied to suit individual tastes.

V A R I A T I O N For an herbal twist, add a little fresh tarragon, parsley, or basil. When you wish a more assertive dressing, vary the oil, vinegar, and herbs, according to the same proportions. Suggested variations might include sherry wine vinegar; tarragon vinegar and ca-pers; or raspberry vinegar and chives, if you omit the mustard.

Y I E L D *1 cup*

This basic light vinaigrette is one of Chez Eddy's most popular dressings. It is excellent to use when you don't want to overpower the flavor of the dominant ingredi-ent in a dish such as Crab Royal (page 96).

SERVING 1 TB.

Calories 48.0

Total Fat 4.6 gm.

Cholesterol 0

Saturated fat 0.58 gm.

Protein 0

Carbohydrates 1.3 gm.

Sodium 9 mg.

BASIC FRUIT SALSA

This generic recipe may be varied depending on your taste and seasonal availability. Some fruits that make interesting salsas include papayas, peaches, plums, nectarines, pineapple, and mango.

½ cup diced fruit
¼ cup crushed fruit
½ cup white wine
¼ cup rice wine vinegar
2 tablespoons red onion, finely chopped
1 pinch sugar
2 tablespoons fresh cilantro, finely chopped
1 teaspoon jalapeño, seeded and finely chopped (or to taste)

Combine all the ingredients. If there is time, let the salsa rest for 20 to 30 minutes to meld flavors.

YIELD *1½ cups*

SERVING ½ C.

Calories 11.0

Total fat 0.1 gm.

Cholesterol 0

Saturated fat 0.01 gm.

Protein 0.1 gm.

Carbohydrates 2.7 gm.

Sodium 0

CHEZ EDDY SPICE BLEND

2 tablespoons chili powder
1 tablespoon black pepper
¼ teaspoon white pepper
1 tablespoon onion powder
1 tablespoon garlic powder
2 tablespoons paprika
2 teaspoons ground cumin
1½ teaspoons fennel seed
1½ teaspoons mustard seed
⅛ teaspoon allspice
Optional: ¼ teaspoon edible dried lavender

Combine all ingredients in the container of a blender or food processor. Process until well mixed. Store in a small jar with a tight-fitting lid.

NUTRITIONAL NOTE This recipe adds virtually no calories, sodium, or fat to the food with which it is prepared.

YIELD *½ cup*

This special blend of spices was developed by Chef Palmer as a substitute for salt. Vary the blend of spices to create your favorite seasoning.

OTHER SAUCES

....

....

Chez Eddy Bordelaise Sauce

Sauce Dijonnaise

Lobster Sauce

Cucumber, Dill, and Crabmeat Sauce

Vincent Sauce

Green Peppercorn Sauce

Cilantro Pesto

Cranberries with Hot-Pepper Jelly

Cumberland Sauce

Horseradish-Gazpacho Sauce

Tomatillo Sauce

Roasted Red Pepper Sauce

Fresh Orange, Mint, and Tarragon Sauce

Orange-Basil Sauce

....

....

Tamarind Sauce

Brandy-Pecan Sauce

Lemon, Mustard, and Herb Marinade

Dry Southwestern Marinade

Zesty Buttermilk Dressing

Chef Denny's Garlic Dressing

Dill Sauce

Picante Vinaigrette

Tangy Grapefruit Vinaigrette

Pico de Gallo

Jicama-Ginger Salsa

Black Bean Salsa

Pineapple Salsa

Spicy Corn Relish

....

CHEZ EDDY BORDELAISE SAUCE

In order to control saturated fat and calories, Chez Eddy omits the bone marrow enrichment traditional to this French sauce. Because of the slowly simmered stock on which our demi-glace is based, however, none of the flavor one expects from a true sauce bordelaise is lost. The sauce is excellent with beef, lamb, venison, and duck.

1 cup demi-glace (pages 45–47)
½ cup dry red wine
2 tablespoons minced shallots
4 sprigs fresh parsley, leaves only, finely chopped
1 teaspoon whole black peppercorns, crushed
2 sprigs fresh thyme, leaves only, finely chopped
2 tablespoons fresh mushrooms, finely diced

Prepare the demi-glace ahead as directed. (See Basic Stocks and Sauces pages 45–47.)

Combine the wine, shallots, parsley, peppercorns, and thyme. Simmer in a small heavy-bottomed saucepan over low heat for 2 to 3 minutes or until reduced to ⅓ of its original volume.

Add the demi-glace and simmer until the sauce is thick enough to coat the back of a spoon. Strain the sauce and return it to the pan, adding the mushrooms. Cook for 2 minutes more or until the mushrooms are tender.

Chez Eddy Bordelaise Sauce may be prepared a day or two in advance and refrigerated; or you may freeze it in serving-size containers. For best results when using the sauce at a later date, add a pinch of finely chopped fresh thyme, then reheat.

YIELD *½ cup*

SERVING 2 TBS.

Calories 4.0
Total fat 0
Cholesterol 0
Saturated fat 0
Protein 0.2 gm.
Carbohydrates 1.0 gm.
Sodium 1.0 mg.

SAUCE DIJONNAISE

6 ounces soubise (page 48)
1 teaspoon fresh tarragon, finely chopped
2 teaspoons Dijon mustard
2 tablespoons white wine
1 tablespoon shallots, finely chopped
1 tablespoon tomato concassé (page 50)
Chicken stock or additional white wine, as needed for
    consistency
Pinch white pepper, to taste

Prepare the soubise ahead as directed. (See Basic Stocks and Sauces, page 48.)

Combine the soubise, tarragon, and mustard in a small bowl and set aside. Heat the white wine in a small, heavy-bottomed saucepan or skillet over medium heat. Add the shallots and cook until translucent, 1 to 2 minutes, stirring often. Add the tomato concassé and bring to a boil. Stir in the soubise mixture and return to a boil. Cook for 30 seconds, stirring constantly. If the sauce appears too thick, thin with heated chicken stock or white wine until the proper consistency is achieved. Remove from the heat, add white pepper, and keep warm until ready to serve.

YIELD *1 cup*

This creamy mustard sauce is our variation of the classic French sauce dijonnaise.

SERVING 2 TBS.
Calories 21.0
Total fat 0.1 gm.
Cholesterol 0
Saturated fat 0.02 gm.
Protein 1.0 gm.
Carbohydrates 3.9 gm.
Sodium 32 mg.

LOBSTER SAUCE

This is a basic sauce used in continental and French cuisine that we have adjusted for heart-healthy use—great over pasta, especially when combined with shrimp.

1½ cups Lobster Bisque (page 43)
4 tablespoons soubise (page 48)
¼ cup cognac

Prepare the Lobster Bisque and soubise ahead as directed. (See Basic Stocks and Sauces, pages 43 and 48.)

Combine the bisque and cognac in a small, heavy-bottomed saucepan. Over medium-high heat, boil gently until reduced to ⅔ its original volume. Reduce the heat, stir in the soubise, and simmer, stirring frequently for 2 to 3 minutes. The sauce should not be thick but should coat the back of a spoon.

YIELD *1½ cups*

SERVING ¼ C.

Calories 8.0

Total fat 0

Cholesterol 0

Saturated fat 0.01 gm.

Protein 0.3 gm.

Carbohydrates 1.5 gm.

Sodium 3.0 mg.

CUCUMBER, DILL, AND CRABMEAT SAUCE

1 teaspoon lemon juice
2 tablespoons nonfat yogurt
1 teaspoon fresh dill, finely chopped
2 tablespoons reduced-calorie mayonnaise
⅓ cup cucumber, peeled, seeded, and finely chopped
¾ cup jumbo lump crabmeat, picked over carefully
Pinch white pepper

In a small nonreactive bowl, whisk together the lemon juice, yogurt, dill, and mayonnaise. Fold in the cucumber and crabmeat and transfer the mixture into a small saucepan. Over medium heat, cook until bubbly, adding white pepper. Keep warm until ready to use. Leftover sauce may be refrigerated for 1 to 2 days.

YIELD *1 cup*

This recipe, which accompanies Sautéed Rainbow Trout (page 208), is also delightful, warm or cold, as a topping for poached salmon, grilled swordfish, or red snapper. In addition, it can be used as a dip or dressing.

SERVING 2 TBS.

Calories 14
Total fat 1.2 gm.
Cholesterol 2.0 mg.
Saturated fat 0.18 gm.
Protein 0.3 gm.
Carbohydrates 0.6 gm.
Sodium 25 mg.

VINCENT SAUCE

This is a spicy mayonnaise, adapted for heart-healthy use, which we like with Crab-and Wild-Rice-Stuffed Tomatoes (page 94). Try it, also, with trout or other low-fat fish or in chicken salad.

½ cup low-fat cottage cheese
½ cup nonfat yogurt
½ cup reduced-calorie mayonnaise
1 teaspoon reduced-sodium soy sauce
1 tablespoon lemon juice
2 tablespoons lime juice
1 tablespoon Dijon mustard
2 teaspoons tarragon vinegar
1 tablespoon fresh tarragon, finely chopped
1 teaspoon fresh parsley, finely chopped
½ teaspoon fresh chervil, finely chopped

In a food processor or blender, combine the cottage cheese, yogurt, and mayonnaise. Process until well mixed. Stir in the soy sauce, lemon and lime juices, mustard, and vinegar. Fold in the herbs. Cover and refrigerate overnight to allow the flavors to blend. Vincent Sauce will keep in the refrigerator for 3 to 5 days. Taste before serving. If needed, add an additional pinch of fresh chervil and tarragon.

YIELD *1¾ cups*

SERVING ½ TB.

Calories 10.0

Total fat 0.7 gm.

Cholesterol 1 mg.

Saturated fat 0.13 gm.

Protein 0.4 gm.

Carbohydrates 0.4 gm.

Sodium 28.0 mg.

GREEN PEPPERCORN SAUCE

½ cup nonfat yogurt
½ cup reduced-calorie mayonnaise
½ cup low-fat cottage cheese
2 tablespoons green peppercorns
1 tablespoon chopped parsley

Combine the yogurt, mayonnaise, and cottage cheese in a blender or food processor and process until smooth. Add the peppercorns and parsley and continue processing until well blended. Transfer the mixture to a container and refrigerate. Serve chilled. This sauce can keep in the refrigerator for 2 to 3 days.

Y I E L D ¾ cup

The Green Peppercorn Sauce, which dresses our Stuffed Chicken Breast (page 107), may also be used as a dip with crudités or as a spread on chicken or turkey sandwiches. Thinned with buttermilk, it makes a piquant salad dressing.

SERVING 2 TBS.

Calories 43.0

Total fat 3.2 gm.

Cholesterol 5 mg.

Saturated fat 0.59 gm.

Protein 1.9 gm.

Carbohydrates 1.5 gm.

Sodium 104.0 mg.

CILANTRO PESTO

This pesto relies on cilantro for its fresh green color and unique flavor. Although nuts such as walnuts, pecans, or pumpkin seeds may be substituted, pine nuts and pumpkin seeds are lowest in fat. Pesto may be served, of course, with pasta (see Shrimp and Pesto over Pasta, page 227), but it is also excellent in soups or, when combined with soubise, as a sauce for grilled tuna or swordfish.

½ cup pine nuts
2 cloves garlic, minced
1 tablespoon olive oil
4 cups cilantro leaves, loosely packed
2 tablespoons lime juice
¼ cup grated Parmesan cheese

Add the pine nuts and garlic to the container of a food processor and process until chunky. With the motor running, slowly add the olive oil. Turn the motor off and add the cilantro, lime juice, and Parmesan. Process again until blended. Transfer to a bowl, cover, and refrigerate until ready to use. Pesto will keep in the refrigerator for approximately 5 days in an airtight container or it may be frozen in serving-size containers for approximately 1 to 2 months.

YIELD ¾ cup

SERVING 2 TBS.

Calories 69.0

Total fat 6.6 gm.

Cholesterol 3 mg.

Saturated fat 1.46 gm.

Protein 3.0 gm.

Carbohydrates 1.1 gm.

Sodium 62.0 mg.

SPICY CORN RELISH

1 Poblano pepper, roasted, peeled, and diced (see Note below)
2 ears fresh corn, shucked and the silk removed
1 tablespoon olive oil
4 tablespoons chopped red onion
2 tablespoons red bell pepper, diced
2 tomatillos, husked, rinsed, and diced
2 teaspoons cider vinegar
Pinch white pepper

Prepare the pepper ahead as directed. Cut the kernels from the ears of corn carefully so they remain whole. Place in a bowl. Heat the olive oil in a nonstick skillet over medium heat. When hot, add the corn kernels and sauté for 2 minutes, stirring frequently. Add the red onion, poblano and bell peppers, tomatillos, vinegar, and pinch of white pepper. Cook for 1 additional minute, stirring, then remove from the heat and set aside.

N O T E To roast the pepper, place it on a broiler pan and broil approximately 6 inches from the heat until blackened on all sides. Remove from heat and place in a plastic bag. Let it rest for 10 minutes. Remove the pepper from the bag, drain and peel off the skin. Make a slit in the pepper and open. Remove the core and cut off the stem. Scrape away the seeds and ribs.

Y I E L D *1 cup*

This relish is especially good with our Chicken Montero (page 161).

SERVING ¼ C.

Calories 70.0

Total fat 3.8 gm.

Cholesterol 0

Saturated fat 0.57 gm.

Protein 12.0 gm.

Carbohydrates 9.4 gm.

Sodium 6.0 mg.

CRANBERRIES WITH HOT-PEPPER JELLY

This assertive cranberry sauce is a good accompaniment for fowl or pork. With its deep red color, it is particularly suitable for holiday menus. Jalapeño pepper jelly is available in most gourmet and specialty food markets.

½ cup granulated sugar
¼ cup cold water
1 package (12 ounces) fresh cranberries (frozen may be substituted, but they should be thawed before use)
½ cup jalapeño jelly

Place the sugar and water in a medium saucepan and stir constantly over medium heat until the sugar dissolves. Add the cranberries and cook, stirring occasionally, until the cranberries pop and the syrup begins to thicken, about 5 minutes. Let cool slightly. Add the jalapeño jelly and stir until completely blended. Let cool completely, then cover and refrigerate. This sauce may be stored in the refrigerator for as long as 1 week. When ready to use, transfer the cranberries to a serving dish and serve chilled.

YIELD *3 cups*

SERVING 1 TB.

Calories 20.0

Total fat 0

Cholesterol 0

Saturated fat 0

Protein 0

Carbohydrates 5.2 gm.

Sodium 1.0 mg.

CUMBERLAND SAUCE

2 teaspoons English (dry) mustard
2 teaspoons cold water
1 teaspoon lemon zest, sliced in ½-inch-long juliennes
1 teaspoon orange zest, sliced in ½-inch-long juliennes
1 tablespoon fresh orange juice
1 tablespoon fresh lemon juice
¼ cup port wine
Pinch ginger, freshly grated
Pinch ground red pepper
1 cup red currant jelly

Stir the English mustard into the water and let soak for 10 to 15 minutes. Blanch the julienned lemon and orange zests by immersing them in boiling water for 2 minutes. Then drain. (Make sure you don't skip this step; if you do, the sauce will be cloudy.)

In a small saucepan, combine the zests with the rehydrated mustard, the orange and lemon juices, the port, ginger, and red pepper. Simmer over low heat for 2 minutes. Stir in the red currant jelly and continue to simmer for 3 additional minutes, until the mixture reaches the consistency of a sauce. It will have been reduced to about 1 cup at this point.

YIELD *1 cup*

This slightly translucent, crimson sauce is a visual delight, while its subdued sweetness, sharpened with citrus, perfectly complements the delicate flavor of quail, pork (such as our Roasted Pork Tenderloin, page 255), and turkey. If it is to be served with sautéed meats, you may use it to deglaze the sauté pan, once the meat has been removed.

SERVING 1 TB.

Calories 51.0

Total fat 0

Cholesterol 0

Saturated fat 0.01 gm.

Protein 0

Carbohydrates 13.2 gm.

Sodium 3.0 mg.

HORSERADISH-GAZPACHO SAUCE

An excellent spicy red sauce for seafood cocktails.

½ cup Basic Tomato Sauce (page 49)
1 tablespoon minced garlic
3 tablespoons diced red onion
4 tablespoons green bell pepper, seeded, and chopped finely
¾ cup cucumber, peeled, seeded, and chopped finely
Fresh grated horseradish to taste (sauce should be spicy)
1 tablespoon sherry wine vinegar
1 tablespoon lemon juice
4 teaspoons olive oil
Pinch ground cumin
½ cup tomato concassé (page 50), preferably made from Roma
  tomatoes

Prepare the tomato sauce ahead as directed.

Combine the tomato sauce with the garlic and onion. Reserve 1 teaspoon each of the green pepper and cucumber. Place the tomato sauce, the remaining green pepper and cucumber, the horseradish, vinegar, lemon juice, olive oil, and cumin in the container of a food processor or blender. Process until blended. Transfer to a container, stir in the reserved cucumber, green pepper, and the tomato concassé, and refrigerate for 20 to 30 minutes to allow flavors to meld.

N O T E Take care not to select horseradish prepared with cream or oil.

Y I E L D *2 cups*

SERVING 2 TBS.

Calories 14.0

Total fat 1.3 gm.

Cholesterol 0

Saturated fat 0.18 gm.

Protein 0.2 gm.

Carbohydrates 1.4 gm.

Sodium 3.0 mg.

TOMATILLO SAUCE

1 cup chicken stock (page 41)
3 fresh Poblano or Anaheim chilies, roasted (follow directions for
  roasting peppers, page 67)
6 fresh tomatillos
¼ cup white onion, diced
½ cup fresh cilantro, whole leaves

Prepare the chicken stock and chilies ahead as directed.

Remove the papery skins from the tomatillos, core them, and cut them in half. In a small saucepan, heat the chicken stock over medium heat until it boils. Add the tomatillos to the chicken stock and return to a boil. Reduce the heat and simmer until tender, about 10 minutes. Remove the tomatillos from the chicken stock and place in a small bowl. Reserve the stock. Place the onion and cilantro in the container of a food processor or blender and process until finely minced. Add the chilies and process again; then add the tomatillos and process until puréed. (If you prefer a chunkier condiment, you may chop the ingredients by hand.) Add the chicken stock to the purée in small amounts, as necessary, until it achieves the consistency of a sauce. The sauce should be smooth and thin enough to film a plate when the plate is rotated.

V A R I A T I O N To make a spicy soup base, thin with several cups of chicken broth. Then you may add zucchini or other bland vegetables and simmer until tender. Serve tomatillo soup with a dash of freshly grated Parmesan cheese.

N O T E When purchasing, select firm, green tomatillos. They may be stored in the crisper of your refrigerator for as long as 2 weeks.

Y I E L D *1¼ cups*

SERVING 2 TBS.
Calories 14.0
Total fat 0.1 gm.
Cholesterol 0
Saturated fat 0.02 gm.
Protein 0.7 gm.
Carbohydrates 3.2 gm.
Sodium 6.0 mg.

ROASTED RED PEPPER SAUCE

*T*his flavorful
sauce is good with
tuna, swordfish, or
poultry.

¼ cup soubise (page 48)
1 cup chicken stock (page 41)
3 roasted red bell peppers (page 67)
4 banana peppers, seeded and chopped
½ medium onion, chopped

Prepare the soubise and chicken stock ahead as directed. (See Basic
Stocks and Sauces, pages 48 and 41.)

Place all the ingredients in a small saucepan over medium heat.
Bring to a boil, reduce the heat, and simmer until the peppers are tender, about 5 to 7 minutes. Transfer to the container of a food processor
or blender and process until smooth.

Y I E L D   *1 cup*

SERVING 2 TBS.

Calories 26.0

Total fat 0.3 gm.

Cholesterol 0

Saturated fat 0.05 gm.

Protein 1.0 gm.

Carbohydrates 5.3 gm.

Sodium 7.0 mg.

FRESH ORANGE, MINT, AND TARRAGON SAUCE

½ cup soubise (page 48)
1 cup fresh orange juice
1 tablespoon white wine
1 teaspoon fresh tarragon, finely chopped
1 teaspoon fresh mint, finely chopped

Prepare the soubise ahead as directed. (See Basic Stocks and Sauces, page 48.)

Pour the orange juice and wine into a small, heavy-bottomed, nonreactive saucepan. Add the herbs and cook over high heat until reduced to ½ cup. Whisk in the soubise. Cook for 1 minute, stirring constantly, until the sauce is thoroughly heated.

YIELD *1 cup*

This is a basic orange-herb sauce that complements either fish or poultry. To vary its effect, you may substitute other fresh herbs such as basil, cilantro, thyme, or rosemary. To achieve a slightly fuller taste, you might add 1 tablespoon of tomato concassé (page 50) before whisking in the soubise.

SERVING 2 TBS.

Calories 22.0

Total fat 0

Cholesterol 0

Saturated fat 0

Protein 0.6 gm.

Carbohydrates 5.0 gm.

Sodium 6.0 mg.

ORANGE-BASIL SAUCE

This sauce is delicious with cold poached chicken and mild fish such as Broiled Wahoo (page 213).

2 tablespoons soubise (page 48)
¼ cup white wine
½ tablespoon fresh basil, finely chopped (use opal basil, if available)
½ cup orange juice
1 tablespoon reduced-calorie mayonnaise
1 tablespoon nonfat yogurt

Prepare the soubise ahead as directed. (See Basic Stocks and Sauces, page 48.)

Combine the white wine and basil in a small saucepan and simmer over medium heat until reduced by half. Add the orange juice and reduce by half again. Stir in the soubise and heat thoroughly. In a small bowl, whisk together the mayonnaise and yogurt and stir into the sauce. Heat through, then remove and keep warm until needed.

YIELD *1 cup*

SERVING 2 TBS.
Calories 31.5
Total fat 1.18 gm.
Cholesterol 0
Saturated fat 0.1 gm.
Protein 0.65 gm.
Carbohydrates 5.45 gm.
Sodium 27.5 mg.

TAMARIND SAUCE

¼ cup tamarind pulp
¼ cup marsala wine
1 cup demi-glace (pages 45–47)
1 clove garlic, minced

Prepare the demi-glace ahead as directed. See Basic Stocks and Sauces, pages 45–47.) Combine all the ingredients in a small saucepan and bring to a simmer. Continue to cook over medium-low heat until the tamarind flesh is thoroughly dissolved into the sauce, about 10 to 12 minutes. Let cool slightly. Purée in a blender or food processor and strain. Serve the warm sauce with game.

N O T E Tamarind pods may be kept in the refrigerator for 2 to 3 weeks; or the pulp may be frozen for 2 to 3 months.

Y I E L D ½ cup

Fresh tamarinds may be found in ethnic and other specialty markets. They resemble long bean pods, with a crackly exterior that should be removed. Inside are beans, which should also be removed, leaving a dark brown, sticky flesh very similar in texture to the interior of a date. The flavor suggests a sour prune. The sauce is delicious with game of all kinds or poultry.

SERVING 2 TBS.

Calories 41.0

Total fat 0.1 gm.

Cholesterol 0

Saturated fat 0.03 gm.

Protein 2.5 gm.

Carbohydrates 7.6 gm.

Sodium 1.0 mg.

BRANDY-PECAN SAUCE

Although delicious with quail, as presented (page 260), this sauce may also be used with chicken or red snapper. If you choose not to deglaze, just add all ingredients to a saucepan and simmer, as directed.

¾ cup demi-glace (page 45–47)
2 tablespoons soubise (page 48)
2 tablespoons chopped pecans
¼ cup cognac (brandy)
1 teaspoon honey

Prepare the demi-glace and soubise ahead as directed. (See Basic Stocks and Sauces, pages 45–48.)

To the pan in which you have sautéed the meat, add pecans and deglaze with cognac, cooking for 1 minute. Stir in the honey, demi-glace, and soubise, and continue to cook, stirring, until it thickens to the consistency of a sauce. Keep warm.

YIELD *1 cup*

SERVING 2 TBS.

Calories 30.0

Total fat 2.2 gm.

Cholesterol 0

Saturated fat 0.18 gm.

Protein 0.5 gm.

Carbohydrates 2.9 gm.

Sodium 2.8 mg.

LEMON, MUSTARD, AND HERB MARINADE

½ cup lemon juice
Zest of 1 lemon, finely chopped
¼ cup Dijon mustard
1 teaspoon fresh thyme, finely chopped
1 teaspoon fresh basil, finely chopped
1 teaspoon fresh rosemary, finely chopped
1 teaspoon fresh oregano, finely chopped
1 teaspoon finely chopped parsley

Combine all the ingredients in a nonreactive bowl and mix by hand with a whisk. Arrange the portions of meat to be marinated in a nonreactive container and add the marinade to cover as much of the meat as possible. Marinate for at least 1 hour. The marinade may also be brushed over the meat as it cooks. This preparation, if covered, will keep in the refrigerator for several days.

NUTRITIONAL NOTE Since this recipe is a marinade, it adds virtually no calories, sodium, or fat to the food with which it is prepared. (Serving 2 Tbs.)

YIELD *1 cup, approximately*

This is a tangy marinade for chicken or lamb. For a more intense flavor, marinate meats overnight. When making larger amounts, the marinade may be prepared in a food processor or blender.

DRY SOUTHWESTERN MARINADE

Dry marinade is another term for spice rub. This one is delicious for grilled or baked chicken, fish, and shrimp. With the addition of ¼ cup of nonfat yogurt, it may be used as a moist marinade for tandoori-style dishes.

1 hot green chili (jalapeño or serrano), seeded and minced
1 clove garlic, minced
1 teaspoon ground cumin
¼ teaspoon chili powder
Pinch ground red pepper
1 tablespoon fresh lime juice

Combine all the ingredients in a nonreactive bowl. Thoroughly rub mixture into the flesh of the meat or seafood. Cover and refrigerate for 2 to 3 hours.

N U T R I T I O N A L   N O T E This recipe adds virtually no calories, sodium, or fat to the food with which it is prepared. (Serving: 2 Tbs.)

Y I E L D *2 tablespoons*

ZESTY BUTTERMILK DRESSING

⅔ cup nonfat yogurt
⅔ cup low-fat buttermilk, strained to remove flakes of butterfat
1 tablespoon fresh parsley, chopped
1 small clove garlic, finely minced
½ teaspoon fresh oregano, chopped
½ teaspoon fresh basil, chopped
2 tablespoons reduced-calorie mayonnaise

Add the yogurt and buttermilk to the container of a blender or food processor and process. Add the remaining ingredients and process again. Refrigerate for at least 1 hour before use.

Y I E L D *2 cups*

SERVING 2 TBS.
Calories 14.0
Total fat 0.6 gm.
Cholesterol 2.0 mg.
Saturated fat 0.12 gm.
Protein 0.8 gm.
Carbohydrates 1.2 gm.
Sodium 24.0 mg.

CHEF DENNY'S GARLIC DRESSING

Assertive with garlic and fresh herbs, this is the dressing we like for Caesar salad. It may be prepared partially in a blender, if you prefer, but the herbs should be incorporated by hand. The dressing is even better if prepared a day ahead.

1 tablespoon Dijon mustard
1 tablespoon reduced-sodium soy sauce
½ teaspoon ground black pepper
2 tablespoons white wine
2 tablespoons red wine vinegar
1 tablespoon lime juice
1 tablespoon olive oil
1 tablespoon corn or canola oil
Pinch fresh chives, finely minced
Pinch fresh chervil, finely chopped
Pinch fresh parsley, finely chopped
Pinch fresh basil, finely chopped
Pinch fresh tarragon, finely chopped
2 cloves garlic, finely minced

Whisk together the mustard, soy sauce, pepper, white wine, vinegar, and lime juice in a nonreactive bowl. Add the oils gradually, stirring constantly with a whisk until the liquid has emulsified. Fold the herbs gently into the dressing. Allow the herbs to steep in the dressing for at least 2 hours before serving. If preparing in advance, cover and store in the refrigerator. When ready to use, bring to room temperature, then shake or stir to serve.

Y I E L D *¾ cup*

SERVING 1 TB.

Calories 24.0

Total fat 2.3 gm.

Cholesterol 0

Saturated fat 0.30 gm.

Protein 0.1 gm.

Carbohydrates 0.5 gm.

Sodium 52.0 mg.

DILL SAUCE

¼ cup reduced-calorie mayonnaise
½ cup nonfat yogurt
¼ cup fresh dill, finely chopped; or 1 tablespoon dried dill
1 tablespoon lemon juice

Whisk all the ingredients together in a small bowl. Chill well before serving. This dressing may be refrigerated for 4 to 5 days.

YIELD *1 cup*

Excellent with our Salmon Crab-cakes (page 104).

SERVING 2 TBS.

Calories 33.0

Total fat 2.4 gm.

Cholesterol 4.0 mg.

Saturated fat 0.44 gm.

Protein 1.4 gm.

Carbohydrates 1.3 gm.

Sodium 78.0 mg.

PICANTE VINAIGRETTE

This spicy dressing may be used as a condiment for beef or fish, or as an accompaniment to chicken fajitas. When used for marinating crudités, it produces crisp vegetables with a gentle bite.

2 tablespoons Tomatillo Sauce (page 71), cooled
2 teaspoons cider vinegar
2 teaspoons fresh cilantro, finely chopped
1 tablespoon lemon juice
1 tablespoon lime juice
1 tablespoon white wine
2 tablespoons canola or corn oil

Prepare the Tomatillo Sauce ahead as directed.

Whisk one tablespoon of the Tomatillo Sauce into the vinegar. Add the cilantro, citrus juices, and wine. Whisk in the oil until an emulsion is formed. Season to taste with a little more Tomatillo Sauce, as desired. Chill and serve.

YIELD *½ cup*

SERVING 1 TB.

Calories 34.0

Total fat 3.4 gm.

Cholesterol 0

Saturated fat 0.44 gm.

Protein 0.1 gm.

Carbohydrates 0.8 gm.

Sodium 1.0 mg.

TANGY GRAPEFRUIT VINAIGRETTE

½ cup fresh grapefruit juice
½ cup champagne vinegar
¼ cup cold water
1 small clove garlic, finely minced
1 teaspoon fresh basil, finely chopped
½ teaspoon fresh thyme, finely chopped
½ teaspoon black pepper
½ teaspoon fresh parsley, finely chopped

Whisk together the grapefruit juice, vinegar, and water in a small non-reactive bowl. Add the garlic, basil, thyme, pepper, and parsley. Mix well and chill until ready to use. It will keep nicely in the refrigerator for several days.

Y I E L D *1 cup*

This tangy dressing has no fat calories. It provides a tart counterpoint to salads composed of bland ingredients like spinach and mushrooms, and, when used with those components, may be garnished with grapefruit sections and walnuts. It also brightens green salads incorporating seafood, as well as making an excellent marinade for fish.

SERVING 1 TB.
Calories 4.0
Total fat 0
Cholesterol 0
Saturated fat 0
Protein 0
Carbohydrates 1.1 gm.
Sodium 0

PICO DE GALLO

This sprightly flavored condiment, basic to Southwestern cooking, is one of the most versatile we know. Try it on fish, meat, or as an addition to seafood salads. We like it with Planked Salmon (page 205), Chicken Fajitas (page 168), and Crab Picante (page 157).

1 cup Roma tomatoes, peeled, seeded, and diced
2 tablespoons red onion, finely chopped
1 tablespoon jalapeño pepper, seeded, ribs removed, and minced
2 tablespoons fresh cilantro, finely chopped

Combine all of the above ingredients in a small nonreactive bowl. Cover and refrigerate. Pico de Gallo will keep in the refrigerator for 3 to 5 days.

YIELD *1¼ cups*

SERVING 2 TBS.

Calories 5.0

Total fat 0

Cholesterol 0

Saturated fat 0.01 gm.

Protein 0.2 gm.

Carbohydrates 1.1 gm.

Sodium 2.0 mg.

JICAMA-GINGER SALSA

1 cup tomato concassé (page 50)
2 teaspoons fresh ginger, finely minced
1 tablespoon scallions, finely chopped
2 tablespoons jalapeño pepper, seeded, ribs removed, and finely minced
1 tablespoon fresh cilantro, finely chopped
2 tablespoons fresh lemon juice
1 tablespoon chopped jicama

Combine the tomato concassé, ginger, scallions, jalapeño, cilantro, lemon juice, and jicama in a nonreactive bowl. Refrigerate for 1 hour. Serve chilled or at room temperature.

YIELD *1 cup*

We like Jicama-Ginger Salsa with mild fish, such as Red Snapper (page 212), trout, salmon, grouper, and catfish.

SERVING 2 TBS.

Calories 13.8

Total fat 0

Cholesterol 0

Saturated fat 0.01 gm.

Protein 0.57 gm.

Carbohydrates 1.9 gm.

Sodium 0.01 mg.

BLACK BEAN SALSA

Black Bean Salsa makes an excellent topping for salads, as well as the Grilled Redfish (page 200) or it may be substituted for Pico de Gallo. It also may be served as a side dish or as one component of a vegetarian plate.

1 cup black beans, cooked according to package directions
⅓ cup tomato concassé (page 50)
⅔ cup white onion, finely diced
¼ teaspoon jalapeño pepper, seeded and diced
4 teaspoons red wine vinegar
2 tablespoons cilantro leaves, chopped
3 tablespoons red bell pepper, diced

Simmer the beans until tender, about 1½ hours. Combine the concassé, onion, jalapeño pepper, vinegar, cilantro, and red bell pepper in a small nonreactive bowl. Add the black beans and toss lightly. Cover and refrigerate until ready to serve.

Y I E L D *2 cups*

SERVING 2 TBS.

Calories 25.0

Total fat 0.1 gm.

Cholesterol 0

Saturated fat 0.03 gm.

Protein 1.5 gm.

Carbohydrates 4.7 gm.

Sodium 1.0 mg.

PINEAPPLE SALSA

¼ cup rice wine vinegar
½ cup white wine
½ cup fresh pineapple, diced
¼ cup fresh pineapple, crushed
2 tablespoons red onion, diced
1 pinch sugar
2 tablespoons fresh cilantro, finely chopped

Bring the vinegar and white wine to a boil in a medium-size, heavy-bottomed saucepan. Reduce the heat and simmer until reduced to one-half its original volume. Stir in all the pineapple, the onion, and the sugar. Simmer until the pineapple and onion are tender, approximately 5 to 7 minutes. Remove from the heat, transfer to a small bowl, and chill. Shortly before serving, stir in the cilantro.

YIELD *1½ cups*

*I*n addition to a topping for Broiled Swordfish (page 203), this salsa is also excellent with fresh tuna.

SERVING 2 TBS.

Calories 6.0

Total fat 0

Cholesterol 0

Saturated fat 0

Protein 0.1 gm.

Carbohydrates 1.7 gm.

Sodium 0

APPETIZERS

....

EVERY MEAL AT CHEZ EDDY begins with a platter of freshly prepared crudités. For some patrons these crisp vegetables, accompanied by our Guacamole Dip (page 102), will be appetizer enough. For others, however, the knowledge that our food is low in calories entices them to try such regionally inspired delicacies as Beggar's Purses with Ancho Chili Sauce (page 91) or Campechana de Marisco (page 97).

Many of the following recipes feature crabmeat. That's because our location near the Gulf of Mexico allows us access to what we consider the finest variety there is: the Gulf Coast Blue Crab, sweet and plump and succulent. Used sparingly, it's the ingredient that makes Crab Pancakes with Jicama-Ginger Salsa (page 95) so luxurious. Mounded generously on a bed of lettuce, bound with a delicate champagne vinaigrette, it becomes Crab Royal (page 96), one of our most popular appetizers.

You may also enjoy a number of these dishes as satisfying main courses, combined with a soup or second appetizer, perhaps, and one of our tempting, guilt-free desserts. Vitello Tonnato (page 100), for example, can herald a special alfresco luncheon, accompanied by a sharply accented Radicchio, Arugula, and Fresh Corn Salad (page 113). Similarly, Salmon Crabcakes (page 104) are delicious following a salad such as one of the several included in this chapter.

If, however, you prefer to compose a meal according to the traditional three-course sequence of appetizer, main course, and dessert, the nutritional analysis accompanying each recipe provides the information you will need to keep within the limits of your particular eating plan.

....

Beggars' Purses with Ancho Chili Sauce

Crab- and Wild-Rice-Stuffed Tomatoes with Vincent Sauce

Crab Pancakes with Jicama-Ginger Salsa

Crab Royal

Campechana de Marisco

Sesame Chicken Fingers LeBlanc with Two Dipping Sauces

Vitello Tonnato

Crudités with Three Dips

Salmon Crabcakes with Dill Sauce

Chez Eddy Hummus

Stuffed Chicken Breast with Green Peppercorn Sauce

Waldorf-Squash Salad

Watercress, Fennel, and Roasted Red Pepper Salad

Lettuce, Jicama, and Orange Salad with Lime Dressing

Chez Eddy House Salad with Almond-Herb Dressing

Radicchio, Arugula, and Fresh Corn Salad

Mixed Field Lettuces with Raspberry Walnut Vinaigrette

Spinach and Mushroom Salad with Zesty Buttermilk Dressing

....

BEGGARS' PURSES WITH ANCHO CHILI SAUCE

CORN CREPES

1 cup nonfat milk
¾ cup all-purpose flour
½ cup water
¼ cup masa harina
2 tablespoons yellow cornmeal
2 teaspoons olive oil
1 tablespoon fresh oregano leaves, finely chopped
¼ cup egg substitute
Nonstick spray

Prepare the crepes as follows: In a food processor or blender, process all the crepe ingredients except for the nonstick spray until smooth. Allow the batter to stand at room temperature for 1 hour, until slightly thickened. The batter should be the consistency of heavy cream. If it is too thick, thin with additional water. Spray a 5-inch crepe pan or skillet with nonstick spray. Heat over medium heat until very hot. Ladle approximately ¼ cup of the batter into the pan and swirl to cover the bottom of the pan. Cook the crepe for about 1 minute, until light brown underneath, then turn. Cook the second side for about 20 seconds. Transfer the crepe to a dish. Repeat the procedure with the remaining batter. Place waxed paper between each crepe while stacking to prevent them from sticking to each other. (Crepes can be prepared up to 2 days ahead, wrapped, and refrigerated. They also freeze well.)

While crepe batter is resting, or after crepes are ready, prepare the Ancho Chili Sauce as directed below.

Y I E L D *20 crepes*

This smashing appetizer is a great do-ahead recipe, perfect for entertaining. The sauce is our version of Santa Fe's famous "red chile." Masa harina, or corn flour, is available in ethnic food markets and in mainstream markets where there is a Hispanic population.

SERVING 1 CREPE
Calories 29.0
Total fat 0.6 gm.
Cholesterol 0
Saturated fat 0.09 gm.
Protein 1.0 gm.
Carbohydrates 4.8 gm.
Sodium 6.0 mg.

ANCHO CHILI SAUCE

2 cups chicken stock (page 41)
8 ancho chilies, enough for a generous ½ cup chili powder
  (see Note below)
2 teaspoons olive or canola oil
3 large cloves garlic, finely diced or crushed
1 tablespoon fresh oregano, finely chopped, or 1 teaspoon dried
1 teaspoon ground cumin
1 teaspoon reduced-sodium soy sauce (optional)
2 teaspoons cornstarch
1 tablespoon cold water

Prepare the chicken stock ahead as directed.

Preheat the oven to 375°F.

Seed the chilies; then grind them in a blender or other grinder until they have been reduced to a relatively fine powder. Take care when handling chilies. Wash hands immediately after and be sure the lid of the blender or grinder is on, so the fumes and fine chili dust will be contained while grinding. (It takes approximately 1 ancho chili to make 1 tablespoon of powder.) Sometimes the chilies will not have been dried to the point where they dissolve into a powder. In that case, just grind them as finely as possible.

Heat the olive oil in a medium saucepan and add the chili powder, stirring constantly. Cook for one minute. Gradually stir in the chicken stock, taking care that no lumps form. Add the garlic, oregano, cumin, and optional soy sauce. Simmer the sauce for 15 minutes, stirring occasionally. At this point, if the sauce is not thick enough to coat the back of a spoon, dissolve the cornstarch in the water and stir it into the sauce. Bring the sauce back to a simmer over low heat, stirring until slightly thickened. It may be prepared up to 1 day ahead, then cooled and refrigerated. Reheat slowly when ready to use.

NOTE Do not substitute American chili powder, which contains other ingredients in addition to the chilies. There are pure ancho chili powders on the market, however, and these may be used.

VARIATION Orange Ancho Chili Sauce: To 1 cup of Ancho Chili Sauce, add ½ cup sweet (not bitter) orange marmalade and ½ cup orange juice. Bring to a simmer over low heat and cook for 10 minutes.

SERVING ¼ C.

Calories 10.0

Total fat 1.1 gm.

Cholesterol 0

Saturated fat 0.14 gm.

Protein 0

Carbohydrates 0.1 gm.

Sodium 20.0 mg.

This sauce may be reduced by half and used as a glaze for chicken or fish, or even duck breast.

Y I E L D *2 cups of sauce*

FILLING

1 large red bell pepper, roasted (page 67)
1 large yellow bell pepper, roasted (page 67)
1 pound grilled chicken breast, cut into ½-inch cubes
8 large fresh chives
Ancho Chili Sauce (opposite page)

Prepare both peppers and the sauce ahead as directed.

When ready to assemble the purses, cut the roasted peppers into thin julienne strips. Combine with the chopped chicken and set aside. Blanch the chives in boiling water for 10 seconds. Rinse under cold water, drain, and pat dry. Place the 12 crepes, spotted sides up, on the work surface and divide the filling among them. Bring up the sides of each crepe to the center, pleating them to enclose the filling. The filled crepes will resemble drawstring purses. Secure the tops of the purses with toothpicks. Tie each with a chive. (If that proves unwieldy, you may cut the green part of a leek into thin strips and use them to tie the purses.)

The purses can be prepared up to 4 hours ahead and refrigerated. Remove from the refrigerator 1 hour before baking. Place the purses in a sprayed nonstick baking pan and cover with foil. Bake in a preheated 350°F oven for 5 minutes to warm. Remove the toothpicks. Heat the Ancho Chili Sauce and divide among 8 plates. Place one purse in the center of each plate and serve immediately.

Y I E L D *20 purses*

SERVING 1 CREPE,
½ OZ. FILLING, AND
¼ C. SAUCE
Calories 54.0
Total fat 1.3 gm.
Cholesterol 12.0 mg.
Saturated fat 0.11 gm.
Protein 5.4 gm.
Carbohydrates 6.1 gm.
Sodium 16.0 mg.

CRAB- AND WILD-RICE-STUFFED TOMATOES WITH VINCENT SAUCE

The ingredients of this versatile cold dish may be prepared a day in advance and assembled when ready to serve. If you prefer, you may substitute cooked shrimp for the crab or omit both for a vegetarian side dish.

4 tablespoons Vincent Sauce (page 64)
4 medium ripe tomatoes, peeled
2 cups wild rice, cooked according to package instructions
12 ounces jumbo lump crabmeat, picked over carefully
½ cup celery, finely chopped
½ cup white onion, diced
½ cup green bell pepper, finely chopped
Garnish: fresh orange slices, raspberries

Prepare the Vincent Sauce as directed.

Cut the tomatoes in half; scoop out the pulp and seeds and discard. If desired, you may carve the edge of each tomato half in a zigzag pattern for a more decorative look. In a medium-size bowl, combine the cooked rice, crabmeat, celery, onion, and bell pepper. Moisten with the Vincent Sauce. Divide the crab mixture evenly among the tomato halves, pressing lightly into the cavities. Serve on a bed of lettuce, garnished with the orange slices and raspberries.

Y I E L D *8 stuffed tomato halves*

SERVING 1 TOMATO HALF WITH ½ TB. SAUCE

Calories 120.5

Total fat 1.7 gm.

Cholesterol 43.5 mg.

Saturated fat 0.26 gm.

Protein 11.78 gm.

Carbohydrates 15.1 gm.

Sodium 160.5 mg.

CRAB PANCAKES WITH JICAMA-GINGER SALSA

Jicama-Ginger Salsa (page 85)
1 cup all-purpose flour
1 tablespoon scallions, finely chopped
1 teaspoon fresh ginger, minced very finely
1 cup skim milk
½ cup egg substitute
2 tablespoons lemon juice
2 teaspoons canola or corn oil
2 cups jumbo lump crabmeat, picked over carefully
Garnish: lemon slices, scallion flowers (page 189)

Prepare the salsa as directed. While the salsa is chilling, combine the flour, scallions, and ginger in a medium bowl. Make a well in the center of the mixture. In a smaller bowl, mix together the milk, egg substitute, lemon juice, and oil, beating lightly with a fork. Pour this mixture into the well in the flour mixture and stir until smooth. Fold in the crabmeat. Preheat a nonstick skillet or griddle until a drop of water sizzles when dropped on the hot cooking surface. Ladle ¼ cup of the batter onto the surface of the skillet or griddle and cook until the edges are dry and the pancake is lightly browned. Turn and brown the other side. Repeat with the remaining batter. Serve immediately or keep warm in the oven.

To serve, arrange 4 pancakes on each plate so they overlap and form a crescent. Place the salsa in the center of the crescent, which should also be the center of the plate. Garnish with scallion flowers.

V A R I A T I O N For a different kind of spicy effect, you might try Horseradish-Gazpacho Sauce (page 70). Or, for a cool alternative, Cucumber Yogurt Dip (page 103) is a refreshing choice.

Y I E L D *24 pancakes, 3 inches in diameter*

The use of two types of heat deepens the flavor of this sauce. Ginger provides a sweeter, less fiery sensation than jalapeño, and the combination creates a lively counterpoint to the mellow crabmeat.

SERVING 4
PANCAKES WITH
2 TBS. SALSA

Calories 159.5

Total fat 3.1 gm.

Cholesterol 43.5 mg.

Saturated fat 0.5 gm.

Protein 14.5 gm.

Carbohydrates 17.1 gm.

Sodium 177.5 mg.

CRAB ROYAL

*E*legantly bound with Champagne Vinaigrette (page 53), this long-time favorite requires absolutely fresh crabmeat. We use Gulf Coast Blue Crab, a local specialty celebrated for its plump texture and sweet flavor, but any first-rate crabmeat will serve. Do not attempt to prepare this dish with canned or frozen varieties.

Champagne Vinaigrette (page 53)
3 cups jumbo lump crabmeat, picked over carefully
2 teaspoons red bell pepper, finely diced
2 teaspoons green bell pepper, finely diced
2 cups chopped fresh spinach
12 whole spinach leaves
4 tablespoons tomato concassé (page 50)
6 cherry tomatoes, halved
4 lemon wedges

Prepare the Champagne Vinaigrette as directed.

In a medium bowl, combine the crabmeat and the bell peppers, tossing with ¼ cup of the vinaigrette to moisten.

Place 3 whole spinach leaves per serving equidistant from each other on an individual salad plate so that they meet in the center of the plate, dividing it into thirds. In the center, where the leaves touch, mound ½ cup of chopped spinach.

Mound ¾ cup of the crabmeat mixture on top of the chopped spinach, sprinkling the top of each portion with 1 tablespoon of the tomato concassé. Garnish by placing one half of a cherry tomato on each whole spinach leaf. Add a lemon wedge to each plate and serve.

Y I E L D *4 cups*

SERVING ¾ C.
CRABMEAT WITH
1 TB. VINAIGRETTE

Calories 150.0

Total fat 6.1 gm.

Cholesterol 85.0 mg.

Saturated fat 0.8 gm.

Protein 19.0 gm.

Carbohydrates 4.3 gm.

Sodium 274.0 mg.

CAMPECHANA DE MARISCO

4 tablespoons Champagne Vinaigrette (page 53)
1 cup fresh jumbo lump crabmeat, picked over carefully
1 cup sea scallops, cooked, drained, and chilled
8 medium shrimp, peeled and deveined, cooked, drained, and
    chilled
½ avocado, cut into cubes
Juice from ½ lemon
1 tablespoon finely chopped cilantro
2 tablespoons tomato concassé (page 50)
2 tablespoons green bell pepper, finely diced
2 tablespoons red onion, finely diced
¼ teaspoon white pepper
Garnishes: 4 slices each, fresh cantaloupe and honeydew melon;
    4 lemon slices; 4 radicchio leaves; 4 cilantro leaves

This light seafood starter is akin to ceviche, but the ingredients are cooked.

Prepare the Champagne Vinaigrette as directed.

Toss the seafood together in a large bowl and set aside. Place the avocado cubes in a medium bowl and squeeze the lemon juice over them. Add the cilantro, tomato concassé, bell pepper, and red onion to the avocado and toss gently. Whisk the white pepper into the champagne vinaigrette, stirring well. Pour the vinaigrette over the avocado mixture, tossing gently, and add to the seafood. Toss again lightly until the seafood and avocado mixtures have been thoroughly combined. Chill well before serving.

Because the campechana will release a little liquid, it is best served in small individual bowls. Line a luncheon plate with radicchio and place the bowl of campechana in the center. Surround it symmetrically with lemon slices, melon slices, and cilantro leaves.

YIELD *4 cups*

SERVING ½ C.
Calories 102.0
Total fat 5.0 gm.
Cholesterol 49.3 mg.
Saturated fat 0.69 gm.
Protein 11.12 gm.
Carbohydrates 2.8 gm.
Sodium 135.0 mg.

SESAME CHICKEN FINGERS LEBLANC WITH TWO DIPPING SAUCES

Honey-Mustard Dip (opposite page)
Basil-Mustard Dip (opposite page)
Four chicken breasts, 4 ounces each, skinned and boned
¼ cup sesame seeds
2 teaspoons olive oil
Red leaf lettuce

Preheat oven to 375°F. Prepare the dips as directed.

Slice the chicken into pieces approximately 2 inches long and ½ inch wide. Press the sesame seeds into the chicken pieces, forming a crust on each. Heat the olive oil in an ovenproof, heavy-bottomed, nonstick skillet or sauté pan, until just below smoking point. Add the chicken fingers and brown on both sides over medium-high heat, taking care not to scorch. When the chicken pieces are browned, place the pan in the oven for 3 to 5 minutes, or until chicken is cooked through. Do not overcook.

While the chicken is cooking, line each plate with a leaf of red leaf lettuce. When the chicken is done, place the chicken fingers on top of the lettuce. Serve with Honey-Mustard Dip and Basil-Mustard Dip on the side.

Y I E L D *12 ounces chicken*

SERVING 3 OZ.
CHICKEN

Calories 212.0
Total fat 9.7 gm.
Cholesterol 72.0 mg.
Saturated fat 1.78 gm.
Protein 28.0 gm.
Carbohydrates 2.1 gm.
Sodium 64.0 mg.

HONEY-MUSTARD DIP

1 tablespoon whole-grain mustard
3 tablespoons honey

Mix mustard with honey in a small bowl, stirring to combine. Chill.

Y I E L D *¼ cup*

SERVING 1 TB.
Calories 51.0
Total fat 0.2 gm.
Cholesterol 0
Saturated fat 0.01 gm.
Protein 0.2 gm.
Carbohydrates 13.3 gm.
Sodium 50.0 mg.

BASIL-MUSTARD DIP

2 tablespoons soubise (page 48)
2 tablespoons white wine or chicken stock (page 41), as needed
  for consistency
1 teaspoon Dijon mustard
1 teaspoon fresh basil, finely chopped

Prepare the soubise and chicken stock ahead as directed. (See Basic
Stocks and Sauces, pages 48 and 41.) Combine the mustard and basil
in a small, heavy-bottomed saucepan. Add the soubise, stirring, and
bring to a simmer over medium heat. Continue to simmer until the
sauce is thick enough to coat a spoon, adding white wine or chicken
stock to thin, if needed. Set aside until ready to serve. (May be served
warm or at room temperature.)

Y I E L D *½ cup*

SERVING 1 TB.
Calories 5.0
Total fat 0.1 gm.
Cholesterol 0
Saturated fat 0.01 gm.
Protein 0.3 gm.
Carbohydrates 0.9 gm.
Sodium 19.0 mg.

VITELLO TONNATO

Vitello Tonnato, traditionally composed of cold veal topped with a rich sauce of puréed tuna and mayonnaise, is a favorite luncheon or supper dish in Italy. We've adapted the recipe for heart-healthy dining by replacing some of the mayonnaise with nonfat alternatives. Many favorite recipes containing mayonnaise may be adjusted in this fashion.

1 bouquet garni (page 39) consisting of:
   1 stalk celery
   ½ white onion
   1 small carrot, peeled
   2 whole cloves
   1 bay leaf
3 cups cold water
1 ounce tarragon vinegar
½ teaspoon black peppercorns
1 pound veal, top round
Tonnato Sauce (next page)
Garnish: 4 lemon slices, 2 tablespoons chopped parsley,
   6 parsley sprigs, 2 tablespoons rinsed capers, 1 tablespoon
   paprika (optional)

Prepare the bouquet garni as directed on page 39. Place the water, vinegar, and peppercorns in a medium-size, heavy-bottomed stockpot or saucepan. Add the bouquet garni and bring to a boil. Add the veal and more water, if necessary, to cover the veal. Return to a boil, then reduce the heat and simmer until the veal is tender, approximately 1 hour. Remove the veal, cool to room temperature, then refrigerate overnight or until completely cold. Reserve 1 to 1½ cups of the veal broth.

Prepare the Tonnato Sauce as directed.

When ready to serve, place the veal, sliced no more than ¼ inch thick, on a platter or individual plates and top with sauce. Garnish with lemon, chopped parsley, parsley sprigs, and additional capers; and sprinkle with paprika, if desired.

Y I E L D *12 ounces veal*

SERVING 3 OZ. VEAL AND 2 TBS. SAUCE

Calories 196.0
Total fat 7.0 gm.
Cholesterol 135.0 mg.
Saturated fat 1.54 gm.
Protein 30.7 gm.
Carbohydrates 0.5 gm.
Sodium 112.0 mg.

TONNATO SAUCE

8-ounce can water-packed tuna, drained and rinsed in a colander
  to remove excess sodium, then drained again
4 tablespoons capers, rinsed and drained
Reserved veal broth
1 tablespoon olive oil
1 tablespoon fresh lemon juice
¼ cup nonfat yogurt
¼ cup reduced-calorie mayonnaise

In a blender or food processor, pureé the tuna, capers, and about 1 cup of the reserved veal broth to make a smooth pureé. Add the olive oil, lemon juice, yogurt, and mayonnaise, and process until combined. Refrigerate until cold.

V A R I A T I O N The dish may be varied by substituting a good deli-style sliced, cooked turkey breast for the veal, in which case it becomes Turkey Tonnato.

Y I E L D *2 cups*

SERVING 2 TBS.

Calories 40.0

Total fat 2.3 gm.

Cholesterol 7.0 mg.

Saturated fat 0.39 gm.

Protein 4.0 gm.

Carbohydrates 0.5 gm.

Sodium 32.0 mg.

CRUDITÉS WITH THREE DIPS

*T*raditionally, at Chez Eddy, dinner guests are greeted with a platter of freshly made crudités, served with our smooth Guacamole Dip. For added interest, we have included here two other low-calorie dips that may be enjoyed with raw vegetables as an appetizer or to round out a cocktail buffet.

For this recipe, choose fresh, tender, seasonal vegetables of varied color, texture, and flavor. Wash, then cut them into manageably sized finger food. As you work, vary their shapes, cutting some into juliennes, some into ovals, some into rosettes or waffles. Generally speaking, the more visual variation, the better.

GUACAMOLE DIP

1 fully ripened avocado
¼ cup low-fat cottage cheese
1 tablespoon lime juice
1½ teaspoons garlic powder
2 teaspoons minced scallions

Halve, seed, and peel the avocado, saving the seed. Cut into chunks. Place in a food processor or blender with the cottage cheese, lime juice, garlic powder, and scallions. Process until smooth, then cover tightly and refrigerate. If you leave the avocado seed in the guacamole until ready to serve, it will prevent the dip from darkening.

Y I E L D *1 cup*

THREE-HERB DIP

4 sprigs fresh parsley (with leaves)
6 tablespoons reduced-calorie mayonnaise
6 tablespoons nonfat yogurt
½ teaspoon fresh chervil, finely chopped
2 teaspoons fresh tarragon, finely chopped
½ shallot, peeled and chopped
½ teaspoon lemon juice
Pinch black pepper

Rinse the sprigs of parsley and chop finely. Wrap the chopped parsley in a soft dish- or tea-towel (neither terry cloth nor cheesecloth); twist

SERVING 1 TB.
GUACAMOLE
Calories 32.0
Total fat 2.8 gm.
Cholesterol 0
Saturated fat 0.48 gm.
Protein 0.8 gm.
Carbohydrates 1.5 gm.
Sodium 16.0 mg.

and wring the parsley in the cloth, squeezing the parsley juice into a bowl. (Reserve the chopped parsley to use as a garnish for the dip.) Whisk all the remaining ingredients together, adding the parsley juice at the end. Chill to allow the flavors to blend.

V A R I A T I O N Three-Herb Dip has many additional uses. Thinned with white wine or buttermilk, it may be served warm with fish or Salmon Crabcakes (page 104). It may also accompany fish terrine.

Y I E L D *1 cup*

CUCUMBER YOGURT DIP

½ cup nonfat yogurt
1 teaspoon lemon juice
1 small clove garlic, minced
2 tablespoons fresh parsley, finely chopped
1 teaspoon chives, minced
Pinch red pepper flakes
½ teaspoon Dijon mustard
½ teaspoon fresh cilantro, finely chopped
½ cup cucumber, peeled, seeded, and finely chopped

Put all ingredients, except for the cucumber, in a bowl and blend well with a whisk. Fold in the cucumber, stirring to combine thoroughly, and store the dip in an air-tight container. Keeps well in the refrigerator for 2 to 3 days.

Y I E L D *1 cup*

SERVING 1 TB.
THREE-HERB DIP

Calories 20.0
Total fat 1.7 gm.
Cholesterol 2.0 mg.
Saturated fat 0.27 gm.
Protein 0.4 gm.
Carbohydrates 0.7 gm.
Sodium 37.0 mg.

SERVING 1 TB.
CUCUMBER
YOGURT DIP

Calories 5.0
Total fat 0
Cholesterol 0
Saturated fat 0.01 gm.
Protein 0.4 gm.
Carbohydrates 0.7 gm.
Sodium 8.0 mg.

SALMON CRABCAKES WITH DILL SAUCE

With a simple variation in size, these delicious crabcakes serve a multitude of purposes. Larger cakes become a main course; smaller ones inhabit a buffet, or nestle between halves of whole-grain bread for a satisfying sandwich (see below).

2 cups poached salmon, flaked (opposite page)
⅓ cup cracker crumbs, from unsalted saltines
¼ cup egg substitute
½ cup fresh parsley, finely chopped
1 tablespoon Dijon mustard
Pinch ground red pepper
4 teaspoons reduced-calorie mayonnaise
2 cups fresh lump crabmeat, picked over carefully
1 tablespoon canola oil
Dill Sauce (page 81)

About 1 hour before proceeding with the recipe, poach the salmon according to directions given below (or use leftover). Let cool and refrigerate.

Combine the cracker crumbs, egg substitute, parsley, mustard, red pepper, and mayonnaise in a large bowl, whisking to blend. Add the salmon and crabmeat and toss together lightly. (Do not overhandle. The salmon and crab should remain somewhat flaky.) Gently shape the mixture into 8 cakes, each about 3 inches in diameter, and refrigerate them for at least one hour.

When ready to proceed, set a nonstick skillet over medium heat. Add 1 tablespoon of oil to coat the bottom of the pan. When the oil is hot, pour it out so that only a film remains. Sauté the cakes until lightly browned on both sides (approximately 3 minutes per side). Serve warm with cool Dill Sauce, 2 tablespoons per serving.

The cakes may be made a day or two in advance and refrigerated. They will keep up to 3 days in the refrigerator and may be frozen for as long as 1 month.

VARIATION Crabcake sandwiches are one of our most popular luncheon items. As you sauté the crabcakes, flatten them with a spatula so they will fit a whole-grain bun. Blot well. Dress the bun with a little dill mayonnaise, made by substituting a mixture of ¾ cup of reduced-calorie mayonnaise plus ¼ cup of yogurt for the yogurt, mayo, and cottage cheese called for in the recipe for Dill Sauce (page 81). Add lemon juice and dill as directed.

SERVING 2
CRABCAKES

Calories 203.0
Total fat 7.6 gm.
Cholesterol 89.6 mg.
Saturated fat 1.38 gm.
Protein 25.7 gm.
Carbohydrates 6.5 gm.
Sodium 302.0 mg.

Place a serving of lettuce leaves and sliced tomato on the side of the sandwich and garnish with peperoncini or fresh fruit.

NUTRITIONAL NOTE Because of their higher concentration of omega-3 fatty acids, we prefer the use of Scottish or Norwegian salmon in our recipes.

YIELD *8 cakes*

POACHED SALMON

Court Bouillon (page 44) or Fish Stock (page 42) or Fish Fumet
 (headnote, page 42) or water
2 salmon steaks, 5 ounces each

Prepare the Court Bouillon or fish stock or fish fumet ahead as directed. (See Basic Stocks and sauces, pages 44 and 42.)

Place the salmon in a heavy-bottomed saucepan or skillet large enough to allow the salmon to be arranged in one layer. Add the liquid to cover. Bring to a simmer over medium heat, then reduce the heat so that bubbles barely reach the surface of the liquid. This slow cooking allows the salmon to cook evenly without breaking apart. Continue to poach for approximately 5 to 7 minutes. The flesh should be just slightly opaque, and spring back lightly when touched with your finger. Salmon should never be overcooked.

CHEZ EDDY HUMMUS

At Chez Eddy, we serve this dip with grilled pita bread as an appetizer. Hummus can also be served as a dip with raw vegetables and low-fat crackers or with chicken, fish or lamb.

1 (15-ounce) can chick-peas
½ teaspoon olive oil
½ cup yellow onion, minced
1 teaspoon garlic, minced
1 teaspoon paprika
Juice from ½ lemon
Cayenne pepper to taste
½ cup nonfat yogurt

Drain the chick-peas, reserving the liquid. Place the chick-peas in a colander and rinse under running water to remove excess salt. Set aside.

Heat the oil in a small nonstick skillet over medium heat. Add onion and garlic and sauté for 1 minute, stirring frequently. Remove from the heat and let cool.

Combine chick-peas, onion, garlic, paprika, lemon juice, and cayenne pepper in the container of a blender or food processor. Purée until smooth. Add the yogurt and process just until blended. The mixture should resemble a slightly chunky dip. If the mixture is too thick, use the reserved liquid to thin to desired consistency. Transfer to a bowl, cover, and chill well before serving. Hummus will keep refrigerated 3 to 4 days.

YIELD *2 cups*

SERVING ¼ C.

Calories 46.0

Total fat 0.6 gm.

Cholesterol 0

Saturated fat 0

Protein 2.3 gm.

Carbohydrates 8.0 gm.

Sodium 100.0 mg.

STUFFED CHICKEN BREAST WITH GREEN PEPPERCORN SAUCE

½ cup carrots, peeled and julienned
2 cups fresh spinach leaves, washed carefully
4 skinless, boneless chicken breast halves, each weighing
    approximately 4 ounces, trimmed of all fat
1 teaspoon fresh thyme, finely chopped
4 cups water or chicken stock (page 41) (optional for poaching)
Green Peppercorn Sauce (page 65)

Blanch the julienned carrots by immersing in 1 cup of boiling water or chicken stock for 2 minutes. Drain quickly and plunge into ice water to halt the cooking process. Drain thoroughly. Place the spinach in a heavy-bottomed saucepan and heat, stirring, until the spinach begins to wilt. Remove the spinach and set aside to cool.

Place the chicken breasts between two sheets of waxed paper or plastic wrap and pound gently with a wooden mallet until each piece has been flattened to a thickness of ⅛ to 1/16 inch. Gently place a thin layer of cooked, cooled spinach down the center of each piece of chicken; place a thin layer of julienned carrots over it and sprinkle with ½ teaspoon of thyme. Then add another layer of spinach over that, pressing the vegetables together so they form a compact cylinder. Roll the sides of the chicken across the filling and tuck the ends in. Tie with string into little rolls, making several loops so the filling is secure.

In a large saucepan, bring 4 cups of water (or stock) to a boil over medium-high heat. Reduce the heat, add the chicken, and simmer gently for 10 minutes. Remove the chicken and chill until cold. Reserve stock for later use. (This is our basic method for poaching chicken.) Slice the chicken into thin rounds and serve with Green Peppercorn Sauce (2 tablespoons per serving).

V A R I A T I O N These chicken rolls, or *paupiettes,* may also be served hot. Two richly flavored sauces for the hot version include Brandy-Pecan Sauce (page 76) and Chez Eddy Bordelaise (page 60). Accompany either one with wild rice or Polenta (page 289) and Mint-Glazed Carrots (page 275).

Y I E L D *12 ounces chicken*

*A*n elegant cold appetizer that serves equally well as a luncheon entrée.

SERVING 3 OZ.
CHICKEN

Calories 154.0

Total fat 3.1 gm.

Cholesterol 72.0 mg.

Saturated fat 0.87 gm.

Protein 27.4 gm.

Carbohydrates 2.7 gm.

Sodium 91.0 mg.

WALDORF-SQUASH SALAD

A crunchy salad that needs no dressing. The fresh, tart taste of the lemon-spiked apples brightens the flavor of the squash that we use here primarily to provide contrasting texture and visual appeal.

1 three-pound spaghetti squash, washed
¼ cup raisins
4 Granny Smith apples
3 tablespoons lemon juice
1 cup diced celery
¼ cup shelled pecans, coarsely chopped
¼ cup shelled walnuts, coarsely chopped
3 tablespoons fresh basil, finely chopped
1 tablespoon dried lemon thyme
Garnish: Bibb lettuce leaves

Bring 4 quarts of water to a boil in a large, heavy-bottomed pot or Dutch oven. Add the squash and boil, uncovered, for 30 to 40 minutes or until soft to the touch.

While the squash is cooking, plump the raisins by placing them in a small saucepan, adding cold water to cover. Bring to a boil, then remove from the heat and let stand for 10 minutes. Drain thoroughly and dry with paper towels. Set aside until needed.

Wash and dice the apples. Place in a large nonreactive bowl and toss with fresh lemon juice to prevent darkening. Add the celery, raisins, nuts, and fresh herbs; toss. Refrigerate to chill.

When the squash is done, drain and pour cold water over it to stop the cooking. Split the squash in half and remove the seeds. Using a fork, scrape the flesh of the squash into a medium-size bowl. It will fall into spaghetti-like threads. Discard the outer shell and chill the squash until ready to assemble.

When ready to serve, gently combine the chilled squash with the apple mixture and serve on individual plates lined with Bibb lettuce.

VARIATION Adding 2½ ounces of lump crab, per person, transforms this dish into a delightful main-course salad.

YIELD *6 cups*

SERVING 1 C.

Calories 148.0

Total fat 6.6 gm.

Cholesterol 0

Saturated fat 0.54 gm.

Protein 2.8 gm.

Carbohydrates 23.0 gm.

Sodium 20.0 mg.

WATERCRESS, FENNEL, AND ROASTED RED PEPPER SALAD

2 bunches watercress
3 bulbs fennel
2 tablespoons lemon juice
3 red bell peppers, roasted (page 67)
Freshly ground pepper, to taste
Chef Denny's Garlic Dressing (page 80)

Remove the tough stems of the watercress, then wash and drain. Tear into bite-size pieces, place in a large bowl, and refrigerate until ready to serve.

Cut the bulb from the feathery stalks of the fennel, reserving the stalks, refrigerated, for another use. Remove the thick tough outer ribs from the bulb. Halve the bulb and remove the tough core inside the bulb. Slice the halves very thinly, lengthwise. In a large nonreactive bowl, combine the fennel and the lemon juice to prevent darkening. Refrigerate until ready to serve. Cut the roasted red peppers into 2-inch julienne strips. Set aside.

Just before serving, divide the watercress among four chilled salad plates. Scatter the fennel and the roasted red peppers over the watercress. Add freshly ground black pepper to taste. Serve with Chef Denny's Garlic Dressing.

N O T E Fresh fennel, a fall and winter crop, can be found in most markets. It looks like a bulbous form of celery, sprouting feathery green leaves that resemble dill. The entire plant is valued for many purposes. It has a licorice-like flavor and a crunchy texture similar to that of celery, both of which are most evident when fennel is eaten raw.

Y I E L D *4 cups*

This intensely flavored, visually dramatic salad juxtaposes the dark sweetness of red bell peppers and the bite of watercress with the anise perfume of fennel, enveloped in a seductive garlic vinaigrette.

SERVING 1 C.

Calories 30.0
Total fat 0.4 gm.
Cholesterol 0
Saturated fat 0.07 gm.
Protein 1.4 gm.
Carbohydrates 6.7 gm.
Sodium 62.0 mg.

LETTUCE, JICAMA, AND ORANGE SALAD WITH LIME DRESSING

Cut the jicama, celery, scallions, and orange rind into very thin pieces to get a mixture of flavors in each forkful.

SERVING 1 C.

Calories 95.0

Total fat 0.4 gm.

Cholesterol 0

Saturated fat 0.07 gm.

Protein 2.7 gm.

Carbohydrates 22.4 gm.

Sodium 23.0 mg.

1 head Boston, red leaf, or limestone lettuce, washed carefully
½ pound jicama, julienned
4 small scallions, sliced crosswise
4 oranges, sectioned, pith removed
2 celery stalks, thinly sliced on the bias
Lime Dressing (see below)
Garnish: 2 tablespoons orange rind, julienned and blanched

Combine the lettuce, jicama, scallions, orange sections, and celery stalks in a bowl. Toss with the dressing and serve, garnished with julienned orange rind.

VARIATION For a main-course dish, add poached or grilled chicken, garnished with toasted almonds or pine nuts.

YIELD *4 cups*

LIME DRESSING

SERVING 1 TB.

Calories 50.0

Total fat 5.5 gm.

Cholesterol 0

Saturated fat 0.7 gm.

Protein 0

Carbohydrates 0.4 gm.

Sodium 1.0 mg.

2 tablespoons fresh lime juice
2 teaspoons lime peel, finely grated
Pinch dry mustard
Pinch ground red pepper
2 tablespoons corn or canola oil
Freshly ground black pepper, to taste

Mix together the lime juice, lime peel, mustard, and red pepper in a small nonreactive bowl. Slowly whisk in the oil to form an emulsion and season the dressing with pepper.

YIELD *5 tablespoons*

CHEZ EDDY HOUSE SALAD WITH ALMOND-HERB DRESSING

2 cups mixed lettuces, such as romaine and red leaf
½ cup red cabbage, julienned
½ cup Red Delicious apples, chopped
½ cup carrots, peeled and julienned
½ cup jicama, julienned
1 medium tomato, cut in wedges
¼ cup sliced cucumbers
½ cup sliced mushrooms
Almond-Herb Dressing (next page)

Wash and dry the lettuces and tear into bite-size pieces. In a large mixing bowl, toss them until they are well combined. Add cabbage, apples, carrots, and jicama, tossing well after each addition. Chill thoroughly.

When ready to serve, mound the salad in the center of a chilled salad plate. Garnish with tomato wedges, cucumber slices, and mushrooms. Serve with Almond-Herb Dressing on the side.

YIELD *4 cups*

This popular salad gains texture and flavor from the hint of sweet apples.

SERVING 1 C. AND 1 TB. DRESSING
Calories 77.0
Total fat 2.0 gm.
Cholesterol 2.0 mg.
Saturated fat 0.29 gm.
Protein 1.9 gm.
Carbohydrates 14.3 gm.
Sodium 40.0 mg.

ALMOND-HERB DRESSING

¼ cup champagne vinegar
½ cup reduced-calorie mayonnaise
¾ cup nonfat yogurt
½ cup honey
1 tablespoon fresh basil, finely chopped
1 tablespoon fresh thyme, finely chopped
1 teaspoon fresh oregano, finely chopped
¼ cup sliced, toasted almonds, finely chopped (page 150)

Using a food processor or blender, combine the vinegar, mayonnaise, yogurt, and honey and process until smooth. Add the herbs and almonds and process again, turning the machine on and off at intervals until just blended. Chill before serving. This dressing will keep in the refrigerator for 3 to 5 days.

Y I E L D *2 cups*

SERVING 1 TB.

Calories 37.0

Total fat 1.7 gm.

Cholesterol 2.0 mg.

Saturated fat 0.24 gm.

Protein 0.6 gm.

Carbohydrates 5.3 gm.

Sodium 26.0 mg.

RADICCHIO, ARUGULA, AND FRESH CORN SALAD

12 radicchio leaves
12 leaves Belgian endive
2 bunches arugula, 3 to 4 ounces
½ cup jicama, julienned
½ cup thinly sliced red onion
½ cup uncooked fresh sweet corn, cut into whole kernels
Beet Vinaigrette (see below)
2 tablespoons garlic chives, finely chopped

Wash and dry the radicchio and endive. Wash the arugula, trim the stems, and pat dry. Toss together lightly the jicama, red onion, and corn. Line one chilled salad plate per serving with three radicchio leaves. Center one leaf of Belgian endive on each and mound arugula in the center of the plate. Sprinkle with ¼ of the jicama mixture. Chill well.

When ready to serve, spoon 1 tablespoon of the Beet Vinaigrette over the salad and sprinkle with garlic chives.

YIELD *4 cups*

BEET VINAIGRETTE

1 small clove garlic
1 small shallot
3 medium-size fresh beets, with greens
⅔ cup beet liquid
5 tablespoons lemon juice
4 tablespoons rice wine vinegar
4 tablespoons water
1 tablespoon Pernod
1½ teaspoons prepared horseradish
1½ teaspoons roasted coriander seeds, finely ground
½ teaspoon ground fennel, roasted

The sweetness of fresh corn, highlighted by this unusual beet-and-fennel dressing, nicely balances the bitter quality of arugula.

(cont.)

2 heaping tablespoons chives, finely chopped
Pinch black pepper

Blanch the garlic and shallot in boiling water for 1 minute. Remove and immerse in ice water until cooled. Drain and set aside. Cut the beet greens 1 inch above the crown. Scrub the beets gently, taking care not to break the skin. Place the beets in a 3-quart saucepan and cover with water. Bring to a boil, reduce the heat, and simmer until the beets are tender, 30 to 35 minutes. Remove from the heat and drain, reserving ⅔ cup of the liquid. Peel the beets.

Place the beets, beet liquid, lemon juice, rice wine vinegar, water, Pernod, shallot, garlic, horseradish, coriander seeds (toss briefly in hot skillet to roast), fennel, chives, and black pepper in the container of a blender and purée until smooth. Strain through a fine sieve or strainer and chill until ready to serve.

Y I E L D *1 cup*

SERVING 1 C. SALAD
WITH 1 TB. DRESSING
Calories 52.0
Total fat 0.5 gm.
Cholesterol 0
Saturated fat 0.09 gm.
Protein 1.9 gm.
Carbohydrates 11.3 gm.
Sodium 8.0 mg.

MIXED FIELD LETTUCES WITH RASPBERRY WALNUT VINAIGRETTE

4 cups mixed field lettuces, such as oak leaf, red leaf, butterhead
½ cup red onion, sliced
¼ cup walnuts, coarsely chopped
Raspberry Walnut Vinaigrette (see below)

Wash and dry the lettuces. Tear into bite-size pieces. In a large mixing bowl, toss together lettuces and onions until well combined. Chill thoroughly.

When ready to serve, mound 1 cup lettuces in the center of four chilled salad plates. Sprinkle each salad with walnuts and 2 tablespoons Raspberry Walnut Vinaigrette.

Y I E L D *4 cups*

RASPBERRY WALNUT VINAIGRETTE

½ cup raspberry vinegar
1 tablespoon Dijon mustard
¼ teaspoon cracked black pepper
¾ teaspoon fresh tarragon, minced
¼ cup honey
1 tablespoon walnut oil
½ cup nonfat yogurt

Combine the vinegar, mustard, black pepper, tarragon, honey, walnut oil, and yogurt in the container of a food processor or blender. Process until smooth.

Y I E L D *1¼ cups*

This delightful salad contrasts the tender flavors of mixed lettuces with tart raspberry vinegar and the nutty taste of walnuts.

SERVING 1 C. SALAD
WITH 2 TBS.
DRESSING
Calories 58.0
Total fat 1.7 gm.
Cholesterol 0
Saturated fat 0.1 gm.
Protein 1.4 gm.
Carbohydrates 11.0 gm.
Sodium 59.0 mg.

SERVING 2 TBS.
Calories 48.0
Total fat 1.5 gm.
Cholesterol 0
Saturated fat 0.11 gm.
Protein 0.7 gm.
Carbohydrates 8.7 gm.
Sodium 54.0 mg.

SPINACH AND MUSHROOM SALAD WITH ZESTY BUTTERMILK DRESSING

Zesty Buttermilk Dressing (page 79)
4 cups shredded spinach
1 cup mushrooms, coarsely chopped
16 spinach leaves, whole, well washed
¼ cup red bell pepper, finely chopped
8 cherry tomatoes, halved

Prepare the buttermilk dressing as directed.

When ready to serve, combine the shredded spinach with the chopped mushrooms in a large bowl. On each chilled salad plate, arrange 4 spinach leaves equidistant from one another so they divide the plate into quarters. They should be touching at their stems. Mound ¼ of the salad mixture in the center of the plate, covering the bottom of each leaf. Sprinkle the salad with 1 tablespoon of red bell pepper. Place 4 cherry tomato halves on each whole spinach leaf. Serve with Zesty Buttermilk Dressing.

Y I E L D *4 cups*

SERVING 1 C. SALAD
WITH 2 TBS.
DRESSING
Calories 40.0
Total fat 1.0 gm.
Cholesterol 2.0 mg.
Saturated fat 0.06 gm.
Protein 3.3 gm.
Carbohydrates 5.9 gm.
Sodium 77.0 mg.

SOUPS

....

TRADITIONALLY, SOUPS APPEAL ON MANY levels. They may begin the meal, inviting the appetite to anticipate with relish what will follow. Or the soup itself may become the light, nutritious lunch or supper so many of us are looking for these days. In any event, whether we choose a clear broth with vegetables or a hearty mixture rich in complex carbohydrates, most of the time we feel confident that we're eating something as low in calories as it is satisfying to the senses.

And at Chez Eddy this is especially true. Unlike traditional soups, ours don't disguise a substantial fat content provided by such things as unskimmed stocks, butter, or flavoring ingredients like bacon or salt pork. In our broths you never see rendered fat as a sheen across the surface of the liquid—a literal oil slick. Even in thicker soups, where the gleam would be absent, you don't have to worry that some starchy ingredient has absorbed an unacceptable amount of fat.

At Chez Eddy, skimmed stocks make our clear soups as light in calories as they are to the taste. Favorites using legumes, such as Southern Black Bean (page 127) or Lentil (page 125), derive their satisfying flavor from innovations in seasoning, not pork. Even our "cream" soups omit the fat, relying on such ingredients as potato purée, a little yogurt, or, in particular, our versatile soubise to provide the unctuous texture, the "creaminess" we expect.

Soups are, also, another reason we urge our readers to take the time to prepare stock from scratch. With stocks on hand, a delectable lunch or appetizer is only as far away as your vegetable crisper. Or, as the dinner hour approaches, you may stir in a little leftover meat or seafood and a handful of pasta to produce a main course faster, and most of the time far better, than take-out.

....

Curried Zucchini Soup

Tomato Bisque with Avocado Sorbet

Chez Eddy Cream of Asparagus Soup with Almonds

Garlic, Mushroom, and Chive Soup

Lemon-Basil Soup

Lentil Soup

Tortilla Soup

Southern Black Bean Soup

Seafood Chowder

Broccoli and Apple Soup

Two-Potato Soup

Caldo Bravo

Salmon Bisque

Cream of Chicken and Watercress Soup

Cream of Pumpkin Soup

Polish Blackberry Soup

Fresh Strawberry Soup

Cold Melon Soup

....

CURRIED ZUCCHINI SOUP

2½ cups chicken stock (page 41)
1 tablespoon olive oil
1½ pounds zucchini, sliced
¾ cup yellow onion, finely chopped
½ teaspoon curry powder, or more, to taste
Pinch ground black pepper, to taste
Garnish: ¼ cup nonfat yogurt

Prepare the chicken stock ahead as directed.

Heat the oil in a medium-size, heavy-bottomed saucepan. Add the zucchini and sauté for 2 minutes. Add the onion and continue to sauté over low heat until the onion is translucent, about 3 minutes. Stir in the curry powder and cook for 1 minute. Add the chicken stock and return to a boil. Reduce the heat, cover, and simmer for 30 minutes. Cool slightly and purée in a blender, adding pepper to taste. Serve hot or cold with a dollop of nonfat plain yogurt.

YIELD *4 cups*

This chilled light soup is perfect for a summer lunch with friends.

SERVING 1 C.

Calories 80.0

Total fat 4.8 gm.

Cholesterol 0

Saturated fat 0.68 gm.

Protein 3.1 gm.

Carbohydrates 7.5 gm.

Sodium 19.0 mg.

TOMATO BISQUE WITH AVOCADO SORBET

This chilled aromatic bisque is best in deep summer, when home-grown tomatoes are available. Its tomato flavor is nicely balanced by the smooth, rich-tasting avocado sorbet. Please note that we have used bread instead of cream to thicken the bisque. This technique is useful in adapting many soups to heart-healthy dining requirements.

SERVING: 1 C. BISQUE
WITH 1 TB. SORBET

Calories 205.0

Total fat 6.7 gm.

Cholesterol 1.0 mg.

Saturated fat 1.14 gm.

Protein 5.8 gm.

Carbohydrates 34.1 gm.

Sodium 169.0 mg.

4 slices stale white bread, crusts removed
1 tablespoon red wine vinegar
4 cloves garlic, finely chopped
1 tablespoon granulated sugar
1 tablespoon olive oil
1½ pounds ripe tomatoes, peeled and seeded (approximately 5 medium tomatoes)
2 cups tomato juice
6 scallions, finely chopped
1 medium cucumber, peeled, seeded, and chopped
2 red bell peppers, seeded and chopped
2 tablespoons fresh basil, finely chopped
Pinch white pepper, to taste
Avocado Sorbet (opposite page)
Garnish: ½-inch ice cubes; whole leaves of fresh basil

Crumble the bread into the container of a food processor. Add the vinegar and process for 1 minute. Add the garlic and sugar and process for an additional minute. With the motor running slowly, add the olive oil, which the bread will absorb. In sequence, add the tomatoes, tomato juice, scallions, cucumber, red pepper, and basil, processing to a smooth consistency after each addition. Strain the mixture into a medium bowl through a fine sieve or a colander lined with several layers of dampened cheesecloth. Whisk in the white pepper to taste and chill.

While the bisque chills, make the avocado sorbet, as directed below.

Serve the soup in chilled bowls. Garnish with a melon ball-size scoop of avocado sorbet in the center, 4 ice cubes, and 2 fresh basil leaves.

YIELD *4 cups*

AVOCADO SORBET

1 avocado, peeled and pitted
2 tablespoons lemon juice
2 tablespoons granulated sugar
1 cup cold water
2 tablespoons fresh basil, finely chopped
¼ cup grated Parmesan cheese
2 tablespoons pine nuts
1 teaspoon garlic, minced

Combine the avocado and the lemon juice in a blender or food processor and process until smooth. In a large bowl, dissolve the sugar in the water, stirring, then add the basil. Pour this liquid into the blender and process again. Add the Parmesan cheese, pine nuts, and garlic and process until smooth. Freeze in an ice cream maker according to the manufacturer's directions.

N O T E Because sorbet crystallizes into a solid mass when held in the freezer for long periods of time, we recommend immediate use. If it must be frozen, you may serve the sorbet by shaving it with a spoon and forming it into balls. The texture will be affected, but the flavor will remain comparable.

Y I E L D *2 cups*

SERVING 1 TB.
Calories 23.0
Total fat 1.9 gm.
Cholesterol 0
Saturated fat 0.38 gm.
Protein 0.5 gm.
Carbohydrates 1.4 gm.
Sodium 12.0 mg.

CHEZ EDDY CREAM OF ASPARAGUS SOUP WITH ALMONDS

The technique used to make this basic cream soup applies equally well to other vegetables. If you prefer a more intense asparagus flavor, omit the soubise.

4 cups chicken stock (page 41)
1 cup soubise (page 48)
1 teaspoon olive oil
1 cup onion, minced
½ cup leek, white part only, carefully washed and chopped
1 cup celery, finely sliced
4 cups peeled asparagus stalks, cut into 1-inch pieces (save the tips for another use)
½ cup white potato, peeled and diced
Pinch white pepper
1 tablespoon lemon juice
Dry sherry, to taste (optional)
Garnish: 2 tablespoons toasted almonds (page 150)

Prepare the chicken stock and soubise ahead as directed. (See Basic Stocks and Sauces, pages 41 and 48.)

Add the olive oil to a 2- to 3-quart heavy-bottomed, nonstick saucepan and place over medium heat. When the oil is hot, add the onion, leek, celery, and asparagus, stirring frequently. Cook until the onion and leek are soft but not browned, approximately 5 minutes. Add the potato and chicken stock and bring to a boil. Reduce the heat and simmer, stirring occasionally, until the potatoes and other vegetables are cooked through, 30 to 45 minutes.

Stir in the soubise and cook approximately 5 minutes until the soup thickens. Cool the soup slightly and process in a blender or food processor until smooth. Add the white pepper and lemon juice to taste or, if you prefer, substitute sherry for lemon juice. Serve hot or cold, garnished with toasted almonds.

Y I E L D *5 cups*

SERVING 1 C.

Calories 132.0

Total fat 3.5 gm.

Cholesterol 1.0 mg.

Saturated fat 0.48 gm.

Protein 7.4 gm.

Carbohydrates 20.9 gm.

Sodium 47.0 mg.

GARLIC, MUSHROOM, AND CHIVE SOUP

4 cups chicken stock (page 41)
1 cup soubise (page 48)
1 teaspoon unsalted margarine, clarified (see Note below)
1 large yellow or white onion, diced
3 cups stale bread (crusts removed), torn, and loosely packed
8 whole cloves garlic
1 bunch chives, finely chopped (reserve 1 tablespoon for
  garnish)
2 cups fresh mushrooms, thinly sliced
½ cup white wine
White pepper, to taste

Prepare the chicken stock and soubise ahead as directed. (See Basic Stocks and Sauces, pages 41 and 48.)

In a 2- to 3-quart, heavy-bottomed nonstick saucepan or pot, melt the margarine over a medium heat. Add the onions and cook until translucent (3 to 4 minutes), stirring frequently. Add the chicken stock, bread, and garlic. Stirring occasionally, cook over a medium heat, uncovered, for 20 to 25 minutes. Cool the mixture slightly, then process in a blender or food processor until smooth. Strain the soup through a fine sieve or colander lined with several layers of dampened cheesecloth.

Return to the pot. Over medium heat, stir in the soubise, chives, mushrooms, and white wine. Cook until the soup thickens and the mushrooms are tender, approximately 5 to 7 minutes. Season with white pepper to taste. Serve garnished with chopped fresh chives.

Y I E L D *5 cups*

N O T E To clarify margarine: In a heavy pan, melt 1 pound of margarine over low heat. Skim off the froth and pour the clear yellow liquid from the pan, leaving a milky residue. Discard the residue. The clear yellow fat can withstand high heat without burning. It will keep for several weeks in the refrigerator or can be frozen for up to 3 months.

Y I E L D *1½ cups*

*E*ven garlic lovers will be surprised at the mellow character it develops in this subtle dish.

SERVING 1 C.

Calories 100.0

Total fat 1.6 gm.

Cholesterol 1.0 mg.

Saturated fat 0.33 gm.

Protein 3.9 gm.

Carbohydrates 17.9 gm.

Sodium 109.0 mg.

LEMON-BASIL SOUP

In this soup, lemon and basil must merely sparkle against the rich essence of chicken. You may further intensify the flavor by poaching the chicken in the stock before reduction. For these reasons, fresh chicken is preferred, although leftover may be used if necessary. Increasing the amount of chicken called for in the recipe transforms this soup into a refreshing main course.

SERVING 1 C.

Calories 82.0

Total fat 3.8 gm.

Cholesterol 16.0 mg.

Saturated fat 0.57 gm.

Protein 7.1 gm.

Carbohydrates 5.2 gm.

Sodium 30.0 mg.

8 cups chicken stock (page 41)
½ leek, white part only, carefully washed and chopped
½ stalk celery, sliced crosswise
½ cup white onion, diced
½ cup carrots, peeled and diced
1 tablespoon olive oil
4 tablespoons fresh basil, finely chopped
4 ounces poached chicken breast, diced
4 tablespoons lemon juice
White pepper, to taste
Garnish: chopped fresh basil or parsley and thin slices of lemon

Prepare the chicken stock ahead as directed.

In a medium-size, heavy-bottomed saucepan or pot, bring the chicken stock to a boil over high heat. Lower the heat and simmer gently until the stock has been reduced by half. Remove from the heat and keep warm.

In a small saucepan or skillet, sauté the leek, celery, onion, and carrots for approximately 5 to 7 minutes in the olive oil until the onion is translucent. Add this mixture to the chicken stock and stir in the basil. Simmer the soup over medium-to-low heat until the carrots are tender, approximately 15 to 20 minutes. Cool slightly and transfer to a blender or food processor. Process until smooth. Strain through a fine sieve or colander lined with dampened cheesecloth. Add the diced chicken and lemon juice and return to the stove. Heat through, stirring in a pinch of white pepper to taste. Garnish with the basil or parsley and float a thin slice of lemon on top.

Y I E L D *4 cups*

LENTIL SOUP

6 cups chicken stock (page 41)
1 tablespoon unsalted margarine, clarified (page 123)
½ cup carrot, peeled and diced
½ cup white or yellow onion, diced
2 cloves garlic, chopped
½ leek, white part only, carefully washed and chopped
½ cup diced celery
1 tablespoon flour
¾ cup beer
2 tablespoons red wine vinegar
1 bay leaf
3 cups dried brown lentils
1 tablespoon honey
1 tablespoon lime juice
Pinch white pepper, to taste
Garnish: 4 tablespoons scallion tops, finely chopped

Prepare the chicken stock ahead as directed.

Heat the clarified margarine in a heavy-bottomed saucepan or Dutch oven over medium heat. Add the carrots, onion, garlic, leek, and celery; dust with flour and stir, reducing the heat. Take care not to scorch. Cover and cook until the vegetables are soft, approximately 10 to 12 minutes. Add the chicken stock and beer. Bring to a boil. Lower the heat and add the vinegar, bay leaf, and lentils. Cover and simmer until the lentils are soft, 30 to 40 minutes. Stir in the honey, lime juice, and pepper, and cook for an additional 3 to 5 minutes. Serve hot, garnished with finely chopped scallion tops.

YIELD *6 cups*

*I*n soups made with legumes, honey and vinegar compensate very nicely for the traditional ham or pork flavorings, which we omit. The resulting dish, which is low in fat and cholesterol, remains a rich source of complex carbohydrates and protein.

SERVING 1 C.
Calories 371.0
Total fat 2.9 gm.
Cholesterol 0
Saturated fat 0.5 gm.
Protein 27.5 gm.
Carbohydrates 62.0 gm.
Sodium 24.0 mg.

TORTILLA SOUP

*A*dd cooked diced chicken breast to this soup for a hearty main course. If you prefer, substitute homemade chicken stock (page 41).

1 teaspoon olive oil
1½ cups minced onion
2 teaspoons garlic, minced
1 teaspoon chili powder
1 tablespoon ground cumin
1 tablespoon tomato paste
½ teaspoon black pepper
2¾ cups canned low-sodium chicken broth
1 (4-ounce) can green chilies, diced
2 cups canned low-sodium tomatoes, diced with juice
4 (6-inch) corn tortillas, diced and toasted in oven until crisp
2 tablespoons fresh cilantro, chopped
Garnish: 1 corn tortilla, julienned and toasted in oven until crisp
    ¼ cup diced fresh tomatoes

Put the olive oil in a 2- to 3-quart nonstick saucepan and place over medium heat. When the oil is hot, add the onion and garlic and cook until the onions are translucent (3 to 4 minutes), stirring frequently. Add the chili powder, cumin, tomato paste, and black pepper and cook for 1 minute. Stir in the chicken broth, chilies, and canned tomatoes and bring to a boil. Reduce heat and add diced tortillas. Simmer 15 to 20 minutes. Cool the mixture slightly, then process in a blender or food processor until smooth. Stir in the cilantro. Garnish each serving with toasted tortilla strips and 1 tablespoon diced fresh tomato.

Y I E L D *5¾ cups*

SERVING 1 C.

Calories 68.0

Total fat 1.0 gm.

Cholesterol 0

Saturated fat 0.1 gm.

Protein 2.5 gm.

Carbohydrates 5.3 gm.

Sodium 131.0 mg.

SOUTHERN BLACK BEAN SOUP

8 cups chicken stock (page 41)
1 cup soubise (page 48)
1½ cups dried black beans
1 tablespoon olive oil
½ cup white onion, chopped
½ cup carrots, peeled and diced
¼ cup celery, finely sliced
1 clove garlic, chopped
1 tablespoon honey
¼ cup sherry wine vinegar
1 tablespoon molasses
White pepper, to taste
Garnish: 4 teaspoons nonfat yogurt and either 1 tablespoon
 diced scallion tops or 1 tablespoon diced red onion

Prepare the chicken stock and soubise ahead as directed. (See Basic Stocks and Sauces, pages 41 and 48.) Wash the beans, cover with water, and soak overnight.

When ready to proceed, bring the chicken stock to a boil in a heavy-bottomed stockpot or Dutch oven. Drain the soaked beans, add them to the chicken stock, and return to a boil. Reduce the heat and simmer until the beans are tender, approximately 3 hours. Heat the olive oil in a heavy saucepan. Add the onions, carrots, celery, and garlic and sauté over a low heat until slightly soft but not browned, 7 to 10 minutes.

Let the cooked beans and liquid cool slightly, then transfer to a food processor or blender and process until smooth. Add the soubise and process again. Return the blended mixture to the pot and bring to a boil over medium heat, stirring frequently. Add the cooked vegetables, then the honey, vinegar, and molasses. Remove from the heat. Stir in the white pepper. Serve hot, garnished with a spoonful of yogurt and a sprinkling of scallion or red onion.

YIELD *4 cups*

This hearty, full-flavored soup is a Chez Eddy favorite. Unlike lentils, black beans must be soaked before proceeding with the recipe.

SERVING 1 C.

Calories 120.0

Total fat 1.5 gm.

Cholesterol 1.0 mg.

Saturated fat 0.25 gm.

Protein 6.8 gm.

Carbohydrates 22.0 gm.

Sodium 23.0 mg.

SEAFOOD CHOWDER

This robust main-course soup with its Provençal aroma is reminiscent of the fish stews celebrated throughout the Mediterranean region.

4 cups fish stock (page 42)
1 cup soubise (page 48)
1½ pounds firm white fish, such as grouper, halibut, redfish, or red snapper, cut in 1-inch chunks
2 tablespoons lime juice
1 tablespoon olive oil
½ cup white potatoes, peeled and diced
½ cup carrots, peeled and diced
½ cup white or yellow onion, diced
¼ cup green bell pepper, diced
1 tablespoon minced garlic
½ cup tomato concassé (page 50)
1½ tablespoons tomato paste
1½ tablespoons fresh basil, finely chopped
¼ teaspoon fresh thyme, finely chopped
1 bay leaf
1 cup fresh mussels, cooked and removed from shells (see Note below)
1 tablespoon honey
Pinch ground red pepper
¼ teaspoon ground black pepper

SERVING 1 C.

Calories 151.0
Total fat 3.5 gm.
Cholesterol 39.0 mg.
Saturated fat 0.52 gm.
Protein 18.7 gm.
Carbohydrates 10.9 gm.
Sodium 112.0 mg.

Prepare the fish stock and soubise ahead as directed. (See Basic Stocks and Sauces, pages 42 and 48).

Toss the fish chunks with the lime juice in a nonreactive container and set aside to marinate.

Heat the oil in a heavy-bottomed stockpot or Dutch oven. Add the potatoes, carrots, onion, green pepper, and garlic, and sauté over medium heat for 5 to 7 minutes. Add the fish stock and bring to a boil. Reduce the heat and add the tomato concassé, tomato paste, basil, thyme, and bay leaf. Simmer until the vegetables are barely tender, approximately 15 minutes. Add the marinated fish chunks, mussels, and soubise to the pot, stirring to combine. Bring to a boil, then reduce

the heat and simmer until the fish is tender. Remove from the heat and stir in the honey, red pepper, and black pepper. Serve hot.

N O T E Purchase live mussels with shells tightly closed. Simmer in water, or steam until the shells open. Discard any mussels whose shells do not open when cooked.

V A R I A T I O N Mussels also make an excellent low-fat appetizer when simmered in wine that has been flavored with chopped garlic, a drop or two of olive oil, and fresh Provençal herbs, such as oregano and thyme.

Y I E L D *8 cups*

BROCCOLI AND APPLE SOUP

4 cups chicken stock (page 41)
2 cups fresh broccoli, stalks only
1 tablespoon unsalted margarine, clarified (page 123)
2 tablespoons fresh thyme, finely chopped
1 cup onion, thinly sliced
½ cup celery, peeled and diced
1 cup Red Delicious or cooking apple, peeled, cored, and
   roughly diced
1 teaspoon ground black pepper
Garnish: 4 tablespoons nonfat yogurt; 2 tablespoons fresh
   parsley, minced

Prepare the chicken stock ahead as directed.

Trim 2 inches from the woody end of each broccoli stalk and peel the outer skin with a vegetable peeler or paring knife. Cut the peeled broccoli into small dice. Melt the margarine in a large pot or Dutch oven and add to it the thyme, onion, celery, and apple. Cover and cook over low heat for 10 minutes. Next, add the broccoli, chicken stock, and pepper and bring to a boil. Reduce the heat and simmer, covered, for 30 minutes. Remove from the heat and cool slightly, then purée in a blender or food processor. Strain the soup through a fine sieve or a colander lined with several layers of dampened cheesecloth. Serve hot or chilled, garnished with a dollop of nonfat yogurt and minced parsley.

Y I E L D *4 cups*

SERVING 1 C.

Calories 73.0

Total fat 3.2 gm.

Cholesterol 0

Saturated fat 0.60 gm.

Protein 2.6 gm.

Carbohydrates 10.1 gm.

Sodium 37.0 mg.

TWO-POTATO SOUP

4 cups chicken stock (page 41)
1 tablespoon olive oil
4 cups leeks, white part only, carefully washed and chopped
1 teaspoon garlic, minced
½ teaspoon ground red pepper
2 cups white potatoes, in ½-inch dice
2 cups sweet potatoes, in ½-inch dice
1 teaspoon curry powder
½ teaspoon garlic powder
Pinch turmeric, to taste
1 tablespoon lemon juice
1 tablespoon fresh mint, minced
Garnish: 3 tablespoons nonfat yogurt; 6 sprigs of mint

Prepare the chicken stock ahead as directed.

Heat the olive oil in a heavy-bottomed saucepan or Dutch oven over medium heat. Add the leeks, garlic, and red pepper, and sauté until the leeks are translucent, 3 to 5 minutes. Add the chicken stock and bring to a boil. Add the white and sweet potatoes and return to a boil. Reduce the heat and simmer gently until the potatoes are tender, approximately 20 to 25 minutes.

Cool slightly. Purée in a blender or food processor until smooth and return to the pot. Bring the purée to a simmer, then reduce the heat; stir in the curry powder, garlic powder, turmeric, lemon juice, and mint. Simmer for another 3 to 5 minutes until the flavors have mingled.

Serve hot or cold with a spoonful of yogurt and a sprig of mint as garnish.

YIELD *6 cups*

An exotic nuance of curry transforms plebian potato soup into a stellar dish, hot or cold.

SERVING 1 C.
Calories 153.0
Total fat 2.7 gm.
Cholesterol 0
Saturated fat 0.39 gm.
Protein 3.2 gm.
Carbohydrates 30.3 gm.
Sodium 28.0 mg.

CALDO BRAVO

This light, clear soup, with its fresh taste of poached fish and vegetables, is best used as a main course.

4 cups fish stock (page 42)
1 tablespoon olive oil
1 cup onion, finely chopped
2½ cloves garlic, minced
1 bay leaf
1 cup tomato concassé (page 50)
1 teaspoon fresh oregano, finely chopped
1 jalapeño pepper, seeded and chopped
2 sprigs fresh parsley, finely chopped
1 tablespoon fresh cilantro, finely chopped
4 steaks from firmly fleshed fish, such as red snapper, tuna, swordfish, or halibut, 4 ounces each
2 tablespoons lemon juice
White pepper, to taste
Garnish: fresh cilantro leaves

Prepare the fish stock ahead as directed.

Heat the oil in a heavy-bottomed saucepan or Dutch oven and sauté the onions, garlic, and bay leaf for approximately 2 to 3 minutes. Add the tomato concassé and cook, stirring constantly, over medium-high heat until the liquid evaporates and the mixture forms a paste. (Take care not to scorch.) Add the oregano and jalapeño and mix well. Add the fish stock, parsley, and fresh cilantro, and bring to a boil, stirring frequently. Reduce the heat, add the fish steaks, and simmer gently for 7 to 10 minutes. Remove from the heat and lift the steaks out of the broth, placing them in warmed individual soup bowls. Stir the lemon juice and white pepper into the hot broth, then pour it over the fish. Garnish with fresh cilantro.

YIELD *5 cups*

SERVING 1 FISH
STEAK AND
¾ C. BROTH
Calories 154.0
Total fat 6.5 gm.
Cholesterol 35.0 mg.
Saturated fat 1.39 gm.
Protein 18.7 gm.
Carbohydrates 4.6 gm.
Sodium 85.0 mg.

SALMON BISQUE

1 quart fish stock (page 42) or 1 quart Court Bouillon
  (optional, page 44)
½ cup soubise (page 48)
4 ounces poached salmon (see below)
1 tablespoon olive oil
1 teaspoon garlic, finely minced
1 cup onions, chopped
1 to 1½ cups raw salmon bone (from a 6- to 7-pound fish, tail
  intact)
½ cup carrots, peeled and finely minced
1 tablespoon fresh dill
½ cup celery, finely minced
½ cup cognac
½ cup tomato paste
½ cup flour

The rich, creamy texture of this bisque derives, once again, from our soubise.

Prepare the fish stock or Court Bouillon and soubise ahead as directed. (See Basic Stocks and Sauces, pages 42, 44, and 48.) If you do not have poached salmon on hand, poach it now in fish stock or Court Bouillon. Remove the salmon and set aside, reserving the stock.

Add the olive oil to a medium-size, heavy-bottomed saucepan and sauté the garlic, onion, and salmon bone for 2 to 3 minutes over medium heat. Add the carrots, dill, and celery, and cook for 5 minutes. Add the cognac and cook for 1 additional minute. Stir in the tomato paste and dust with flour, stirring to combine. Add the reserved fish stock and soubise and cook for 5 minutes, stirring, until slightly thickened. Remove from the heat and strain through a fine sieve, discarding the solids. Return to the pan and bring to a simmer. Stir in the poached salmon and heat thoroughly.

N O T E The use of raw bones in this recipe adds intensity of flavor. Ask your fish market for any extra salmon bones they may have on hand.

Y I E L D *4 cups*

SERVING 1 C.
Calories 168.0
Total fat 5.6 gm.
Cholesterol 16.0 mg.
Saturated fat 0.82 gm.
Protein 9.2 gm.
Carbohydrates 20.5 gm.
Sodium 44.0 mg.

CREAM OF CHICKEN AND WATERCRESS SOUP

If you increase the amount of chicken, this becomes an attractive main-course soup.

6 cups chicken stock (page 41)
1½ cups soubise (page 48)
5 ounces skinless, boneless chicken breast, finely diced
2 bunches watercress leaves, carefully washed and chopped
White pepper to taste
Garnish: 2 tablespoons nonfat yogurt

Prepare the chicken stock and soubise ahead as directed. (See Basic Stocks and Sauces, pages 41 and 48.)

Bring the chicken stock to a boil and reduce to ½ its original volume. You will have approximately 3 cups. Add the chicken and simmer for 5 minutes. Stir in the watercress and the soubise, cooking for 1 more minute. Season with pepper. Serve garnished with a spoonful of yogurt.

Y I E L D   *4 cups*

SERVING 1 C.

Calories 98.0

Total fat 0.5 gm.

Cholesterol 22.0 mg.

Saturated fat 0.17 gm.

Protein 11.6 gm.

Carbohydrates 11.0 gm.

Sodium 66.0 mg.

CREAM OF PUMPKIN SOUP

6 cups chicken stock (page 41)
1 yellow onion, finely chopped
3 shallots, finely chopped
1 small leek, white part only, finely chopped
2 medium potatoes, peeled and finely chopped
3 ribs of celery, sliced
2 carrots, peeled and chopped
1 tablespoon corn oil
¼ cup Madeira
1 sprig fresh thyme or 1 teaspoon dried thyme
2 teaspoons fresh chervil, finely chopped, or 1 teaspoon dried
  chervil
1 bay leaf
1 small pumpkin, peeled, seeded, and cut into cubes
  (approximately 1 cup puréed pumpkin)
½ cup evaporated skim milk
Garnish: paprika

Prepare the chicken stock ahead as directed.

In a 2-quart saucepan, sauté the onion, shallots, leek, potatoes, celery, and carrots in the corn oil until soft. Add the Madeira, cover and cook over low heat for about 5 minutes. Add the chicken stock, herbs, and pumpkin, and bring to a boil. Reduce heat and simmer for 30 minutes. Strain the mixture into a bowl, reserving the liquid. Remove the bay leaf and transfer the remaining solids to the container of a blender or food processor. Process until smooth, adding the reserved liquid in small amounts until you achieve the desired consistency. Stir in the evaporated milk, combining thoroughly, and return the soup to the pan. Serve hot, garnished with paprika.

YIELD *8 cups*

You may present this striking fall specialty in a hollow pumpkin shell on a platter garnished with seasonal vegetables.

SERVING 1 C.

Calories 69.0

Total fat 1.9 gm.

Cholesterol 2.0 mg.

Saturated fat 0.27 gm.

Protein 1.9 gm.

Carbohydrates 11.9 gm.

Sodium 14.0 mg.

POLISH BLACKBERRY SOUP

*A*t *Chez Eddy,*
this attractive dish
is also a popular
choice for dessert.

1 pint fresh blackberries, rinsed and drained
½ cup granulated sugar
2 cups cold water
2 small lemons, thinly sliced
1 stick cinnamon
2 whole cloves
2 cups nonfat yogurt
Garnish: a small dollop of yogurt, 1 whole blackberry, and
        2 fresh mint leaves per serving

In a medium-size saucepan over medium-high heat, combine the berries, sugar, water, lemons, cinnamon, and cloves. Bring to a boil, then reduce the heat and simmer 10 minutes. Remove the cinnamon and cloves, and purée the berry mixture in a food processor or blender until smooth. Strain through a sieve and chill. Add the yogurt, mixing well. Refrigerate. When ready to serve, add a small dollop of yogurt to each bowl of soup, top with a whole blackberry, and flank with two mint leaves.

Y I E L D *6 cups*

SERVING 1 C.

Calories 131.0

Total fat 0.3 gm.

Cholesterol 2.0 mg.

Saturated fat 0.09 gm.

Protein 4.7 gm.

Carbohydrates 28.5 gm.

Sodium 58.0 mg.

FRESH STRAWBERRY SOUP

2 pints fresh strawberries
4 green Granny Smith apples
1 cup fresh orange juice
1 cup red wine
1 cup nonfat yogurt
Liquid fructose, to taste (optional)
Garnish: fresh mint leaves

Wash, hull, and halve the strawberries. Peel and core the apples, then cut them into dice. Add the diced apples to the container of a blender or food processor and purée. Strain through a fine sieve. In similar fashion, purée and strain the strawberries. Pour the purée into a medium-size bowl and stir in the orange juice, red wine, and yogurt. Add the apple purée, mixing thoroughly to combine. Sweeten with fructose, if desired, and chill thoroughly. Garnish with fresh mint leaves.

Y I E L D *4 cups*

*T*his fairly tart, rosy concoction makes a delectable first course.

SERVING 1 C.

Calories 226.0

Total fat 1.2 gm.

Cholesterol 1.0 mg.

Saturated fat 0.18 gm.

Protein 4.9 gm.

Carbohydrates 42.7 gm.

Sodium 51.0 mg.

COLD MELON SOUP

The essence of summer in a bowl, this light starter also makes an unusual dessert.

3 cups cantaloupe, peeled and finely chopped
1 cup fresh orange juice
1 tablespoon fresh lime juice
1½ tablespoons honey
1 cup champagne or dry white wine
Garnish: fresh mint leaves

Add half the cantaloupe along with the two juices and the honey to the container of a blender or food processor. Process until smooth. Stir in the champagne or wine and the remainder of the melon. Cover and chill for several hours. Serve garnished with fresh mint.

VARIATION For a different visual effect, you may purée all the cantaloupe and garnish with small balls of honeydew melon.

YIELD *5 cups*

SERVING 1 C.

Calories 119.0

Total fat 0.4 gm.

Cholesterol 0

Saturated fat 0.17 gm.

Protein 1.3 gm.

Carbohydrates 22.7 gm.

Sodium 25.0 mg.

MAIN-COURSE
SALADS

·····················:::::·····················

THE COMPOSED SALAD PLAYS A UNIQUE role in fine dining. With meat or seafood, and sometimes a starch, added to a delicate mixture of crisp greens, this mainstay of the luncheon menu has become a popular choice for light dinners all year round. Particularly when dressed in intense flavors and bound with a minimum of oil, such main-course salads provide a deep satisfaction with relatively few calories. In fact, it's not at all uncommon for Chez Eddy patrons to follow Grilled Thai Chicken Salad (page 143) or Seafood-Pasta Salad (page 150), for example, with a luscious dessert for a total of less than 500 calories.

The key in composing such hearty salads is to view the seafood, meat, or pasta as a base tone against which to establish a melody line consisting of complementary vegetables or perhaps a mellow dressing, sparked with striking, even surprising, accents. This broad concept allows you to play variations on an ethnic theme, such as Chez Eddy Sliced Beef Salad with Five-Spice Dressing (page 154), or indulge in eclectic improvisations in the manner of Chicken Salad Enrico (page 145). In this chapter we have provided only a representative sampling. The possible combinations are endless.

....

Chicken-Pasta Salad with Spicy Garlic Dressing

Béarnaise-Chicken Salad

Grilled Thai Chicken Salad

Chicken-Barley Salad

Chicken Salad Enrico with Mango Vinaigrette

Southwestern Chicken Salad

Grilled Tuna Niçoise

Warm Scallop Salad with Tomato Coulis and Mint

Seafood-Pasta Salad with Curry-Cumin Dressing

Country Garden Pasta Salad

Chez Eddy Sliced Beef Salad with Five-Spice Dressing

Grilled Chicken Caesar Salad

Crab Picante

....

CHICKEN-PASTA SALAD WITH SPICY GARLIC DRESSING

3 skinless, boneless chicken breasts, 4 ounces each, halved, poached (page 107), and cut into 1-inch cubes
2 red bell peppers, roasted (page 67), cut into julienne strips
Spicy Garlic Dressing (see below)
4 scallions, thinly sliced
¼ cup parsley, finely chopped
2 tablespoons capers, drained, rinsed, and drained again
4 cups fusilli (corkscrew) pasta, cooked
Garnish: 12 tomato slices, 12 cucumber slices

The pungent dressing lends zip to this substantial salad.

Prepare the chicken breasts, peppers, and dressing as directed.

In a large bowl, toss the chicken, peppers, scallions, parsley, and capers with ½ cup of the dressing. Add the cooled pasta and toss well. Garnish: with sliced cucumber and tomatoes.

VARIATION You may substitute water-packed, twice-rinsed tuna for the chicken, if you wish. Drain carefully before adding to the salad

YIELD *6 cups*

SPICY GARLIC DRESSING

¼ cup nonfat yogurt
¼ cup reduced-calorie mayonnaise
2 medium cloves garlic, minced
Pinch ground black pepper, to taste
Pinch ground red pepper, to taste
1 tablespoon corn or canola oil
2 tablespoons champagne vinegar

In a small bowl, whisk together the yogurt, mayonnaise, garlic, peppers, oil, and vinegar. Set aside until needed.

YIELD *1 cup*

SERVING 1 C. SALAD WITH 2 TBS. DRESSING
Calories 245.0
Total fat 7.4 gm.
Cholesterol 40.0 mg.
Saturated fat 1.28 gm.
Protein 17.7 gm.
Carbohydrates 26.5 gm.
Sodium 103.0 mg.

BÉARNAISE-CHICKEN SALAD

*H*ere, moist chunks of chicken are bound with a low-fat tarragon mayonnaise, spiked with white wine. We call it béarnaise after the traditional tarragon-flavored sauce, usually served warm, but we omit the egg yolks and butter.

2 skinless, boneless chicken breasts, 8 ounces each, halved, poached (page 107), and cut into 1-inch cubes
¼ cup raisins
1 cup celery, cut diagonally into thin slices
2 tablespoons scallions, finely chopped
¼ cup reduced-calorie mayonnaise
¼ cup nonfat yogurt
1 tablespoon dry white wine
¼ cup parsley, finely chopped
1½ teaspoons fresh tarragon, finely chopped, or ½ teaspoon dried tarragon
Pinch white pepper, to taste
Garnish: red leaf lettuce leaves, fresh tarragon leaves, fresh strawberries (halved), and 2 tablespoons toasted almonds

Prepare the chicken breasts as directed.

Cover the raisins in boiling water and soak until they are plump, about 5 to 10 minutes. Drain thoroughly and dry with paper towels. Combine the raisins, chicken, celery, and scallions in a large bowl. In a small bowl, whisk together the mayonnaise, yogurt, wine, parsley, tarragon, and pepper. Add ½ cup of this dressing to the chicken mixture and toss gently to coat. Cover and refrigerate.

When ready to serve, place one leaf of red leaf lettuce in the middle of each chilled salad plate. Mound the cool chicken salad off center so that most of the leaf is exposed. Arrange two strawberry halves at the base of the chicken salad. Garnish with a sprig of fresh tarragon and toasted almonds. This salad will keep in the refrigerator for 2 to 3 days.

V A R I A T I O N This chunky chicken salad makes a fine filling for sandwiches. Slip ¼ cup into each half of a split pita bread, and garnish with tarragon and red leaf lettuce, as above.

Y I E L D *4 cups*

SERVING 1 C.
CHICKEN SALAD
WITH 2 TBS.
DRESSING
Calories 213.0
Total fat 6.2 gm.
Cholesterol 76.0 mg.
Saturated fat 1.37 gm.
Protein 27.9 gm.
Carbohydrates 10.4 gm.
Sodium 158.0 mg.

GRILLED THAI CHICKEN SALAD

Thai Dressing (see below)
2 skinless, boneless chicken breasts, 8 ounces each, halved
6 cups romaine lettuce leaves, torn into bite-size pieces
½ cup scallions, white part only, chopped
½ cup diced red onion
½ cup cilantro leaves, finely chopped
Garnish: leaves of red leaf lettuce, ½ cup tomato concassé
  (page 50), toasted sesame seeds (see Note below)

Prepare the Thai Dressing as directed. Grill the chicken (page 161) until cooked through, approximately 6 to 7 minutes, turning once after 4 minutes. Combine the romaine, scallions, red onion, and cilantro in a large bowl, tossing to mix well.

When ready to serve, line 4 plates with red leaf lettuce. Add the tossed greens. Remove the chicken and slice it on the bias. Arrange over the greens, drizzle each serving with 1 tablespoon of Thai Dressing, top with tomato concassé, and sprinkle with sesame seeds.

N O T E To toast sesame seeds, place on a baking sheet in a 350°F oven and toast until lightly brown, 3 to 5 minutes, being careful not to let them burn.

Y I E L D *4 servings*

THAI DRESSING

½ cup rice wine vinegar
¼ cup olive oil
2½ tablespoons reduced-sodium soy sauce
½ tablespoon crushed red pepper flakes

Place the ingredients in a jar with a tight-fitting lid and shake well to mix. Refrigerate until needed. Will keep in the refrigerator for 5 to 7 days.

Y I E L D *1 cup*

SERVING 3 OZ.
CHICKEN AND 1 ¼ C.
MIXED GREENS WITH
1 TB. DRESSING

Calories 216.0

Total fat 8.1 gm.

Cholesterol 72.0 mg.

Saturated fat 1.55 gm.

Protein 29.2 gm.

Carbohydrates 6.0 gm.

Sodium 138.0 mg.

SERVING 1 TB.

Calories 31.0

Total fat 3.4 gm.

Cholesterol 0

Saturated fat 0.46 gm.

Protein 0.1 gm.

Carbohydrates 0.5 gm.

Sodium 65.0 mg.

CHICKEN-BARLEY SALAD

This colorful salad is surprisingly substantial.

1 skinless, boneless chicken breast (8 ounces), halved, poached (page 107), and cut into ¾-inch chunks
2 cups barley, cooked according to package directions, without salt, drained, and cooled
¼ cup red onion, finely diced
¼ cup scallions, finely diced
¼ cup cooked asparagus, finely sliced
¼ cup snow peas, cooked and cut in half crosswise
¼ cup Champagne Vinaigrette (page 53)
¼ cup roasted red bell pepper (page 67), drained well and cut into ½-inch juliennes
16 leaves of Belgian endive
16 whole cooked asparagus, cooled
16 tomato wedges
1 cup mixed greens, chopped (romaine or red leaf)

Prepare the chicken breast as directed.

In a large bowl, combine the cooked barley, red onion, scallions, sliced asparagus, and snow peas, mixing thoroughly. Add the chicken and toss gently. Sprinkle the mixture with the vinaigrette, tossing to coat evenly. Just before serving, fold in the roasted red bell pepper.

For each serving, garnish each chilled dinner plate with 4 leaves of Belgian endive and 4 whole asparagus spears equidistant from each other, so that the plate is divided into quadrants. Place one tomato wedge on top of each endive leaf. Mound ¼ cup of the chopped mixed greens in the center of the plate. Mound 1 cup of the salad mixture on top of the mixed greens and serve.

N O T E Roasted peppers are added only moments before serving so their red color will not be absorbed by the salad. They should be kept on waxed paper, blotted periodically, then blotted again carefully before use. The salad mixture may be prepared a day in advance. Add the dressing and peppers when ready to serve.

Y I E L D *6 cups*

SERVING 1 C.

Calories 345.0

Total fat 5.1 gm.

Cholesterol 24.0 mg.

Saturated fat 0.85 gm.

Protein 17.8 gm.

Carbohydrates 59.0 gm.

Sodium 37.0 mg.

CHICKEN SALAD ENRICO WITH MANGO VINAIGRETTE

2 skinless, boneless chicken breasts, 8 ounces each, halved,
 poached (page 107), cut into 1-inch cubes, and chilled
Mango Vinaigrette (see below)
2 ripe mangoes, peeled, seeded, and cut into ½-inch cubes
12 honeydew melon balls
12 cantaloupe melon balls
Garnish: 8 radicchio leaves, 8 red leaf lettuce leaves, and
 1 tablespoon cilantro, finely chopped

Prepare the chicken breasts and Mango Vinaigrette as directed.

While the dressing chills, toss together the chicken, mangoes, honeydew, and cantaloupe in a large nonreactive bowl. Add the vinaigrette to coat lightly and toss well again.

When ready to serve, arrange 2 radicchio leaves and 2 red leaf lettuce leaves alternately on each of 4 large chilled plates so that the plates are divided into quadrants. Place the salad in the center of the plate and garnish with chopped cilantro leaves.

YIELD *4 cups*

MANGO VINAIGRETTE

1 ripe mango
2 tablespoons rice wine vinegar
1 teaspoon sesame seed oil
1 teaspoon olive oil
½ teaspoon curry powder
2 tablespoons white wine

Peel, seed, and cut the mango into chunks. Add all the ingredients to the container of a blender or food processor. Process until smooth. Refrigerate.

YIELD *1 cup*

The fresh, sweet flavor of this salad is perfect for a summer supper or lunch on a hot day.

SERVING 1 C. SALAD
WITH ¼ C. DRESSING
Calories 208.0
Total fat 5.9 gm.
Cholesterol 72.0 mg.
Saturated fat 1.36 gm.
Protein 28.0 gm.
Carbohydrates 36.9 gm.
Sodium 80.0 mg.

SOUTHWESTERN CHICKEN SALAD

Spicy pumpkin seeds add a little kick to this cool mixture of chicken, avocado, and Southwestern seasonings.

2 skinless, boneless chicken breasts, 8 ounces each, halved, poached (page 107) and cut into 1-inch chunks
1 avocado, pitted, peeled, and diced
4 tablespoons fresh lime juice
1 cup tomato concassé (page 50)
½ cup red onion, finely chopped
½ cup cilantro, finely chopped
½ teaspoon lime zest, grated
1 teaspoon olive oil
¼ teaspoon ground cumin
¼ teaspoon chili powder
1 cup red cabbage, finely shredded
1 cup green cabbage, finely shredded
Garnish: 2 tablespoons Spicy Pumpkin Seeds (opposite page)

Prepare the chicken breasts as directed and refrigerate.

Toss the avocado with 2 tablespoons of the lime juice in a large non-reactive bowl. Add the tomato concassé, red onion, and cilantro. In a small nonreactive container, whisk together the remaining lime juice, lime zest, olive oil, cumin, and chili powder. Add to the avocado mixture and toss gently. Fold in the chicken and refrigerate for at least 1 hour to allow the flavors to blend.

When ready to serve, arrange alternating portions of shredded red and green cabbage on each chilled salad plate. Spoon the salad into the center, sprinkling the top with Spicy Pumpkin Seeds. This salad may be kept in the refrigerator for 2 to 3 days.

YIELD *2½ cups*

SERVING ½ C. SALAD
WITH 2 TBS.
PUMPKIN SEEDS
Calories 197.0
Total fat 8.4 gm.
Cholesterol 58.0 mg.
Saturated fat 1.66 gm.
Protein 23.4 gm.
Carbohydrates 7.7 gm.
Sodium 65.0 mg.

SPICY PUMPKIN SEEDS

2 cloves garlic, minced
2 tablespoons olive oil
4 teaspoons cumin
2 teaspoons paprika
1 teaspoon ground red pepper
1 cup pumpkin seeds, shelled and unsalted

Preheat the oven to 400°F. In a small, heavy-bottomed skillet, sauté the garlic in the olive oil, without browning. Strain the oil and discard the garlic. Return the garlic-flavored oil to the skillet. Add the cumin, paprika, and red pepper and cook over low heat, stirring occasionally, about 1 minute. Place the pumpkin seeds on a baking sheet, scrape the spice mixture over the seeds, and toss to coat evenly. Spread the seeds in a single layer and bake in the oven for about 5 minutes, or until they turn light brown. The seeds will pop and dance during baking. They burn easily, so take care not to scorch. Cool to room temperature and store in an airtight container. They may be kept in the refrigerator for 1 to 2 weeks without loss of flavor.

N O T E Pumpkin seeds are available, shelled and unsalted, from specialty or gourmet markets, or you may prepare your own, as follows: Remove seeds from a pumpkin. Rinse the seeds thoroughly and dry them on paper towels. Spread the seeds in a single layer on a sheet pan and place in a warm, sunlit area for several hours. The sheet pan acts as a solar collector, accelerating the drying process. After they are dried, shell the seeds and proceed with recipe.

GRILLED TUNA NICOISE

*Y*ou can also use canned water-packed tuna or grilled or sautéed chicken breast.

4 tuna steaks, 4 ounces each
2 tablespoons balsamic vinegar
1 teaspoon Spice Blend (see page 55)
4 cups mixed greens, such as romaine, butterhead, red leaf, radicchio
8 medium red potatoes, steamed until tender, quartered, chilled
½ pound fresh green beans, steamed al dente, chilled
2 plum tomatoes, quartered
1 lemon cut into 8 wedges
½ cup Balsamic Vinaigrette (see below)

Sprinkle the tuna steaks with balsamic vinegar and Spice Blend and refrigerate 1 hour. Grill or broil tuna about 2 minutes on each side. Tuna should be slightly pink in the middle.

To assemble salad, mound greens on 4 dinner plates. Arrange potato wedges, green beans, tomatoes, and lemon wedges around outside of the greens. Place warm tuna steaks on top of the greens and drizzle each serving with 2 tablespoons Balsamic Vinaigrette.

Y I E L D *4 servings*

BALSAMIC VINAIGRETTE

¾ cup nonfat yogurt
½ cup balsamic vinegar
¼ teaspoon garlic, minced
¾ teaspoon cracked black pepper
1 tablespoon Dijon mustard
2 tablespoons olive oil

Place the yogurt in a medium bowl and set aside. Combine the balsamic vinegar, garlic, pepper, mustard, and olive oil in a medium bowl. Whisk together until smooth. Slowly pour the balsamic vinegar mixture into the yogurt and whisk until smooth. Chill well before serving. This will keep refrigerated for 3 to 5 days.

Y I E L D *1¼ cups*

WARM SCALLOP SALAD WITH TOMATO COULIS AND MINT

2 cups Fresh Tomato Coulis (page 51)
2 tablespoons fresh mint, finely chopped
1 tablespoon olive oil
1 pound sea scallops, well drained, then patted dry
3 bunches watercress, carefully washed and large stems removed
Pinch coarsely cracked black pepper, to taste

Combine the Fresh Tomato Coulis with the mint and refrigerate. Heat the oil in a nonstick skillet and sauté the scallops over medium-high heat until done, about 1 minute. They should be barely opaque throughout and slightly resilient to the touch. Remove from the heat and keep warm.

Dry the watercress and divide it equally among the individual salad or luncheon plates. Arrange the scallops in a circle, spooning the Tomato Coulis into the center of each circle. Season with pepper.

V A R I A T I O N   To present this salad as a cold dish, cook the scallops up to 6 hours ahead and refrigerate. When ready to serve, mix the scallops with the coulis and present on the bed of chilled watercress.

Y I E L D   *4 cups*

We like the contrast of warm, sweet scallops with cold, peppery watercress and mint-studded Tomato Coulis. This dish, however, may be eaten chilled (see Variation below).

SERVING 1 C.

Calories 115.0
Total fat 2.2 gm.
Cholesterol 33.0 mg.
Saturated fat 0.27 gm.
Protein 17.9 gm.
Carbohydrates 5.6 gm.
Sodium 212.0 mg.

SEAFOOD-PASTA SALAD WITH CURRY-CUMIN DRESSING

The seafood in this fragrant dish should be quite visible. You may use either shrimp or jumbo lump crab, but do not chop the shrimp too finely. We've chosen fusilli for the pasta, because creamy dressings cling well to its long spiral shape.

Curry-Cumin Dressing (opposite page)
2 cups cooked seafood, such as shrimp or jumbo lump crabmeat
4 teaspoons scallions, finely chopped
3 cups fusilli (corkscrew) pasta, cooked al dente
3 cups mixed greens, chopped (red leaf lettuce or romaine)
Garnish: alfalfa sprouts; 8 cherry tomatoes, halved; 4 teaspoons
  sliced toasted almonds (see below)

Prepare the dressing and toast the almonds as directed.

When the dressing is ready, add the seafood, scallions, and cooked pasta to a large bowl and toss. Add enough of the dressing to coat the salad mixture lightly and toss again. Chill.

When ready to serve, place a small bundle of sprouts on the edge of a chilled dinner plate. Arrange ½ cup of chopped lettuce in the center of the plate. Mound the salad mixture on top of the lettuce. Garnish with 3 cherry tomato halves and sprinkle with 1 tablespoon of toasted almonds.

TO TOAST ALMONDS Spread sliced almonds on a baking sheet and toast in a 300°F oven for 5 to 7 minutes, or until golden. Take care not to scorch.

NOTE Any pasta will absorb color and flavor from the dressing, both of which will intensify the longer the dressed pasta is held. In fact, many people prefer the stronger effect. This salad keeps well in the refrigerator for 2 to 3 days. Or you may refrigerate the ingredients and combine them when ready to serve.

YIELD *6 cups*

SERVING ¾ C. PASTA
AND 3 OZ. SEAFOOD
WITH 2 TBS.
DRESSING
Calories 195.0
Total fat 4.9 gm.
Cholesterol 111.0 mg.
Saturated fat 0.58 gm.
Protein 16.3 gm.
Carbohydrates 23.0 gm.
Sodium 169.0 mg.

CURRY-CUMIN DRESSING

¾ cup reduced-calorie mayonnaise
1¼ cups nonfat yogurt
4 teaspoons ground cumin
½ teaspoon ground red pepper
2 teaspoons curry powder

Mix all ingredients together in a medium-size bowl and chill.

Y I E L D *2 cups*

SERVING 2 TBS.

Calories 22.0

Total fat 1.7 gm.

Cholesterol 2.0 mg.

Saturated fat 0.27 gm.

Protein 0.6 gm.

Carbohydrates 0.9 gm.

Sodium 40.0 mg.

COUNTRY GARDEN PASTA SALAD

The success of this dish depends on the texture of the vegetables, which must be crunchy in contrast to the tender resistance of the pasta. Do not overcook either component.

1 cup fresh vegetables, such as carrots and zucchini, cut into matchsticks; and broccoli and snow peas, cut into bite-size pieces
2 tablespoons fresh basil, finely chopped
1 cup Creole Mustard Dressing (opposite page)
4 cups small-shell pasta, cooked al dente
Garnish: 12 slices fresh pineapple, 12 slices ripe tomato, 2 tablespoons Parmesan cheese

Bring 4 cups of water to a boil in a large, heavy-bottomed pot and add the vegetables, blanching them for 1 to 2 minutes, or until barely tender. Drain the vegetables in a colander, then plunge them into a large bowl of ice water to stop the cooking. Cool and drain well.

At least 1 hour before serving, add the vegetables, the basil, and ¼ cup of dressing to the pasta. Toss gently until thoroughly combined and refrigerate. When ready to serve, place ¼ of the salad mixture on each chilled dinner plate, garnished with 3 slices of pineapple and 3 tomato slices. Sprinkle with Parmesan cheese just before serving.

V A R I A T I O N You may, of course, substitute your favorite vegetables for the ones given above. The salad ingredients may be prepared a day in advance and refrigerated separately. Merely add diced poached chicken breast to transform this into an even more substantial main course.

Y I E L D *4 cups*

SERVING 1 C. SALAD
WITH 1 TB. DRESSING
Calories 136.0
Total fat 5.4 gm.
Cholesterol 1.0 mg.
Saturated fat 0.91 gm.
Protein 3.7 gm.
Carbohydrates 18.6 gm.
Sodium 77.0 mg.

CREOLE MUSTARD DRESSING

¼ cup whole-grain or Creole mustard
2 medium cloves garlic, minced
¼ cup lemon juice
2 tablespoons sherry wine vinegar
¼ teaspoon pepper, coarsely ground
⅓ cup olive oil

In a medium-size nonreactive bowl, combine the mustard, garlic, lemon juice, vinegar, and pepper. Whisk in the olive oil to form an emulsion and refrigerate until ready to use.

Y I E L D *1 cup*

SERVING 1 TB.

Calories 44.0

Total fat 4.7 gm.

Cholesterol 0

Saturated fat 0.62 gm.

Protein 0.2 gm.

Carbohydrates 0.7 gm.

Sodium 49.0 mg.

CHEZ EDDY SLICED BEEF SALAD WITH FIVE-SPICE DRESSING

The exotic flavor of Chinese five-spice gives this cold beef dish a distinctive twist.

1 pound beef tenderloin, all fat carefully trimmed
2 tablespoons reduced-sodium soy sauce
1 clove garlic, minced
2 tablespoons brown sugar
2 tablespoons rice wine vinegar
¼ teaspoon Chinese five-spice powder (see Note)
½ cup nonfat yogurt
¼ cup reduced-calorie mayonnaise
6 cups romaine lettuce leaves, torn into bite-size pieces
Pinch freshly ground white pepper, to taste
Garnish: 4 scallions, finely sliced; 4 sprigs watercress

Bring 3 quarts of water to a boil. Add the beef and boil for 15 to 18 minutes (rare or very rare). Boil longer if you desire more fully cooked meat.

While the meat cooks, bring to a boil in a small saucepan the soy sauce, garlic, brown sugar, and vinegar. Reduce the heat and simmer for about 1 minute. Add the five-spice powder and let cool.

When the beef is done, remove it from the water and let it rest at room temperature for about 15 minutes. When cool, slice along the grain into ½-inch slices; then slice across the grain into 2½- to 3-inch julienne strips. Refrigerate for 10 minutes. (Meat should not be too cold when served.)

Finish the dressing by combining the yogurt with the mayonnaise in a small bowl. Stir in the cooled soy sauce and vinegar mixture, mixing thoroughly. Cover and refrigerate for 15 to 20 minutes.

When ready to serve, line 4 plates with lettuce. Arrange strips of beef in a crown over the lettuce and drizzle each serving with 1 tablespoon of the dressing. Season the meat with freshly ground pepper and sprinkle it with sliced scallions. Place a sprig of watercress in the center of the crown.

SERVING 3 OZ. BEEF
WITH 1 TB. DRESSING

Calories 193.0

Total fat 9.1 gm.

Cholesterol 72.5 mg.

Saturated fat 3.5 gm.

Protein 24.5 gm.

Carbohydrates 2.0 gm.

Sodium 133.0 mg.

NOTE Five-spice powder and rice wine vinegar are available on many grocery shelves and at most Asian markets. Five-spice powder typically contains clove, star anise, anise seed, cinnamon or cassia, and Szechuan peppercorns, although some versions contain cardamom or orange peel. Rice wine vinegar has a mild, sweet flavor, but take care to avoid brands containing MSG.

YIELD *4 servings*

GRILLED CHICKEN CAESAR SALAD

2 skinless, boneless chicken breasts, 8 ounces each, halved
1 tablespoon rice wine vinegar
1 teaspoon Spice Blend (see page 55)
1 large head romaine lettuce, washed, drained, and torn into
  bite-size pieces
1 small cucumber, peeled, seeded, and diced
1 cup unseasoned croutons
½ cup Caesar Dressing (see below)
2 plum tomatoes, quartered
½ medium red onion, thinly sliced

Sprinkle chicken breasts with rice wine vinegar and Spice Blend and refrigerate 1 hour before grilling. Grill the chicken for approximately 5 minutes per side. Let chicken cool to room temperature and cut into julienne strips.

In a large bowl combine chicken, lettuce, cucumber, croutons, and ½ cup Caesar Dressing. Toss well. Arrange on 4 chilled plates. Garnish with tomatoes and red onion.

Y I E L D *4 servings*

CAESAR DRESSING

¼ cup red wine vinegar
1 tablespoon prepared mustard
1 tablespoon olive oil
Juice of ½ lemon
1 cup reduced-calorie mayonnaise
1 cup nonfat yogurt
1½ tablespoons cracked black pepper
¼ cup Parmesan cheese, grated
1 tablespoon garlic, minced

Combine the vinegar, mustard, olive oil, and lemon juice in a medium bowl. Whisk in the remaining ingredients until well blended. Chill well before serving. The dressing will keep refrigerated 1 week.

Y I E L D *2¾ cups*

SERVING 3 OZ.
CHICKEN, 2 TBS.
DRESSING, 1 C.
GREENS, AND ¼ C.
CROUTONS
Calories 251.0
Total fat 8.0 gm.
Cholesterol 79.0 mg.
Saturated fat 1.8 gm.
Protein 31.0 gm.
Carbohydrates 12.5 gm.
Sodium 246.0 mg.

SERVING 2 TBS.
Calories 48.0
Total fat 4.3 gm.
Cholesterol 5.0 mg.
Saturated fat 0.8 gm.
Protein 1.1 gm.
Carbohydrates 1.5 gm.
Sodium 98.0 mg.

CRAB PICANTE

3 cups jumbo lump crabmeat, picked over carefully
Cilantro Vinaigrette (see below)
¼ cup Pico de Gallo (page 84)
2 cups romaine lettuce, chopped
Garnish: leaves of red leaf lettuce, slices of ripe cantaloupe and
   honeydew melon, fresh strawberries (halved)

In a large bowl, toss the crabmeat gently with ¼ cup of the vinaigrette
and ¼ cup Pico de Gallo.

   When ready to serve, place a whole lettuce leaf on one side of a
chilled dinner plate with the base of the leaf in the center. Arrange
2 slices of cantaloupe and 3 of honeydew just off center so that they
touch the base of the lettuce leaf, making a circle. In that circle place
½ cup of chopped lettuce and mound the dressed crabmeat on top.
Garnish with fresh strawberry halves, pointing outward toward the
edge of the plate, touching the crabmeat at their base.

YIELD *4 cups*

The mellow succulence of lump crab is nicely balanced by this slightly astringent treatment, perfumed with jalapeño.

SERVING ¾ C. CRAB
SALAD WITH 1 TB.
DRESSING
Calories 118.0
Total fat 4.9 gm.
Cholesterol 85.0 mg.
Saturated fat 0.62 gm.
Protein 17.7 gm.
Carbohydrates 0.2 gm.
Sodium 237.0 mg.

CILANTRO VINAIGRETTE

2 teaspoons cider vinegar
2 teaspoons cilantro, finely chopped
1 tablespoon lemon juice
2 tablespoons corn or canola oil
1 tablespoon white wine

Whisk together the vinegar, cilantro, lemon juice, oil, and white wine.

YIELD *½ cup*

SERVING 1 TB.
Calories 31.0
Total fat 3.4 gm.
Cholesterol 0
Saturated fat 0.43 gm.
Protein 0
Carbohydrates 0.2 gm.
Sodium 0

POULTRY

....

THE TASTY AND VERSATILE CHICKEN breast provides a delightful foil for a multitude of salsas, marinades, and sauces. In this chapter, we offer some of our favorite preparations, spicy ones, such as Chicken Montero, served with our Spicy Corn Relish (page 67), and pungent Grilled Chicken Pepita (page 164), which incorporates chilies and tomatillos into a pumpkin-seed base. But there are mild recipes, too, reveling in the nuances of our reduced demi-glace, spiked with citrus and fresh herbs.

So varied, indeed, are these delights that sometimes we tend to forget that poultry means more than chicken. For example, duck, turkey, and poussin also find low-caloric treatments in the recipes that follow. Turkey, of course, is well known—although the traditional holiday bird appears more often on weekday dinner plates as its distinctive flavor wins new admirers. The less familiar poussin is simply baby chicken, which offers a more fragile taste and is, therefore, best presented simply.

The inclusion here of duck, however, may be a surprise, especially to people who associate it with dishes that focus on its significant fat layer, rendered crispy and caloric. Yet, when trimmed correctly, duck breast can be delectably lean. Simply grilled over charcoal, or presented with our five-spice sauce and served rare, duck is a revelation to heart-wise carnivores of every stripe.

....

Chicken Montero

Grilled Chicken with Orange-Cilantro Sauce

Grilled Chicken Pepita

Chicken Brochette with Tarragon Sauce

Chez Eddy Chicken Fajitas

Grilled Chicken Tabbouleh

Roasted Turkey Breast with Thyme Sauce

Grilled Poussin with Poached Pear-and-Wine Sauce

Sautéed Duck Breast with Five-Spice Peach Sauce

Stir-Fried Chicken with Sweet and Sour Sauce

Sautéed Duck Breast with Raspberry-Vinegar Sauce

....

CHICKEN MONTERO

2 skinless, boneless chicken breasts, 8 ounces each, halved and
  pounded to an even thickness
Spicy Corn Relish (page 67)
Garnish: 4 tablespoons julienned jicama; ½ teaspoon ground red
  pepper

Prepare the grill with nonstick spray. Make a fire with your preferred
material, charcoal briquettes and/or aromatic wood such as mesquite,
hickory, or pecan. Let the fire burn down to hot coals. Grill the chicken
over the hot coals for approximately 5 minutes per side, turning once.
It will be done when the flesh loses its soft texture and springs back to
the touch. Keep warm while you prepare the relish as directed.

   When ready to serve, place ¼ cup of corn relish on each plate. Top
with the grilled chicken. Spread 1 tablespoon jicama over each breast
and dust with red pepper if more heat is desired (you can use paprika
for color, if not).

N O T E The chicken may be broiled, if you prefer not to grill.

Y I E L D *4 servings*

This dish provides rich contrasts of color, texture, and flavor. The piquant relish may also be served as a side dish, with other chicken recipes or with seafood.

SERVING 3 OZ.
CHICKEN AND
¼ C. RELISH
Calories 210.0
Total fat 6.8 gm.
Cholesterol 72.0 mg.
Saturated fat 1.48 gm.
Protein 27.6 gm.
Carbohydrates 19.4 gm.
Sodium 69.0 mg.

GRILLED CHICKEN WITH ORANGE-CILANTRO SAUCE

We are very fond of cilantro, or coriander leaf, with chicken and fish dishes. Here it imparts a little mystery to this sunny, uncomplicated orange sauce.

Orange-Cilantro Sauce (opposite page)
2 skinless, boneless chicken breasts, 8 ounces each, halved
2 tablespoons cumin seeds
1¼ cups nonfat yogurt
Pinch ground black pepper, to taste
1 tablespoon fresh cilantro, chopped
4 to 5 tablespoons fresh orange juice mixed with 1 teaspoon
   olive oil
Garnish: 4 thin slices fresh navel orange; 4 sprigs fresh cilantro

Prepare the Orange-Cilantro Sauce as directed.

Wrap the chicken breasts with plastic wrap and pound with a mallet or rolling pin lightly to flatten them. Toast the cumin seeds in a skillet over medium-high heat, tossing until lightly browned. Let cool, then pulverize, either with a mortar and pestle or in a food processor. Rub the chicken lightly with 2 teaspoons of the cumin.

For the marinade, combine 1¼ cups yogurt with 2 teaspoons cumin, the pepper, and the cilantro. Marinate the chicken in the refrigerator for 6 hours or longer.

Remove the marinated chicken from the refrigerator and allow it to come to room temperature before grilling. Meanwhile, prepare the grill as directed on previous page. When the fire is ready, brush off the excess marinade and grill the chicken 4 to 5 minutes per side or until done, basting with the mixture of orange juice and olive oil as it cooks.

When ready to serve, nap plate with a little sauce, rotating so that cilantro leaves will be visible. Add chicken to the corner of the sauce, garnished with a slice of fresh orange and a sprig of cilantro.

N O T E The chicken may be broiled, if you prefer not to grill.

Y I E L D *12 ounces chicken*

SERVING 3 OZ. CHICKEN WITH 2 TBS. SAUCE

Calories 186.0
Total fat 4.1 gm.
Cholesterol 72.0 mg.
Saturated fat 1.0 gm.
Protein 26.8 gm.
Carbohydrates 15.7 gm.
Sodium 64.0 mg.

ORANGE-CILANTRO SAUCE

½ cup demi-glace (pages 45–47)
1 cup fresh orange juice
1 tablespoon cognac
1 teaspoon granulated sugar
1½ teaspoons orange zest
3 tablespoons fresh cilantro leaves, whole

Prepare the demi-glace ahead as directed. (See Basic Stocks and Sauces, pages 45–47.)

Pour the orange juice into a medium-size, heavy-bottomed saucepan and reduce over low heat to ½ its original volume. Add the cognac, sugar, orange zest, and demi-glace and reduce again to ½ the volume. Add the fresh cilantro and simmer until a smooth consistency is achieved. This sauce is also excellent with red snapper, swordfish, or tuna.

Y I E L D *½ cup*

SERVING 2 TBS.

Calories 32.0

Total fat 0

Cholesterol 0

Saturated fat 0

Protein 0.4 gm.

Carbohydrates 7.7 gm.

Sodium 1.0 mg.

GRILLED CHICKEN PEPITA

An unusual ingredient in this spicy dish is distinctively flavored epazote, which grows wild in Mexico and the American Southwest. In either fresh or dried forms, it can be found primarily in Hispanic markets.

2 skinless, boneless chicken breasts, 8 ounces each, halved
Green Pumpkin-Seed Sauce (see below)
Nonstick spray
Garnish: 8 leaves of fresh cilantro

Prepare the grill with nonstick spray. Make a fire with your preferred material, charcoal briquettes and/or aromatic wood such as mesquite, hickory, or pecan. Let the fire burn down to hot coals. Grill the chicken about 5 minutes per side, turning once. It will be done when the flesh springs back to the touch. Keep warm while you prepare the sauce as directed on opposite page.

When ready to serve, nap each dinner plate with the sauce, add the grilled chicken, and garnish with 2 leaves of fresh cilantro.

N O T E If you wish, you may begin the preparation by marinating the chicken in Dry Southwestern Marinade (see page 78).

Y I E L D *4 servings*

GREEN PUMPKIN-SEED SAUCE

1½ cups chicken stock (page 41)
1 cup pumpkin seeds, shelled and unsalted (see Note, page 147)
4 leaves of romaine lettuce, roughly chopped
4 tomatillos, chopped
1 clove garlic, roughly chopped
½ medium white or yellow onion, chopped
1 tablespoon ripe avocado (use the rest to make Guacamole, page 102)
1 serrano chili pepper, seeded and chopped
¼ cup water
4 tablespoons fresh cilantro, whole leaves
2 tablespoons fresh epazote (see sidebar)
½ teaspoon ground cumin
1 tablespoon olive oil

SERVING 3 OZ.
CHICKEN WITH
2 TBS. SAUCE

Calories 202.0
Total fat 8.0 gm.
Cholesterol 72.0 mg.
Saturated fat 1.74 gm.
Protein 28.9 gm.
Carbohydrates 3.2 gm.
Sodium 67.0 mg.

Prepare the chicken stock ahead as directed.

Place the pumpkin seeds in the container of a food processor and process until finely ground. Remove from the processor and set aside. Add to the processor the lettuce, tomatillos, garlic, onion, avocado, chili, and water and process until the ingredients form a smooth paste. Add the fresh cilantro, epazote, and cumin, processing thoroughly once more.

Heat the olive oil in a medium-size, nonstick skillet over medium heat. Add the puréed mixture, reduce the heat, and simmer, stirring, until the ingredients are cooked through (approximately 3 to 5 minutes). Stir in the reserved ground pumpkin seeds and the chicken stock. Bring to a boil, stirring occasionally. Remove from the heat and keep warm until ready to serve.

V A R I A T I O N This strongly flavored dish may also be prepared with fish, such as tuna, swordfish, or mackerel.

Y I E L D *1 cup*

SERVING 2 TBS.

Calories 62.0

Total fat 5.0 gm.

Cholesterol 0

Saturated fat 0.89 gm.

Protein 2.5 gm.

Carbohydrates 3.2 gm.

Sodium 4.0 mg.

CHICKEN BROCHETTE WITH TARRAGON SAUCE

A tangy sauce, heady with fresh tarragon, enlivens this adaptation of an old favorite.

Nonstick spray
Tarragon Sauce (opposite page)
2 medium-size green bell peppers, seeded
2 medium-size red bell peppers, seeded
1 white onion (a sweet onion such as Vidalia or Texas 10/15 is best)
2 skinless, boneless chicken breasts, 8 ounces each, halved
2 cups cooked white or brown rice, or couscous (bulgar wheat), prepared according to package directions

Prepare the grill with nonstick spray. Make a fire with your preferred material, charcoal briquettes and/or aromatic wood such as mesquite, hickory, or pecan. Let the fire burn down to hot coals.

While the fire is heating, prepare the sauce as directed on opposite page. Keep warm until needed. Bring 4 cups of water to a rapid boil. While the water is heating, cut the peppers in half. Remove the ribs and seeds, including the white pith. Cut the peppers into 1½-inch sections. Cut the onion into 1½-inch sections. Blanch the onion and peppers in the boiling water for 1 to 2 minutes. Remove and plunge into an ice-water bath to stop the cooking process. Drain.

Cut each chicken breast into 1-inch cubes. Beginning with the green bell pepper, thread alternate pieces of chicken, onion, and red and green bell pepper along four 10-inch stainless steel or bamboo skewers, ending with the red bell pepper. Grill over the hot coals for approximately 8 minutes, turning every so often, until done.

When ready to serve, make a bed of rice or couscous on a heated platter and slip the meat and vegetables across it, removing the skewers. Nap the meat with the sauce and serve immediately.

N O T E The chicken may be broiled, if you prefer not to grill.

Y I E L D *4 brochettes*

TARRAGON SAUCE

1 cup demi-glace (pages 45–47)
½ cup white wine
1 tablespoon lemon juice
2 tablespoons fresh tarragon, finely chopped

Prepare the demi-glace ahead as directed. (See Basic Stocks and Sauces, pages 45–47.)

Heat a medium-size, heavy-bottomed saucepan over medium heat. Add the demi-glace, white wine, lemon juice, and tarragon. Simmer, stirring occasionally, until the mixture coats the back of a spoon. This sauce is also delicious with veal, quail, pheasant, and mild fish, such as red snapper.

Y I E L D *½ cup*

SERVING 3 OZ.
CHICKEN AND
½ C. RICE WITH
2 TBS. SAUCE
Calories 278.0
Total fat 3.6 gm.
Cholesterol 72.0 mg.
Saturated fat 0.96 gm.
Protein 29.4 gm.
Carbohydrates 30.1 gm.
Sodium 67.0 mg.

CHEZ EDDY CHICKEN FAJITAS

The term fajitas properly refers to skirt steak, marinated and grilled, wrapped in a flour tortilla along with grilled onions, pico de gallo, and other delicious condiments. To reduce saturated fat, we have substituted marinated chicken breast, which may be either grilled or sautéed, served with traditional accompaniments and our reduced-calorie version of guacamole. This recipe is not difficult to prepare. Its complexity is largely one of assembly.

1 cup demi-glace (pages 45–47)
Approximately 1½ cups marinade (see below)
Ingredients for marinade:
    1 tablespoon ground cumin
    2 tablespoons fresh oregano, finely chopped
    1 tablespoon ground black pepper
    1 teaspoon chili powder
    1 teaspoon fresh thyme, finely chopped
    2 tablespoons Worcestershire sauce
    2 teaspoons Tabasco sauce
    1 tablespoon reduced-sodium soy sauce
    1 cup red wine
    2 tablespoons corn or canola oil
    1 tablespoon shallots, finely chopped
2 skinless, boneless chicken breasts, 8 ounces each, halved
Approximately 1 cup Pico de Gallo (page 84)
8 tablespoons Guacamole Dip (page 102)
8 whole-wheat or white flour tortillas (widely available in packages)
1 large white onion, sliced crosswise, separated into rings
4 leaves of red leaf lettuce
2 cups black beans, cooked according to package directions
Garnish: 8 peperoncinis (pickled Tuscan peppers)

Prepare the demi-glace ahead as directed. (See Basic Stocks and Sauces, pages 45–47.)

In a large nonreactive bowl, combine the ingredients for the marinade and whisk until well blended. Add the chicken, mixing well. Cover and refrigerate for at least 2 hours.

While the chicken marinates, prepare the Pico de Gallo as directed and refrigerate. Prepare the guacamole and refrigerate. Wrap the tortillas in foil and place in an oven set at low heat. Add the demi-glace and onion rings to a nonstick skillet and bring to a boil. Reduce the heat and simmer until the demi-glace is reduced by half its original volume. The onions should appear to be glazed and the sauce should coat the back of a spoon. Keep warm until needed.

Remove the chicken from the marinade and drain well. Either prepare a grill or, if you prefer to sauté the chicken, heat a nonstick skillet over medium-high heat. Add the chicken and sauté, or grill over hot coals, until done, 7 to 10 minutes. Remove the chicken and keep warm.

When ready to serve, place a leaf of red leaf lettuce on the side of a dinner plate. Place 2 tablespoons each of guacamole and Pico de Gallo on the leaf. Mound ⅓ cup of black beans beside it. Slice chicken into ½-inch-wide strips and place on the remaining part of the plate. Arrange the onions on top and spoon sauce over them. Garnish with two peperoncini. Serve warm tortillas on the side.

V A R I A T I O N If you wish to serve our fajitas with rice instead of black beans, you may substitute the Black Bean Salsa (page 86) for the Pico de Gallo. (Pico de Gallo, however, is an excellent nonfat topping for all types of fish and chicken.) If grilling the chicken, you may also grill the onions and add them to the reduced demi-glace. In addition, Dry Southwestern Marinade (page 78) makes a tasty substitute for the marinade given in the recipe.

Y I E L D *12 ounces chicken with 8 tortillas*

SERVING 3 OZ.
CHICKEN WITH
2 TBS. SAUTÉED
ONIONS, 2
TORTILLAS, ½ C.
BLACK BEANS, 2 TBS.
PICO DE GALLO, AND
2 TBS. GUACAMOLE
Calories 523.0
Total fat 7.7 gm.
Cholesterol 72.0 mg.
Saturated fat 2.01 gm.
Protein 38.9 gm.
Carbohydrates 18.8 gm.
Sodium 169.0 mg.

GRILLED CHICKEN TABBOULEH

1 tablespoon rice wine vinegar
1 teaspoon Spice Blend (see page 55)
1 teaspoon fresh mint, minced
1 teaspoon fresh cilantro, minced
2 skinless, boneless chicken breasts, 8 ounces each, halved
3 cups Tabbouleh (see below)

Combine vinegar, Spice Blend, mint, and cilantro in a medium bowl. Add chicken breasts, turning to coat thoroughly, and refrigerate 1 hour before cooking. Grill the chicken for approximately 5 minutes per side.

To serve, arrange ¾ cup tabbouleh salad on 4 dinner plates. Add grilled chicken breast and serve with Lemon-Garlic Roasted Potatoes (page 291).

YIELD *4 servings*

TABBOULEH

½ cup bulgar
2 medium tomatoes, seeded and diced
4 green onions, minced
1 cucumber, peeled, seeded, and diced
1 bunch parsley, minced
Juice of 1 lemon
1 teaspoon olive oil
1 teaspoon garlic, minced
White pepper to taste
2 tablespoons fresh mint, chopped

Rinse bulgar and drain. Cover with cold water and let stand 1 hour. Drain well, pressing out moisture.

In a medium bowl, combine bulgar, tomatoes, onions, cucumber, and parsley and toss well. Add lemon juice, olive oil, garlic, pepper, and mint. Mix lightly.

Cover and refrigerate at least 2 hours before serving. The tabbouleh will keep 2 to 3 days in the refrigerator.

YIELD *3½ cups*

SERVING 3 OZ.
CHICKEN AND
¼ C. TABBOULEH

Calories 263.0
Total fat 8.9 gm.
Cholesterol 82.0 mg.
Saturated fat 2.4 gm.
Protein 33.4 gm.
Carbohydrates 13.3 gm.
Sodium 73.0 mg.

SERVING ¼ C.

Calories 70.0
Total fat 1.38 gm.
Cholesterol 0
Saturated fat 0.2 gm.
Protein 4.3 gm.
Carbohydrates 13.3 gm.
Sodium 3.0 mg.

ROASTED TURKEY BREAST WITH THYME SAUCE

One uncooked turkey breast, weighing 4 to 5 pounds
White pepper to taste
¾ cup Thyme Sauce (see below)

Prepare the Thyme Sauce as directed and keep warm. Preheat the oven to 325°F. Wash the turkey breast and pat dry with paper towels. Season with white pepper and place on a rack in a shallow roasting pan. Roast to an internal temperature of 170°F on a meat thermometer. When ready to serve, remove the turkey skin and slice the turkey. Place 3 ounces of turkey on each warmed dinner plate and spoon 2 tablespoons of the sauce over it.

N O T E It is best to purchase fresh turkey, if possible. But avoid self-basting varieties since they have been injected with fats as well as other additives in many cases.

Y I E L D *24 ounces turkey*

THYME SAUCE

¾ cup demi-glace (pages 45–47)
¼ cup red wine
1 tablespoon fresh thyme, finely chopped (may be omitted when herbed stuffing is used)
1 cup mushrooms, thinly sliced

Prepare the demi-glace ahead as directed. (See Basic Stocks and Sauces, pages 45–47.)

Add the red wine and thyme to a small, heavy-bottomed saucepan. Cook over medium heat for 1 minute. Add the demi-glace and mushrooms and simmer until reduced to a saucelike consistency, about 6 to 8 minutes. The sauce should coat the back of a spoon.

N U T R I T I O N A L N O T E This sauce adds only 3 calories, no sodium and only 0.01 gram of fat to the food with which it is prepared.

Y I E L D *¾ cup*

This dish would make something special out of any meal. If you wish to serve it for a holiday dinner, accompany it with our Herbed-Bread Stuffing (see page 293), and omit the thyme called for in the sauce.

SERVING 3 OZ.
TURKEY AND
2 TBS. SAUCE
Calories 134.0
Total fat 2.7 gm.
Cholesterol 59.0 mg.
Saturated fat 0.87 gm.
Protein 25.3 gm.
Carbohydrates 0
Sodium 54.0 mg.

GRILLED POUSSIN WITH POACHED PEAR-AND-WINE SAUCE

The delicate flavor of poussin, or baby chicken, makes it the perfect foil for this whole wine sauce. Halving the recipe allows you to present it as the main course of an elegant little dinner for two.

Poached Pear-and-Wine Sauce (see below)
2 poussins, approximately 1 pound each (see Note on opposite page)
White pepper, to taste
Nonstick spray
Garnish: parsley sprigs

Prepare the Pear-and-Wine Sauce as directed. Keep warm.

Make a fire with your preferred material, charcoal briquettes and/or aromatic wood such as mesquite, hickory, or pecan. Let the fire burn down to hot coals.

Wash the poussin and pat dry. Split in half, or have the butcher do this for you in advance. Season with white pepper. When the fire is ready, prepare the grill with nonstick spray. Grill the poussin, turning once. The poussin is done when the juices run clear when the thigh is pierced.

When ready to serve, place the poussin on a heated platter. Garnish with parsley. Serve the Poached Pear-and-Wine Sauce on the side.

N O T E The chicken may be broiled, baked, or roasted, if you prefer not to grill.

Y I E L D *12 ounces poussin*

POACHED PEAR-AND-WINE SAUCE

¾ cup demi-glace (page 45–47)
¼ cup white wine
¼ cup red wine
2 sprigs fresh thyme
2 whole cloves
2 tablespoons cider vinegar
3 Bosc pears, peeled, cored, and sliced

SERVING 3 OZ.
POUSSIN WITH
2 TBS. SAUCE
Calories 199.0
Total fat 6.5 gm.
Cholesterol 76.0 mg.
Saturated fat 1.73 gm.
Protein 24.8 gm.
Carbohydrates 9.3 gm.
Sodium 73.0 mg.

Prepare the demi-glace ahead as directed. (See Basic Stocks and Sauces, pages 45–47.)

Combine the white wine, red wine, thyme, cloves, and vinegar in a medium-size, heavy-bottomed saucepan. Bring to a boil and add the pears. Reduce the heat and simmer gently, until the pears are tender. Cool slightly. Remove the cloves and sprigs of thyme. Place the pears and liquid in the container of a food processor. Add the demi-glace and process until smooth. Pour the purée back into the saucepan. Cook over medium heat, stirring occasionally, until reduced by half or a saucelike consistency is formed. Serve warm. This sauce is also good with veal, pheasant, quail, or breast of chicken.

N O T E Although the poussin makes a more attractive presentation with the skin on, you should remove the skin before you begin to eat.

Y I E L D *1 cup*

SERVING 2 TBS.

Calories 37.0

Total fat 0.2 gm.

Cholesterol 0

Saturated fat 0.01 gm.

Protein 0.2 gm.

Carbohydrates 9.3 gm.

Sodium 0

SAUTÉED DUCK BREAST WITH FIVE-SPICE PEACH SAUCE

Breast of duckling, cooked rare and anointed with this voluptuous sauce, calls for the simplest accompaniments. We suggest steamed green beans with almonds and wild rice.

1 cup Five-Spice Peach Sauce (opposite page)
2 whole duck breasts, approximately ½ pound each
2 teaspoons olive oil
Garnish: warm slices of fresh peaches (if available) and kiwi

Prepare the Five-Spice Peach Sauce as directed.

Skin the duck breasts, removing all cartilage and fat. Split them in half, making four lean portions.

Preheat the oven to 400°F. Meanwhile, heat the olive oil in an oven-proof heavy-bottomed skillet until almost smoking. Quickly sear the duck breasts on each side, about 1 minute. Place the skillet containing the duck breasts into the preheated oven for 3 to 4 minutes. When done, remove from the oven and keep warm while you make the sauce.

When ready to serve, slice the duck breasts diagonally into 1-inch-thick slices. Place 2 tablespoons of the sauce on a warmed dinner plate and add the sliced duck breast. Garnish with slices of warmed peach and kiwi.

N O T E Buy whole ducks at the market. The butcher will debone them for you, if you ask. Reserve the bones and remainder of the duck for other recipes, including duck demi-glace, stocks, and soups. Leaving the skin and fat on the duck breasts until ready to use will keep them from drying out.

Y I E L D *4 servings*

SERVING 3 OZ. DUCK BREAST
Calories 208.0
Total fat 9.43 gm.
Cholesterol 75.0 mg.
Saturated fat 5.03 gm.
Protein 18.9 gm.
Carbohydrates 11.8 gm.
Sodium 63.4 mg.

FIVE-SPICE PEACH SAUCE

½ cup demi-glace (page 45–47)
4 teaspoons honey
4 tablespoons fresh orange juice
4 tablespoons white wine
1 cup Five-Spice Peach Purée (see recipe below)

Prepare the demi-glace ahead as directed. (See Basic Stocks and Sauces, pages 45–47.)

Heat the pan in which the duck was seared. Add the honey and cook until large bubbles break the surface. Deglaze with the fresh orange juice and white wine. Add 1 cup of the purée and the demi-glace, simmering until the mixture coats the back of a spoon. Serve immediately with the duck.

Y I E L D *2 cups*

FIVE-SPICE PEACH PURÉE

1 cup pitted peaches, fresh if possible, or if canned, packed in
  juice
1 tablespoon lemon juice
1 tablespoon Chinese five-spice powder (see Note, page 155)
¼ cup white wine
1 tablespoon honey

Purée the ingredients in a food processor or blender until smooth.

Y I E L D *1 cup*

SERVING 2 TBS.

Calories 23.0

Total fat 0

Cholesterol 0

Saturated fat 0

Protein 0.1 gm.

Carbohydrates 6.1 gm.

Sodium 0

STIR-FRIED CHICKEN WITH SWEET AND SOUR SAUCE

2 skinless, boneless chicken breasts, 8 ounces each, halved
1 teaspoon fresh ginger, minced
1 teaspoon fresh garlic, minced
1½ teaspoons sesame oil
1 tablespoon sake or rice wine vinegar
1 teaspoon cornstarch
1 red onion cut into 1-inch chunks (about 1 cup)
½ cup celery, sliced on bias
½ cup carrots, blanched and sliced on bias
1½ cups Sweet and Sour Sauce (opposite page)
½ cup broccoli florets, blanched
½ cup snow peas, blanched
½ cup frozen green peas, thawed

Cut chicken into julienne strips. Combine ginger, garlic, ½ teaspoon sesame oil, sake, and cornstarch in a medium bowl. Add chicken strips and refrigerate 2 hours before cooking.

In a large skillet, heat remaining 1 teaspoon sesame oil until smoking. Add chicken and stir-fry about 1½ to 2 minutes. Stir in onion, celery, and carrots; cook another minute. Stir in sauce, broccoli, snow peas, and green peas. Cook until thoroughly heated. Serve with steamed rice.

Y I E L D *4 servings*

SERVING 3 OZ.
CHICKEN AND
1 C. VEGETABLES
WITH SAUCE

Calories 268.0
Total fat 4.9 gm.
Cholesterol 73.0 mg.
Saturated fat 1.0 gm.
Protein 29.2 gm.
Carbohydrates 21.4 gm.
Sodium 98.0 mg.

SWEET AND SOUR SAUCE

1 cup fresh orange juice
1 tablespoon brandy
1 tablespoon honey
1 tablespoon tomato paste
1 tablespoon fresh ginger, minced
½ teaspoon sesame oil
2 tablespoons cornstarch
½ cup low-sodium chicken broth

Combine orange juice, brandy, honey, tomato paste, ginger, and sesame oil in a medium saucepan. Bring to a boil. Dissolve cornstarch in chicken stock and add to the sauce. Cook 1 minute and remove from heat. The sauce may be made ahead and refrigerated.

YIELD *1½ cups*

SAUTÉED DUCK BREAST WITH RASPBERRY-VINEGAR SAUCE

The tart perfume of vinegar infused with raspberries deepens the taste of this wine sauce.

SERVING 3 OZ. DUCK BREAST

Calories 161.0

Total fat 9.33 gm.

Cholesterol 75.0 mg.

Saturated fat 5.0 gm.

Protein 18.3 gm.

Carbohydrates 0

Sodium 63.4 mg.

2 whole duck breasts, approximately 1 pound each
2 teaspoons olive oil
Freshly ground pepper, to taste
Raspberry-Vinegar Sauce (see below)
Garnish: grated orange zest and fresh mint leaves

Prepare the Raspberry-Vinegar Sauce as directed.

Prepare and cook the duck breasts as directed in the recipe for Sautéed Duck Breast with Five-Spice Peach Sauce (page 175). When ready to serve, slice the breasts diagonally, season with pepper, and place on 4 warm dinner plates. Nap each portion of duck with 2 tablespoons of the sauce, sprinkle on a little grated orange zest, and decorate with 2 mint leaves.

YIELD *4 servings*

RASPBERRY-VINEGAR SAUCE

1 cup demi-glace (pages 45–47)
¼ cup raspberry vinegar
½ cup port wine

Prepare the demi-glace ahead as directed. (See Basic Stocks and Sauces, pages 45–47.)

Add the vinegar and port wine to a small, heavy-bottomed saucepan. Simmer until reduced by half its volume. Add the demi-glace and simmer until reduced to a saucelike consistency. This sauce should have a glazed appearance and coat the back of a spoon.

YIELD *4 ounces*

SERVING 2 TBS.

Calories 20.0

Total fat 2.3 gm.

Cholesterol 0

Saturated fat 0.3 gm.

Protein 0

Carbohydrates 0

Sodium 0

FISH

....

THE BOUNTY OF FRESH LOCAL fish with which we on the Texas Gulf Coast are blessed has been joined in recent years by a variety flown in from around the world. Many of these new arrivals originate in cold waters and thus offer dramatic contrasts of flavor and texture, stimulating new thinking about how to prepare fish, which is, after all, one of the best foods for heart-healthy dining.

For generations, fish cookery in Texas has been influenced by the proximity of Louisiana. Her heritage of Creole and Acadian cuisine is nearly as familiar to us as our own chili con carne. In some respects Chez Eddy's culinary feet remain entwined among the cypress stumps of Louisiana's bayous; but we have discovered that our palates resonate as well to the dry desert heat of the great Southwest. The chili-spiked relishes called salsas are part of that heritage, taking their inspiration from the spicy cuisine of Mexico. In strength of flavor, they are the perfect accent to many of the more robust fish, such as tuna, swordfish, and marlin; in terms of their acid content, they complement the oilier salmon and cape bluefish.

Although the benefits of consuming fish oil remain unclear, many physicians suggest incorporating fattier fish, such as salmon and swordfish, into the diet on a regular, if moderate, basis. From a culinary point of view, we agree, although we find these denizens of colder waters most delicious when their natural fat content is offset by an acid or pepper.

Whatever fish we prepare, however, our intention remains one of enhancing its natural fresh flavor rather than masking it with a heavy sauce. We vary the salsas as well as other treatments in the recipes that follow to fit the specific variety of fish, but, in fact, most may be used interchangeably. You may also vary the preparation, substituting broiled or baked for grilled, or the reverse, as you prefer.

A final reminder: All of our fish fillets and steaks are boneless and skinless.

....

Salmon Antonio

Swordfish with Almond Skordalia

Baked Grouper with Three-Peppers Sauce

Baked Catfish Creole

Lemon Sole with Ginger Sauce and Fresh Oysters

Broiled Tuna with Fresh Mint Salsa

Pan-Steamed Tuna with Tomatillo Sauce

Marinated Cape Bluefish with Tequila-Lime Sauce

Broiled Salmon in Three-Citrus Sauce

Baked Redfish with Sautéed Red Onion and Cilantro

Poached Salmon with Spinach and Orange-Basil Vinaigrette

Grilled Redfish with Black Bean Salsa

....

....

Grilled Fish Mayan

Broiled Swordfish with Salsa

Broiled Salmon Dijonnaise

Planked Salmon with Pico de Gallo

Broiled Salmon or Swordfish with Red Pepper Salsa

Sautéed Rainbow Trout with Cucumber, Dill, and
Crabmeat Sauce

Baked Red Snapper with Roasted Red Peppers
and Sun-Dried Tomatoes

Seared Red Snapper with Criolla Relish

Baked Red Snapper with Jicama-Ginger Salsa

Broiled Wahoo with Orange-Basil Sauce

....

SALMON ANTONIO

This spicy brown sauce provides a bold alternative to the many light citrus sauces that are more common with fish. It is one of Dr. Gotto's favorites.

⅔ cup demi-glace (pages 45–47)
⅓ cup red wine
2 tablespoons green peppercorns
Nonstick spray
4 salmon fillets, 4 ounces each

Prepare the demi-glace ahead as directed. (See Basic Stocks and Sauces, pages 45–47.)

Preheat the broiler.

In a small, heavy-bottomed saucepan, stir the red wine and peppercorns into the demi-glace. Simmer over medium heat, stirring occasionally, until the liquid is reduced to ½ cup. Keep warm until needed.

When the broiler is preheated, spray the rack with nonstick vegetable spray and broil the salmon 4 inches from the heat for about 5 to 7 minutes, or until opaque throughout, turning once, if necessary. It should just spring back when touched. Remove fish from the heat and immediately place the salmon fillets on a warmed platter or dinner plate and drizzle 2 tablespoons of sauce, per portion, over them.

Y I E L D *12 ounces fish*

SERVING 3 OZ. FISH
WITH 2 TBS. SAUCE
Calories 161.0
Total fat 7.2 gm.
Cholesterol 62.0 mg.
Saturated fat 1.11 gm.
Protein 22.5 gm.
Carbohydrates 0
Sodium 50.0 mg.

SWORDFISH WITH ALMOND SKORDALIA

Almond Skordalia (next page)
Oil or nonstick spray
4 swordfish steaks, 4 ounces each
Garnish: sprigs of fresh parsley

Prepare the Almond Skordalia as directed.

While the sauce chills, make a fire using your preferred material and let the fire burn down to hot coals. Prepare the grill by brushing with oil or, as an alternative to grilling directly on the rack, spray a hinged wire grill with nonstick cooking spray. Place the fish in the grill on the rack about 5 inches from the coals. Turning once, grill the fish for about 3 to 4 minutes per side or until resilient to the touch.

When ready to serve, remove the fish to a heated platter and place 1 tablespoon of skordalia on top of each swordfish steak. Garnish with sprigs of fresh parsley.

Y I E L D   *12 ounces fish and 1¼ cups sauce*

The smooth taste of cold, creamy skordalia sauce is a provocative counterpoint to the sharp flavor of swordfish. This entree may also be served with Pico de Gallo (page 84) or Black Bean Salsa (page 86).

SERVING 3 OZ. FISH
AND 2 TBS. ALMOND
SKORDALIA
Calories 198.0
Total fat 9.0 gm.
Cholesterol 47.0 mg.
Saturated fat 1.88 gm.
Protein 24.2 gm.
Carbohydrates 3.9 gm.
Sodium 203.0 mg.

ALMOND SKORDALIA

¼ cup almonds, sliced
2 cloves garlic, finely minced
¼ cup breadcrumbs
⅓ cup reduced-calorie mayonnaise
⅓ cup nonfat yogurt
⅓ cup low-fat cottage cheese
1 teaspoon lemon juice
½ teaspoon Dijon mustard
1 tablespoon parsley, finely chopped
1 tablespoon cold water
Ground pepper, to taste

Grind the almonds in a food processor or blender. Add the remaining ingredients to the machine and process until combined. Chill for 1 hour.

V A R I A T I O N We like to use Pineapple Salsa (page 87) as a slightly astringent accompaniment to the skordalia.

Y I E L D *1¼ cups*

SERVING 2 TBS.

Calories 66.0

Total fat 4.6 gm.

Cholesterol 4.0 mg.

Saturated fat 0.68 gm.

Protein 2.6 gm.

Carbohydrates 3.9 gm.

Sodium 105.0 mg.

BAKED GROUPER WITH THREE-PEPPERS SAUCE

Three-Peppers Sauce (next page)
4 grouper fillets, 4 ounces each
1 tablespoon lemon juice
Cold water
Garnish: 1 tablespoon parsley, finely chopped

Prepare the Three-Peppers Sauce as directed.

Preheat the oven to 350°F. Place the grouper fillets in a large non-stick pan and squeeze lemon juice over them. Add water to the pan until the fillets are covered to a depth of approximately ¼ inch. Cover with foil or parchment paper and bake for approximately 10 to 15 minutes or until the fish springs back lightly to the touch.

When ready to serve, place the fish on a warm serving platter, drizzle the sauce over it, and sprinkle with parsley.

YIELD *12 ounces fish*

In recent years, grouper has become a popular addition to Houston menus. It is a large fish, reminiscent of red snapper in flavor, but a little firmer in texture. Note that the sauce in this recipe is reduced to the point where it merely glazes the peppers.

SERVING 3 OZ.
GROUPER WITH
2 TBS. SAUCE
Calories 120.0
Total fat 2.9 gm.
Cholesterol 40.0 mg.
Saturated fat 0.50 gm.
Protein 21.3 gm.
Carbohydrates 1.0 gm.
Sodium 46.0 mg.

THREE-PEPPERS SAUCE

½ cup demi-glace (pages 45–47)
½ cup green bell peppers, cut into 1½-inch julienne pieces
½ cup yellow bell peppers, cut into 1½-inch julienne pieces
½ cup red bell peppers, cut into 1½-inch julienne pieces
½ cup red onion, julienned
1 tablespoon unsalted margarine, clarified (page 123)

Prepare the demi-glace ahead as directed. (See Basic Stocks and Sauces, pages 45–47.) In a medium nonstick skillet, sauté the bell peppers and onion in the margarine until soft. Add the demi-glace and reduce over medium heat until it attains the consistency of a sauce. The peppers should appear glazed.

YIELD *1¼ cups glazed peppers*

SERVING 2 TBS.

Calories 20.0

Total fat 1.5 gm.

Cholesterol 0

Saturated fat 0.36 gm.

Protein 0.3 gm.

Carbohydrates 2.2 gm.

Sodium 2.0 mg.

BAKED CATFISH CREOLE

Creole Sauce (next page)
4 catfish fillets, 4 ounces each
Nonstick spray
Garnish: 4 tablespoons finely chopped parsley

Prepare the Creole Sauce as directed.

Preheat the oven to 375°F. Place the catfish in a baking dish you have sprayed with nonstick vegetable spray. Add the Creole Sauce and bake uncovered about 20 minutes or until the fish springs back to the touch.

When ready to serve, remove the fish fillets to a warmed platter and pour the sauce over them. Garnish with chopped parsley.

Y I E L D   *12 ounces fish*

Firm-fleshed and fine-textured with a distinctive sweet flavor, catfish is one of our most common fresh-water fish. Recently, it has become plentiful in markets, farm-raised varieties being available all year. It may be used in any recipe calling for lean fish.

SERVING 3 OZ.
CATFISH WITH
ABOUT ½ C. SAUCE
Calories 161.0
Total fat 6.7 gm.
Cholesterol 66.0 mg.
Saturated fat 1.37 gm.
Protein 21.2 gm.
Carbohydrates 3.3 gm.
Sodium 83.0 mg.

CREOLE SAUCE

½ tablespoon olive oil
½ cup tomatoes, peeled and diced
¼ cup onions, finely chopped
¼ cup celery, finely chopped
¼ cup green bell pepper, finely chopped
1 teaspoon garlic, finely minced
Creole seasonings:
   ¾ teaspoon fresh oregano, finely chopped
   ½ teaspoon fresh thyme, finely chopped
   ½ teaspoon fresh basil, finely chopped
   Pinch white pepper (for additional heat, increase amounts of
     all 3 peppers)
   Pinch black pepper
   Pinch red pepper
   Pinch paprika
¾ cup chicken stock (page 41)
1 tablespoon tomato paste

Heat the oil in a large skillet over medium heat. Add the tomatoes, onions, celery, bell pepper, garlic, and seasonings, stirring thoroughly to combine. Cook until the onions are translucent, about 5 minutes. Stir in the stock and tomato paste and bring to a boil. Reduce the heat and simmer, stirring occasionally, until the vegetables are tender, about 20 minutes.

N O T E If you add garlic powder to the seasoning mixture, it may be rubbed into fish or chicken as a Cajun blackening spice.

Y I E L D *1½ cups*

SERVING ¼ C.

Calories 30.0

Total fat 1.8 gm.

Cholesterol 0

Saturated fat 0.25 gm.

Protein 0.6 gm.

Carbohydrates 3.3 gm.

Sodium 12.0 mg.

LEMON SOLE WITH GINGER SAUCE AND FRESH OYSTERS

Ginger Sauce (next page)
1 tablespoon olive oil
4 lemon sole fillets, 4 ounces each
Garnish: 6 scallions, washed and cleaned. Cut the scallions into
   2-inch lengths, making ½-inch lengthwise incisions beginning at
   each end, and place in ice water, where they will curl into a
   beautiful flower garnish.

Prepare the Ginger Sauce as directed.

When the sauce is ready, add the olive oil to a nonstick skillet until almost smoking. Rotate the skillet so the oil coats the bottom, pouring off any excess. Return the skillet to the heat and add the fillets. Sauté the fillets quickly over medium heat for 1 to 2 minutes on each side or until they spring back lightly to the touch. Remove to a heated platter or individual dinner plates.

When ready to serve, nap each fillet with 2 tablespoons of sauce, including 2 oysters, and garnish with scallion flowers.

Y I E L D *12 ounces fish*

The subtle interplay of oysters and fresh ginger in the sauce intensifies the delicate flavor of this fish.

SERVING 3 OZ. FISH
WITH 2 TBS. SAUCE
AND 2 OYSTERS

Calories 147.0

Total fat 5.4 gm.

Cholesterol 64.0 mg.

Saturated fat 0.9 gm.

Protein 21.4 gm.

Carbohydrates 1.9 gm.

Sodium 158.0 mg.

GINGER SAUCE

½ teaspoon garlic, finely chopped
1 teaspoon fresh ginger, finely chopped
1 teaspoon scallions, finely chopped
1 teaspoon olive oil
1 tablespoon white wine
1 teaspoon red wine vinegar
1 tablespoon Worcestershire sauce
½ cup plus 3 tablespoons cold water
1 tablespoon reduced-sodium soy sauce
1½ teaspoons sugar
2 teaspoons cornstarch
8 fresh shucked oysters, with liquor

Combine the garlic, ginger, and scallions in a small bowl and set aside. Heat the olive oil in a small, heavy-bottomed sauté pan or skillet over medium heat. Add the garlic mixture and cook for 10 seconds, stirring frequently.

Stir in the white wine, vinegar, Worcestershire sauce, 3 tablespoons water, soy sauce, and sugar and boil for 2 minutes, stirring occasionally. Whisk the cornstarch and remaining water together in a small bowl and add this to the pan. Return to a boil. Add the oysters with their liquor and cook until the oysters curl, approximately 1 minute. Remove from the heat and keep warm until ready to serve.

Y I E L D *1 cup*

SERVING 2 TBS.

Calories 18.0
Total fat 0.7 gm.
Cholesterol 6.0 mg.
Saturated fat 0.13 gm.
Protein 0.9 gm.
Carbohydrates 1.9 gm.
Sodium 69.0 mg.

BROILED TUNA WITH FRESH MINT SALSA

Fresh Mint Salsa (next page)
2 tablespoons olive oil
¼ cup white wine
½ teaspoon white pepper
2 to 3 tablespoons fresh mint, finely chopped
4 tuna steaks, 4 ounces each
Nonstick spray
Garnish: fresh mint leaves and thin slices of lemon

Prepare the Mint Salsa as directed.

Whisk together the olive oil, white wine, white pepper, and mint in a nonreactive bowl and set aside. Place the tuna in a single layer in a shallow nonreactive pan or dish. Pour this marinade over the tuna. Cover and refrigerate for at least 1 hour.

Preheat the broiler. Spray the rack of the broiling pan with nonstick spray. When the broiler is hot, remove the tuna steaks from the marinade and wipe off any excess with paper towels. Broil the tuna approximately 4 inches from the heat for 3 to 4 minutes per side, turning once.

When ready to serve, arrange 1 serving of fish on each heated dinner plate and spoon 2 tablespoons of salsa over it. Garnish with fresh mint leaves and lemon slices.

Y I E L D *12 ounces tuna*

We prefer to have our fresh tuna steaks trimmed of dark meat, which has a stronger taste and tends to cook unevenly. Tuna is also an excellent choice when grilling and, in fact, may be grilled in this recipe, if you prefer.

SERVING 3 OZ. TUNA
AND 2 TBS. SALSA

Calories 163.0

Total fat 5.3 gm.

Cholesterol 42.0 mg.

Saturated fat 1.38 gm.

Protein 25.7 gm.

Carbohydrates 1.5 gm.

Sodium 45.0 mg.

FRESH MINT SALSA

2 tablespoons fresh mint, finely chopped
2 shallots, finely diced
1½ cups tomato concassé (page 50)
2 cloves garlic, finely diced

Combine the mint, shallots, tomato concassé, and garlic in a small bowl. Refrigerate until ready to use.

Y I E L D *1½ cups salsa*

SERVING 2 TBS.

Calories 7.0

Total fat 0

Cholesterol 0

Saturated fat 0.01 gm.

Protein 0.3 gm.

Carbohydrates 1.5 gm.

Sodium 2.0 mg.

PAN-STEAMED TUNA WITH TOMATILLO SAUCE

Tomatillo Sauce (page 71)
1 tablespoon olive oil
4 tuna steaks, 4 ounces each
Garnish: finely chopped parsley or finely chopped fresh cilantro

Prepare the Tomatillo Sauce as directed.

Add the olive oil to a nonstick skillet and heat until almost smoking. Rotate the skillet so the oil coats the bottom, pouring off any excess. Add the tuna, quickly searing one side; turn, and quickly sear the second side. Cover the pan and lower the heat. Let the fish steam in its own juices over low heat about 2 minutes, or until resilient to the touch.

When ready to serve, nap each warmed dinner plate with 2 tablespoons of the sauce. Top with the tuna steaks, garnished with finely chopped parsley or cilantro.

YIELD *12 ounces tuna*

*A*lthough it resembles a small green tomato, the tomatillo is not a member of the same family. In fact, this native of Mexico is related to the cape gooseberry. Its flavor suggests the tartness of lemons, with an undertone of apples, a taste we find particularly pleasing in contrast to robust, meaty fish such as tuna.

SERVING 3 OZ. FISH
WITH 2 TBS. SAUCE
Calories 200.0
Total fat 8.8 gm.
Cholesterol 42.0 mg.
Saturated fat 1.85 gm.
Protein 26.1 gm.
Carbohydrates 3.2 gm.
Sodium 49.0 mg.

MARINATED CAPE BLUEFISH WITH TEQUILA-LIME SAUCE

Bluefish is a cold-water variety rich in omega-3 fatty acids. Because of its high oil content, it tastes best when accompanied by an astringent sauce, such as the Tequila-Lime Sauce given on the opposite page. For similar reasons, this sauce also goes well with tuna or swordfish.

Tequila-Lime Sauce (opposite page)
2 cloves garlic, finely chopped
2 tablespoons lemon juice
1 tablespoon oyster sauce (see Note below)
1 tablespoon olive oil
4 cape bluefish fillets, 4 ounces each
Nonstick spray
Garnish: thin slices of fresh lime and whole cilantro leaves

Prepare the Tequila-Lime Sauce as directed. Combine the garlic, lemon juice, oyster sauce, and olive oil in a small bowl. Arrange the fish fillets in a shallow nonreactive dish so they form a single layer and pour the marinade over them. Cover and refrigerate overnight or for at least 4 hours.

Prepare the grill with nonstick spray. Make a fire with your preferred material, charcoal briquettes and/or aromatic wood such as mesquite, hickory, or pecan. Let the fire burn down to hot coals. When ready to proceed, remove the fish from the marinade and wipe off the excess. Grill the fish 3 to 5 minutes on each side or until the thickest portion is resilient to the touch.

Nap each warmed dinner plate with 2 tablespoons of the sauce. Place the fish on top of the sauce and serve garnished with thin slices of lime and fresh cilantro leaves.

N O T E Oyster sauce, found in most Oriental markets and gourmet shops, is made from dried oysters and contains soy sauce, which is high in sodium. To control the sodium content of recipes, use only small amounts. You may also dilute with water.

Y I E L D 12 ounces fish

SERVING 3 OZ. FISH WITH 2 TBS. SAUCE

Calories 113.0
Total fat 1.3 gm.
Cholesterol 50.0 mg.
Saturated fat 0.79 gm.
Protein 17.6 gm.
Carbohydrates 1.9 gm.

TEQUILA-LIME SAUCE

¼ cup demi-glace (pages 45–47)
¼ cup soubise (page 48)
½ cup lime juice
½ cup white tequila
1 teaspoon granulated sugar

Prepare the demi-glace and soubise ahead as directed. (See Basic Stocks and Sauces, pages 45–47.)

Combine the lime juice, tequila, sugar, and demi-glace in a small, heavy-bottomed saucepan or skillet and bring to a boil over medium-high heat. Stir in the soubise and continue cooking, stirring occasionally, until the mixture is reduced to 1 cup. Remove from the heat and keep warm until needed.

Y I E L D *1 cup*

SERVING 2 TBS.
Calories 8.0
Total fat 0
Cholesterol 0
Saturated fat 0.01 gm.
Protein 0.3 gm.
Carbohydrates 1.9 gm.
Sodium 5.0 mg.

BROILED SALMON IN THREE-CITRUS SAUCE

It is the distinctive flavor of jalapeño, not its heat, that melds the tart and sweet elements of this sauce.

4 salmon fillets, 4 ounces each
Juice of 1 small orange, plus 1 teaspoon grated zest
Juice of 1 small lemon, plus 1 teaspoon grated zest
Juice of 1 small lime, plus 1 teaspoon grated zest
½ small white onion, minced
½ teaspoon honey
1 small jalapeño pepper, seeded and minced
Nonstick spray
Garnish: 1 lime, peeled and cut into thin slices; 4 sprigs of watercress

Arrange the salmon fillets in a single layer in a small nonreactive pan or dish. In a small nonreactive bowl, mix together the three citrus juices and zests, the onion, honey, and jalapeño. Pour over the salmon. Marinate, covered, in the refrigerator for 3 hours or overnight. Occasionally turn the fish so all areas come into contact with the marinade.

Preheat the broiler. Prepare the rack of a broiler pan by spraying with a nonstick spray.

Lift the salmon fillets out of the marinade and wipe off the excess, reserving the marinade. Place the fillets on the broiler rack and broil approximately 4 inches from the heat for about 4 to 6 minutes per side, turning once. When cooked, the salmon should just spring back to the touch. Do not overcook.

When ready to serve, heat the marinade until it begins to bubble. Pour the hot marinade over the salmon and garnish with slices of lime and sprigs of watercress.

Y I E L D   *12 ounces fish*

SERVING 3 OZ. FISH
WITH SAUCE
Calories 189.0
Total fat 7.3 gm.
Cholesterol 62.0 mg.
Saturated fat 1.13 gm.
Protein 22.9 gm.
Carbohydrates 7.3 gm.
Sodium 53.0 mg.

BAKED REDFISH WITH SAUTÉED RED ONION AND CILANTRO

1 tablespoon olive oil
1 medium red onion, quartered, thinly sliced
1 jalapeño, seeded and diced
Juice and zest of 1 lemon
1 bunch fresh cilantro leaves, finely chopped (reserve several
    whole leaves)
4 redfish fillets, 4 ounces each
¼ cup cold water
Garnish: lemon nests (lemon zest removed with a zester and
    formed into nests the size of a whole lemon); whole leaves of
    cilantro (see above)

Preheat the oven to 350°F.

Heat the olive oil in a heavy-bottomed skillet and add the red onion.
Sauté the onion for 2 minutes, then stir in the jalapeño, lemon juice
and zest, and cilantro. Cook for 1 additional minute and remove from
the heat.

Place the redfish in a shallow baking dish. Add the water and spread
equal amounts of the sautéed mixture over each fillet. Cover with foil
or parchment paper and bake for 15 to 20 minutes.

When ready to serve, place each redfish fillet in the center of a dinner plate. To the side of the plate, arrange a garnish of 1 lemon nest
flanked by 2 whole cilantro leaves.

YIELD *12 ounces fish*

The lemon nests used as a garnish in this dish would also make an attractive accompaniment for grilled or broiled fish.

SERVING 3 OZ. FISH
WITH 2 TBS. RED
ONION MIXTURE
Calories 153.0
Total fat 5.3 gm.
Cholesterol 46.0 mg.
Saturated fat 0.75 gm.
Protein 21.1 gm.
Carbohydrates 4.5 gm.
Sodium 88.0 mg.

POACHED SALMON WITH SPINACH AND ORANGE-BASIL VINAIGRETTE

*I*f *you don't have court bouillon on hand, substitute canned low-sodium chicken broth for the poaching liquid. Strain and reserve the liquid from the poached fish for soups, or freeze to use for poaching later.*

4 salmon fillets, 4 ounces each, poached (page 105)
1 pound fresh spinach, washed and drained, tough stems removed
½ cup Orange Basil Vinaigrette (opposite page)
Garnish: fresh orange slices

Poach salmon as directed. Remove to a warm platter, cover, and keep warm until ready to serve. Place spinach in a heated dry skillet over medium heat and turn carefully until wilted (1 to 2 minutes). Place ½ cup spinach on a heated dinner plate. Place 1 salmon fillet on top and drizzle with 2 tablespoons Orange Basil Vinaigrette. Garnish with fresh orange slices and serve immediately.

Y I E L D *4 servings*

SERVING 3 OZ. FISH,
½ C. SPINACH,
2 TBS. VINAIGRETTE
Calories 182.0
Total fat 7.7 mg.
Cholesterol 47.0 mg.
Saturated fat 0.8 gm.
Protein 17.0 gm.
Carbohydrates 4.0 gm.
Sodium 37.0 mg.

ORANGE-BASIL VINAIGRETTE

½ cup fresh orange juice
¼ cup rice wine vinegar
1 tablespoon sugar
1 tablespoon sesame oil
1 tablespoon sesame seeds, toasted (page 143)
1 tablespoon green onion, minced
3 tablespoons fresh basil, chopped

Combine all the ingredients except the fresh basil in a small bowl (the mixture will keep refrigerated for 5 to 6 days). Add the chopped fresh basil just before serving.

YIELD *1 cup*

If you're lucky enough to find them, try adding different flavors of basil for a variety of flavors—for example, sweet basil, lemon basil, or cinnamon basil.

SERVING 2 TBS.
VINAIGRETTE
Calories 46.0
Total fat 2.3 gm.
Cholesterol 0
Saturated fat 0.3 gm.
Protein 0.3 gm.
Carbohydrates 4.0 gm.
Sodium 0

GRILLED REDFISH WITH BLACK BEAN SALSA

The pungent flavor of this salsa is a perfect counterpoint to any fish or chicken dish. If redfish is difficult to find, you may substitute red snapper, grouper, tuna, or swordfish.

Black Bean Salsa (page 86)
¼ cup olive oil
2 tablespoons cilantro leaves, chopped
2 tablespoons lime juice
1 jalapeño pepper, seeded, split lengthwise
1 teaspoon black pepper, cracked
1 clove garlic, chopped
4 redfish fillets, 4 ounces each
Garnish: slices of fresh papaya or mango or fresh strawberry
   halves on red leaf lettuce

Prepare the Black Bean Salsa as directed.

   Combine the olive oil, cilantro, lime juice, jalapeño pepper, black pepper, and garlic in a nonreactive bowl. Arrange the fish in a nonreactive shallow dish so it forms a single layer. Pour the marinade over the fish, cover, and refrigerate for at least 1 hour.

   Prepare the grill. When the fire is ready, remove the fish from the marinade and wipe off the excess. Place the fish on the heated grill and cook, turning twice, so that each piece is clearly marked with a diamond pattern (2 to 3 minutes per side).

   When ready to serve, spoon 2 tablespoons of the salsa over each serving of the fish. Garnish with sliced fruit or strawberry halves on red leaf lettuce.

VARIATION For added visual pizazz, nap the plate with Roasted Red Pepper Sauce (page 72) and garnish salsa with diced red bell pepper.

YIELD *12 ounces fish*

SERVING 3 OZ. FISH
WITH 2 TBS. SALSA

Calories 128.0

Total fat 1.9 gm.

Cholesterol 46.0 mg.

Saturated fat 0.30 gm.

Protein 21.8 gm.

Carbohydrates 4.7 gm.

Sodium 83.0 mg.

GRILLED FISH MAYAN

3 tablespoons annato seeds, soaked overnight in ½ cup water
½ tablespoon black peppercorns
¾ teaspoon ground allspice
1 whole head of garlic, roasted and peeled (see page 294), plus
    4–5 cloves raw garlic
½ tablespoon dried oregano
½ teaspoon ground cumin
¼ teaspoon ground cloves
½ cup orange juice
¼ cup grapefruit juice
¼ cup cider vinegar
4 fish fillets, 4 ounces each (any firm fish, such as trout, red
    snapper, grouper)
1 cup Pickled Red Onions (next page)
Garnish: 1 lime, cut into wedges, and 4 plum tomatoes, sliced

Combine soaked and drained annatto with peppercorns, allspice, roasted garlic, raw garlic, oregano, cumin, cloves, orange juice, grapefruit juice, and vinegar in the container of a food processor or blender. Process until smooth. Transfer the mixture to a large bowl and add the fish, turning to coat surfaces. Cover and refrigerate for 1 to 2 hours. Remove the fish and reserve the marinade.

    Grill or broil the fish 3 to 4 minutes on each side, being careful not to overcook and brushing liberally with the marinade mixture. Arrange on heated serving plates and garnish with pickled onions, lime wedges, and sliced tomatoes.

Y I E L D *4 servings*

*T*he hard, brick-red seed of the annatto tree is called achiote. You may purchase achiote in Latin American, Caribbean, or Philippine markets.

SERVING 3 OZ. FISH,
¼ C. ONIONS

Calories 123.0

Total fat 1.5 gm.

Cholesterol 40.0 mg.

Saturated fat 0.3 gm.

Protein 22.6 gm.

Carbohydrates 3.4 gm.

Sodium 49.0 mg.

PICKLED RED ONIONS

2 medium red onions, sliced into thin rings
1 cup water
½ cup rice wine vinegar or white vinegar
1 teaspoon black peppercorns
½ teaspoon juniper berries
Pinch allspice
1 tablespoon sugar

Place onion rings in a medium bowl and set aside. Combine remaining ingredients in a medium saucepan and bring to a boil. Cook 1 minute and remove from heat. Let cool and pour over onions. Refrigerate for 2 hours before serving.

YIELD *1½ cups*

BROILED SWORDFISH WITH SALSA

Pineapple Salsa (page 87)
Nonstick spray
4 swordfish steaks, 4 ounces each
2 teaspoons olive oil
Garnish: sprigs of cilantro and cherry tomatoes

Prepare the Pineapple Salsa as directed.

Preheat the broiler. Spray the rack of a broiling pan with a nonstick spray. Place the fish on the broiler rack and brush lightly with olive oil. Broil the fish 4 inches from the heat, without turning, until the fish springs back lightly to the touch. Remove from the heat and transfer to a warmed platter or individual dinner plates. Distribute 2 tablespoons of chilled salsa per serving lengthwise over the fish. Garnish with cilantro and cherry tomatoes.

VARIATION For a colorful variation, you may nap the plate with Cilantro Pesto (page 66), thinned with a little chicken stock or white wine, before topping the swordfish with the salsa.

YIELD *12 ounces fish*

*A*s this pineapple salsa provides more zing than sweetness, it stands up well to the assertive taste of swordfish.

SERVING 3 OZ. FISH
WITH 2 TBS. SALSA
Calories 158.0
Total fat 7.1 gm.
Cholesterol 43.0 mg.
Saturated fat 1.5 gm.
Protein 21.7 gm.
Carbohydrates 1.7 gm.
Sodium 98.0 mg.

BROILED SALMON DIJONNAISE

The rich taste of salmon is nicely balanced by the assertive character of this creamy mustard sauce.

Sauce Dijonnaise (page 61)
4 salmon fillets, 4 ounces each
Garnish: parsley or fresh cilantro, finely chopped

Prepare the Sauce Dijonnaise as directed.

Preheat the broiler. Arrange the salmon in a shallow heat-resistant pan or dish. Broil the fish 4 inches from the heat for about 5 to 7 minutes, turning once, or until the thickest portion springs back to the touch. Remove from the heat.

When ready to serve, nap each warmed dinner plate with 2 tablespoons of the sauce. Place a salmon fillet on top and sprinkle with finely chopped fresh parsley or cilantro.

Y I E L D *12 ounces fish*

SERVING 3 OZ. FISH
WITH 2 TBS. SAUCE
Calories 182.0
Total fat 7.3 gm.
Cholesterol 62.0 mg.
Saturated fat 1.13 gm.
Protein 23.5 gm.
Carbohydrates 3.9 gm.
Sodium 82.0 mg.

PLANKED SALMON WITH PICO DE GALLO

½ cup Pico de Gallo (page 84)
4 salmon fillets, 4 ounces each
1 ashwood plank, washed and charred (see Note below)
1 teaspoon olive oil
Garnish: dried seaweed, cut into 3-inch-long strips, each ¼ inch
    wide by 3 inches long (dried seaweed can be found in specialty
    markets)

Prepare the Pico de Gallo as directed.

Preheat the broiler. Place the fish, flat side down, on the surface of
the plank, which you have rubbed with the olive oil. Broil 4 inches from
the heat, for 5 to 7 minutes, or until the thickest portion of the fish
springs back lightly to the touch.

When ready to serve, remove salmon to heated dinner plates.
Moisten dried seaweed strips so they are pliable, and arrange them
across fish to resemble grill marks. Serve Pico de Gallo on the side.

N O T E You will need an ashwood plank measuring approximately
10 x 5 x 1 inches to fit the 4 salmon fillets called for in this recipe. The
plank must not be larger than the fish, or the edges will burn. Thus, if
you plan to halve this recipe, invest in planks of different sizes. Such
planks are available from a hardwood lumber company, which will trim
the edges to your specifications. Although pecan or hickory may be
used, we find that ashwood gives the best flavor.

Wash and dry the planks thoroughly after purchase; then blacken
them under the broiler before use. Although the planks may be reused
for many years, you will not have to wash them again. Nevertheless,
after each use you should remove any residue of the cooked fish with a
brush; then char briefly under the broiler to sterilize.

Y I E L D *12 ounces fish*

*I*n this unusual recipe, the aromatic qualities of ashwood impart a delicate, smoky flavor to the fish.

SERVING 3 OZ. FISH WITH 2 TBS. PICO DE GALLO

Calories 166.0
Total fat 7.7 gm.
Cholesterol 62.0 mg.
Saturated fat 1.12 gm.
Protein 22.7 gm.
Carbohydrates 1.1 gm.
Sodium 52.0 mg.

BROILED SALMON OR SWORDFISH WITH RED PEPPER SALSA

*A*gain, a slightly
astringent sauce to
balance an oilier
fish.

Red Pepper Salsa (opposite page)
4 salmon or swordfish fillets, 4 ounces each
Nonstick spray
Garnish: zest of one lemon, julienned, and sprigs of fresh cilantro

Prepare the Red Pepper Salsa as directed. Preheat the broiler. Place the fish in a shallow heat-resistant dish or pan. Spray the rack of the broiling pan with nonstick spray and broil the fish 4 inches from the heat for about 7 to 10 minutes, turning once. The fish should just spring back when touched.

When ready to serve, place the fish on a heated platter or dinner plate and spoon 2 tablespoons of salsa attractively across the top of each steak. Garnish with julienned lemon zest and sprigs of fresh cilantro.

Y I E L D *12 ounces fish*

SERVING 3 OZ. FISH
WITH 2 TBS. SALSA

Calories 163.0

Total fat 4.5 gm.

Cholesterol 43.0 mg.

Saturated fat 1.2 gm.

Protein 21.9 gm.

Carbohydrates 1.8 gm.

Sodium 99.0 mg.

RED PEPPER SALSA

1 medium red bell pepper, roasted (page 67)
2 teaspoons fresh oregano, finely chopped
2 tablespoons red wine vinegar
½ jalapeño pepper, seeded and minced (for additional jalapeño, if
   desired)
½ cup tomato concassé (page 50)
¼ cup red onion, finely chopped
1 clove garlic, finely minced

Prepare the pepper as directed.

Soak the oregano in the red wine vinegar in a small nonreactive bowl for 10 minutes. Meanwhile, cut the bell pepper into ½-inch strips and dice. Mix together thoroughly the bell pepper, jalapeño pepper, tomato concassé, red onion, garlic, oregano, and red wine vinegar in a nonreactive container. Set aside.

Y I E L D *1 cup salsa*

SERVING 2 TBS.

Calories 8.0
Total fat 0.1 gm.
Cholesterol 0
Saturated fat 0.01 gm.
Protein 0.3 gm.
Carbohydrates 1.8 gm.
Sodium 1.0 mg.

SAUTÉED RAINBOW TROUT WITH CUCUMBER, DILL, AND CRABMEAT SAUCE

The delicate perfume of dill weed gently enhances the flavor of this light fish.

Cucumber, Dill, and Crabmeat Sauce (page 63)
1 tablespoon canola or corn oil
2 whole rainbow trout, 7 to 10 ounces each, boned

Prepare the Cucumber, Dill, and Crabmeat Sauce as directed.

Heat the oil in a large, heavy-bottomed nonstick skillet, rotating the skillet so the oil coats the bottom of the pan. Pour out any excess. Return the skillet to the heat and add the trout. If the skillet is not large enough to hold 2 trout, use 2 pans so all the fish can be prepared at the same time. Sauté quickly, turning when the edges become opaque, 2 to 3 minutes. The fish is done when the thickest portion loses its translucency and springs back lightly to the touch. When fish are cooked, remove the heads and divide the body of the fish into 4 fillets.

Remove the fish to a warm platter or individual dinner plates. Spoon 2 tablespoons of sauce over each piece of fish and garnish with chopped parsley.

N O T E Although whole boned rainbow trout is now generally available in fish markets, you will probably need to remove additional bones after cooking. Use tweezers.

Y I E L D *4 trout fillets*

SERVING 3 OZ. FISH
WITH 2 TBS. SAUCE

Calories 186.0
Total fat 9.4 gm.
Cholesterol 65.0 mg.
Saturated fat 1.5 gm.
Protein 22.9 gm.
Carbohydrates 1.3 gm.
Sodium 79.0 mg.

BAKED RED SNAPPER WITH ROASTED RED PEPPERS AND SUN-DRIED TOMATOES

2 medium-size red bell peppers, roasted (page 67) and diced
1 tablespoon demi-glace (pages 45–47)
¼ cup dehydrated sun-dried tomatoes
1 whole red snapper, 3 to 4 pounds, cleaned and carefully
  washed
1 tablespoon lemon juice
2 tablespoons olive oil
½ teaspoon white pepper
½ cup cold water
½ clove garlic, finely chopped
Garnish: lemon, thinly sliced; fresh cilantro, finely chopped

Use dehydrated sun-dried tomatoes, not the kind that are packed in oil.

Prepare the peppers and demi-glace ahead as directed. (See Basic Stocks and Sauces, pages 000.)

Place the sun-dried tomatoes in a small bowl and cover with water. Soak until they are plump and tender, then drain, cut into strips and set aside.

Preheat the oven to 425°F. Pat the fish dry and rub with the lemon juice, 1 tablespoon of the olive oil, and pepper. Place in a nonstick shallow baking pan and add the water. Spray aluminum foil with nonstick spray and cover the pan. Bake for 20 to 30 minutes or until the fish springs back to the touch. Remove from the oven and keep warm.

Heat a medium-size, heavy-bottomed skillet or saucepan over medium heat. Add the remaining olive oil. Rotate the pan so the oil covers the bottom and drain off the excess. Return to the heat, add the garlic and cook for 10 seconds, stirring. Stir in the red peppers, sun-dried tomatoes, and demi-glace. Heat until the mixture begins to bubble; remove from the heat and keep warm.

When ready to serve, transfer the whole fish to a warmed platter. Cover with sauce and garnish with lemon slices and cilantro.

Y I E L D *12 ounces fish*

SERVING 3 OZ. FISH
WITH 2 TBS. SAUCE
Calories 133.0
Total fat 3.3 gm.
Cholesterol 40.0 mg.
Saturated fat 0.56 gm.
Protein 22.7 gm.
Carbohydrates 2.0 gm.
Sodium 62.0 mg.

SEARED RED SNAPPER WITH CRIOLLA RELISH

4 red snapper fillets, 4 ounces each
1 teaspoon Spice Blend (page 55)
Nonstick spray
1 cup Criolla Relish (opposite page)
Garnish: lemon slices

Sprinkle fish with Spice Blend and set aside. Preheat oven to 350°F. Oil an ovenproof nonstick skillet lightly with nonstick spray and heat until smoking. Add fish fillets and sear quickly, about 1 minute on each side.

Place in oven for approximately 3 to 4 minutes to finish cooking. Place fish on heated plates and garnish with Criolla Relish and lemon slices.

Y I E L D *4 servings*

SERVING 3 OZ. FISH,
¼ C. RELISH

Calories 127.0

Total fat 2.0 gm.

Cholesterol 40.0 mg.

Saturated fat 0.3 gm.

Protein 23.0 gm.

Carbohydrates 3.0 gm.

Sodium 165.0 mg.

CRIOLLA RELISH

4 plum tomatoes, seeded and diced
1 cucumber, peeled, seeded, and diced
1 small green bell pepper, seeded and diced
1 small red bell pepper, seeded and diced
1 small red onion, diced
1 teaspoon fresh garlic, minced
1 tablespoon capers, rinsed
1 teaspoon fresh dill, chopped
1 teaspoon fresh parsley, chopped
1 tablespoon Dijon mustard
1 tablespoon red wine vinegar
Tabasco to taste

Combine tomatoes, cucumber, diced green and red peppers, onion, garlic, capers, dill, and parsley in a large bowl. Toss well. In a small bowl, stir together mustard, vinegar, and Tabasco and fold into vegetable mixture. Cover and refrigerate 2 hours before serving. The relish will keep refrigerated for 1 to 2 days.

YIELD *1¾ cups*

SERVING ¼ C.
Calories 18.0
Total fat 0.4 gm.
Cholesterol 0
Saturated fat 0
Protein 0.63 gm.
Carbohydrates 3.0 gm.
Sodium 192.0 mg.

BAKED RED SNAPPER WITH JICAMA-GINGER SALSA

Jicama is a crunchy, sweet tuber from South America that looks like a large, knobby turnip with rough, earth-colored skin. It can be used raw or cooked, and may replace water chestnuts in recipes.

Jicama-Ginger Salsa (page 85)
½ cup white wine
Juice of ½ lemon
4 red snapper fillets, 4 ounces each
Garnish: 4 sprigs fresh cilantro

Prepare the Jicama-Ginger Salsa as directed.

Preheat the oven to 425°F. Combine the white wine and lemon juice in a nonreactive container and pour a little of the mixture into an oven-proof dish. Add the snapper fillets and pour the remaining wine mixture over them. Cover with foil or parchment and bake in the oven for 10 to 15 minutes, or until the fish springs back lightly to the touch.

When ready to serve, place one serving of snapper on a heated dinner plate and spoon ¼ cup of the salsa attractively over the fish. Garnish with a sprig of fresh cilantro.

YIELD *12 ounces fish*

SERVING 3 OZ. FISH
WITH 2 TBS. SALSA

Calories 123.0
Total fat 1.6 gm.
Cholesterol 40.0 mg.
Saturated fat 0.33 gm.
Protein 22.9 gm.
Carbohydrates 3.4 gm.
Sodium 53.0 mg.

BROILED WAHOO WITH ORANGE-BASIL SAUCE

Orange-Basil Sauce (page 74)
1 medium-size yellow squash
1 medium-size zucchini squash
4 wahoo fillets, 4 ounces each
Nonstick spray

Prepare the Orange-Basil Sauce as directed.

Peel the squashes, cutting the peelings into lengthwise strips. Reserve the flesh of the squash for use in another recipe. Cut the long peelings into still thinner strips resembling spaghetti and blanch for 1 to 2 minutes. Drain and set aside.

Preheat the broiler. Spray the rack of a shallow broiling pan with nonstick spray and place the wahoo in the pan. Broil the fish for about 7 to 10 minutes, turning once. The fish should just spring back when touched.

When ready to serve, nap the plate with Orange-Basil Sauce, rotating the plate to spread the sauce thinly. Arrange the wahoo fillets on the sauce and top with the squash julienne strips.

Y I E L D *12 ounces fish*

Wahoo is the top grade of mackerel, found predominantly in Hawaii, the Bahamas, and the area around Bermuda. A mild fish, much leaner than king mackerel, its fine white circular flakes make it particularly delightful with delicate sauces like this one.

SERVING 3 OZ. FISH
AND 2 TBS. SAUCE
Calories 179.5
Total fat 3.78 gm.
Cholesterol 42.0 mg.
Saturated fat 0.04 gm.
Protein 27.7 gm.
Carbohydrates 6.2 gm.
Sodium 104.5 mg.

S H E L L F I S H

....

BONELESS AND QUICK-COOKING, SHELLFISH is increasingly becoming one of our nation's most popular foods. Fortunately for heart-healthy concerns, some varieties, such as oysters, mussels, clams, and scallops, are extremely low in fat and cholesterol. Others, however, such as shrimp and crawfish—and, to a lesser degree, crab—are higher in cholesterol, and should be enjoyed in moderate amounts.

We meet this challenge by combining the richer shellfish with items such as pasta and fruit, which contain no cholesterol or saturated fat. Our Risotto with Seafood (page 228) is precisely such a dish, merely studding the plump, creamy grains of rice with nuggets of shrimp and scallops. We attempt to keep factors like this in mind as we create our dishes, and we urge that you do the same in composing your menus.

Along these lines, therefore, you may substitute one kind of shellfish for another in many of these recipes. Where we have specific suggestions in this regard, we have pointed them out. Again, the more acidic treatments are recommended to accompany the richer shellfish, by way of balance.

....

*Brochette of Sea Scallops with Red and Green Peppers
and Fresh Dill Sauce*

Sautéed Sea Scallops with Pernod and Julienne of Vegetables

Crab Marsala

Crabmeat Enchiladas with Green Chili Sauce

Crabmeat Tostados

Sautéed Oysters with Vermouth-Cream Sauce and Fettuccine

Blackened Shrimp with Cajun Rémoulade

Angel-Hair Pasta with Crabmeat and Tomatoes

Stir-Fried Sea Scallops with Crunchy Vegetables

Shrimp and Pesto over Pasta

Risotto with Seafood

Grilled Shrimp with Black Bean and Ginger Sauce

Sautéed Shrimp with Champagne-Saffron Sauce

Blackened Shrimp Balsamico

Fresh Lobster and Papaya with Cold Curry Sauce

....

BROCHETTE OF SEA SCALLOPS WITH RED AND GREEN PEPPERS AND FRESH DILL SAUCE

½ cup Dill Sauce (page 81)
2 cups cooked rice (page 285)
1 to 2 medium-size red bell peppers
1 to 2 medium-size green bell peppers
Nonstick spray
1 pound whole sea scallops, rinsed and drained

A colorful and delicious dish that is very low in fat.

Prepare the Dill Sauce and rice ahead as directed.

Bring 4 cups of water to a rapid boil. While the water is heating, cut the peppers in half. Remove the ribs and seeds, including the white pith. Cut the peppers into triangles or squares approximating the size of the scallops. Blanch the peppers in the boiling water for 1 to 2 minutes. Remove and plunge into an ice-water bath to stop the cooking process. Drain.

Make a fire with preferred materials. Let the fire burn down to hot coals. Prepare the grill by spraying the rack with nonstick spray. On 8 metal or bamboo skewers, alternate slices of red and green bell pepper with the scallops until the skewer is filled. Grill these brochettes over the hot coals until the scallops are opaque and slightly resilient to the touch, about 2 to 3 minutes per side.

When ready to serve, spoon a layer of rice onto a warmed platter. Arrange the brochettes across the bed of rice and gently remove the skewers. Serve with cool Dill Sauce on the side.

VARIATION You may add shrimp to the brochettes, if you desire. Marinating the seafood in Lemon, Mustard, and Herb Marinade (page 77) adds a little zing.

YIELD *8 brochettes, 2 cups rice, and ½ cup dressing*

SERVING 2 BROCHETTES AND ½ C. RICE WITH 2 TBS. DRESSING

Calories 253.0
Total fat 3.6 gm.
Cholesterol 44.0 mg.
Saturated fat 0.59 gm.
Protein 23.8 gm.
Carbohydrates 29.2 gm.
Sodium 274.0 mg.

SAUTÉED SEA SCALLOPS WITH PERNOD AND JULIENNE OF VEGETABLES

Anise-flavored ingredients, such as fennel or the Pernod called for in this recipe, make a distinctive contribution to many seafood dishes.

3 tablespoons soubise (page 48)
¼ cup Pernod
1 tablespoon shallots, finely chopped
2 tablespoons finely chopped mixed fresh herbs, such as oregano, tarragon, and thyme
3 tablespoons nonfat yogurt
2 tablespoons reduced-calorie mayonnaise
2 teaspoons olive oil
1 pound whole sea scallops, rinsed and drained
¼ cup carrots, julienned
½ cup leeks, julienned
½ cup onion, julienned
White pepper, to taste

Prepare the soubise ahead as directed. (See Basic Stocks and Sauces, page 48.)

In a heavy-bottomed sauté pan, place the Pernod, shallots, and herbs. Simmer over a medium heat until reduced by ½ its original volume. Stir in the soubise, yogurt, and mayonnaise, and heat thoroughly. Keep warm while you prepare the scallops.

Heat the oil in a heavy-bottomed sauté pan or nonstick skillet. Add the scallops and sauté until opaque and slightly resilient to the touch.

Blanch the julienned vegetables in 4 cups of boiling water for 2 minutes. Remove and plunge briefly into ice water to stop the cooking process. Do not allow to chill. Drain and set aside until needed. (They may be rewarmed, if necessary, by tossing in a saucepan with a little chicken stock over medium heat.)

When ready to serve add the sauce to the scallops and heat thoroughly, seasoning to taste with white pepper. Arrange the scallops and sauce attractively on each warm dinner plate. Top with the julienned vegetables.

Y I E L D   *12 ounces scallops and 1 cup sauce*

SERVING 3 OZ. SEA
SCALLOPS WITH
2 TBS. SAUCE
Calories 182.0
Total fat 5.5 gm.
Cholesterol 43.0 mg.
Saturated fat 0.79 gm.
Protein 21.7 gm.
Carbohydrates 10.3 gm.
Sodium 258.0 mg.

CRAB MARSALA

1 cup demi-glace (pages 45–47)
1 teaspoon olive oil
3 cloves garlic, finely chopped
¾ cup marsala wine
1 pound jumbo lump crabmeat, picked over carefully
2 cups cooked rice
Garnish: 16 julienne strips of red pepper, roasted (page 67);
  8 fresh cilantro leaves; 2 tablespoons chives, finely chopped

Prepare the demi-glace ahead as directed. (See Basic Stocks and Sauces, pages 45–47.)

Heat the oil in a heavy-bottomed saucepan over medium-low heat. Add the garlic and sauté for 30 seconds. Do not brown. Add the wine and demi-glace and simmer over medium heat until the sauce coats the back of a spoon. Fold in the crabmeat and heat until bubbly.

When ready to serve, place ½ cup of rice on each heated dinner plate. Form a well in the center of the rice ring, leaving the center of the plate clear. Fill the center with ¼ of the crabmeat and sauce and garnish as follows: On opposite sides of the rice ring, arrange red pepper strips in the form of an X. You will have two X's per plate. Place the cilantro leaves on the edge of the plate at each X. Sprinkle with fresh chives.

YIELD *16 ounces crabmeat and 1 cup sauce*

Marsala wine augments the natural sweetness of crab in this adaptation of a Creole sauté. It may be served as either a main course or an appetizer.

SERVING 4 OZ.
CRABMEAT AND
½ C. RICE WITH
¼ C. SAUCE
Calories 243.0
Total fat 3.3 gm.
Cholesterol 113.0 mg.
Saturated fat 0.45 gm.
Protein 25.1 gm.
Carbohydrates 26.0 gm.
Sodium 316.0 mg.

CRABMEAT ENCHILADAS WITH GREEN CHILI SAUCE

Our creamy, pale-green sauce flecked with bits of tomato is not the incendiary New Mexican dish, but it gives a provocative zip to mellow lump crabmeat.

Green Chili Sauce (opposite page)
8 corn tortillas
1 teaspoon olive oil
1 teaspoon garlic, finely chopped
1 teaspoon jalapeño pepper, seeded and finely chopped
2 tablespoons tomato concassé (page 50)
2 tablespoons scallions, finely sliced crosswise
1 pound jumbo lump crabmeat, picked over carefully
Pinch white pepper, to taste
Nonstick spray
3 tablespoons skim mozzarella cheese
3 tablespoons nonfat yogurt
Garnish: chopped cilantro; paprika

Prepare the Green Chili Sauce as directed.

To make the tortillas more pliable, heat them as follows: Preheat oven to 350°F. Wrap the tortillas in foil and place in the oven until heated through, approximately 10 to 15 minutes.

In a heavy-bottomed saucepan, heat the olive oil. Add the garlic, jalapeño, and tomato concassé and sauté for about 30 seconds. Stir in the scallions and fold in the crabmeat. Heat the mixture thoroughly and season with white pepper. Divide the crabmeat equally among the warm tortillas. Carefully roll the tortillas around the filling and place in an ovenproof dish that you have sprayed with nonstick spray. Pour the sauce over the rolled tortillas. Sprinkle with mozzarella cheese and dot each with approximately 1 teaspoon of yogurt. Bake in the oven at 350°F until heated through, approximately 15 to 20 minutes. Garnish with chopped cilantro and a dusting of paprika.

VARIATION As a variation, you may replace the crab with coarsely chopped cooked shrimp.

YIELD *8 enchiladas*

SERVING 2 ENCHILADAS WITH 2 TBS. SAUCE

Calories 327.0
Total fat 8.61 gm.
Cholesterol 117.0 mg.
Saturated fat 1.52 gm.
Protein 30.7 gm.
Carbohydrates 31.8 gm.
Sodium 473.0 mg.

GREEN CHILI SAUCE

4 tablespoons soubise (page 48)
¼ cup white onion, finely chopped
1 teaspoon finely chopped garlic
2 tablespoons jalapeño pepper, seeded and finely chopped
3 tomatillos
2 teaspoons olive oil
6 tablespoons tomato concassé (page 50)
4 tablespoons nonfat yogurt
½ cup chicken stock (page 41)

Prepare soubise ahead as directed. (See Basic Stocks and Sauces, page 52.)

Sauté the onion, garlic, jalapeño, and tomatillos in the hot olive oil for approximately 3 minutes, until the onion is translucent. Stir in the tomato concassé and cook for 2 additional minutes. Mix in the soubise, yogurt, and chicken stock, heating until bubbly. Keep warm until needed.

N O T E Primarily for reasons of texture, we always seed our jalapeños.

Y I E L D *1½ cups*

CRABMEAT TOSTADOS

These make a great party hors d'oeuvre, appetizer, or light lunch.

⅓ cup red onion, finely diced
½ cup tomato, seeded and diced
1 teaspoon seeded and minced jalapeño pepper
2 tablespoons fresh cilantro, minced
1 pound jumbo lump crabmeat, picked over carefully
Juice from ½ lemon
½ cup nonfat yogurt
½ teaspoon ground cumin
½ teaspoon chili powder
½ teaspoon sugar
¼ teaspoon black pepper
¼ teaspoon coriander
3 drops Tabasco
8 Tostados (see below)

Combine onion, tomato, jalapeño, and cilantro in a large bowl; mix well. Add crabmeat and toss gently. Stir together lemon juice, yogurt, cumin, chili powder, sugar, black pepper, coriander, and Tabasco in a small bowl. Fold into the crabmeat mixture. To serve, place 1 tablespoon crabmeat mixture on each tostado.

If desired, serve with Black Bean Salsa (page 86), Pico de Gallo (page 84) and Guacamole (page 102). The crab mixture will keep refrigerated up to 2 days.

Y I E L D *3½ cups*

TOSTADOS

8 (6-inch) corn tortillas

Preheat oven to 350°F. Cut three 2-inch circles from each tortilla with a cookie cutter. Place circles on a cookie sheet and toast in oven until crisp, 3 to 5 minutes.

Y I E L D *24*

SERVING 4 TBS.
CRABMEAT
MIXTURE,
4 TOSTADOS
Calories 100.0
Total fat 1.5 gm.
Cholesterol 25.0 mg.
Saturated fat 0
Protein 8.4 gm.
Carbohydrates 13.0 gm.
Sodium 150.0 mg.

SAUTÉED OYSTERS WITH VERMOUTH-CREAM SAUCE AND FETTUCCINE

½ cup soubise (page 48)
1 pound fresh or dried fettuccine
⅓ cup dry white vermouth
1 tablespoon minced shallots
¼ cup tomato concassé (page 50)
1 tablespoon fresh cilantro, finely chopped
White pepper
24 medium oysters, shucked
Garnish: chopped fresh cilantro or parsley; finely chopped lemon zest

Prepare the soubise ahead as directed. (See Basic Stocks and Sauces, page 48.)

Bring 4 quarts of water to a boil; add the fettuccine, reduce heat, and cook until al dente.

Meanwhile, simmer the vermouth, shallots, tomato concassé, and cilantro in a medium-size, heavy-bottomed saucepan over medium heat for 2 to 3 minutes. Stir in the soubise and continue to cook until bubbly. Add white pepper to taste. Add the oysters and simmer until their edges begin to curl.

When ready to serve, toss the fettuccine with the oysters and sauce, and arrange on warm dinner plates or in individual bowls. Garnish with chopped parsley (or cilantro) and lemon zest.

YIELD *4 servings*

Oysters and cream are a favorite combination. Here, we've replaced the cream with soubise and brightened the resulting sauce with crushed tomatoes and a splash of vermouth.

SERVING 1 C. FETTUCCINE AND 3 OZ. OYSTERS WITH ¼ C. SAUCE

Calories 294.0
Total fat 2.75 gm.
Cholesterol 47.25 mg.
Saturated fat 0.55 gm.
Protein 16.35 gm.
Carbohydrates 50.88 gm.
Sodium 118.75 mg.

BLACKENED SHRIMP WITH CAJUN RÉMOULADE

16 jumbo shrimp, shelled and deveined, tails intact (about
   1 pound)
1 teaspoon Spice Blend (page 55)
2 teaspoons olive oil
2 cups Cajun Rémoulade (see below)

Sprinkle shrimp with Spice Blend and set aside. Place olive oil in heavy nonstick sauté pan and heat over high heat until just below the smoking point. Add shrimp and sear on each side about 1 minute or until shrimp blackens. Remove from pan immediately. Serve warm or chilled, combining 4 shrimp on a plate with 2 tablespoons Cajun Rémoulade.

YIELD *16 shrimp*

*T*his spicy version of rémoulade sauce can be served with other fish or shellfish instead of the traditional cocktail sauce.

CAJUN RÉMOULADE

2 tablespoons each, whole-grain and Dijon mustards
2 tablespoons tomato paste
1 tablespoon white wine vinegar
½ tablespoon paprika
½ cup celery, chopped
2 tablespoons green onion, minced
½ tablespoon garlic, minced
2 tablespoons egg substitute
½ cup nonfat yogurt
Juice from ½ lemon
½ cup fresh parsley, minced
Tabasco to taste

Place all ingredients in the container of a blender or food processor. Process until smooth. Chill well before serving. The sauce can be kept refrigerated for up to 7 days.

YIELD *2 cups*

ANGEL-HAIR PASTA WITH CRABMEAT AND TOMATOES

4 quarts water, for cooking pasta
1 teaspoon olive oil
2 tablespoons white onion, chopped
1 teaspoon garlic, minced
3 ripe tomatoes, peeled, seeded, and chopped
2 tablespoons tomato paste
½ cup white wine
1 cup chicken stock (page 41)
1 tablespoon fresh parsley, finely chopped
1 tablespoon fresh basil, finely chopped
1 pound jumbo lump crabmeat, picked over carefully
2 tablespoons scallions
White pepper, to taste
1 pound fresh angel-hair pasta, to make 4 cups
Garnish: fresh basil or parsley, chopped

Bring water to a boil. Meanwhile, heat the oil in a nonstick saucepan. Add the onion and garlic and sauté until the onion is translucent. Add the tomatoes and tomato paste and cook for 5 minutes. Stir in the white wine, chicken stock, parsley, basil, and crabmeat, and simmer for 10 minutes over low heat. Stir in the scallions and add white pepper. Remove from heat and keep warm.

When the water is ready, add the angel-hair pasta and reduce the heat. Cook for 2 to 3 minutes, or until al dente. Do not overcook, or the pasta will become gummy. Drain the pasta and add it to the hot sauce, tossing to combine. Serve immediately, garnished with chopped basil or parsley.

Y I E L D *4 cups pasta with 2 cups sauce*

This light sauce, aromatic with garlic and fresh basil, is surprisingly intense.

SERVING 1 C. PASTA
WITH ½ C. SAUCE
Calories 229.0
Total fat 2.1 gm.
Cholesterol 0
Saturated fat 0.29 gm.
Protein 7.7 gm.
Carbohydrates 45.3 gm.
Sodium 15.0 mg.

STIR-FRIED SEA SCALLOPS WITH CRUNCHY VEGETABLES

4 teaspoons cornstarch
1 cup canned low-sodium chicken broth
1½ tablespoons dry sherry
4 teaspoons reduced-sodium soy sauce
1 medium yellow onion, cut into wedges and layers separated
3 stalks celery, sliced diagonally into ½-inch pieces
1 cup fresh green beans, cut into 1-inch pieces
1 cup fresh broccoli, cut into 2-inch pieces
1 medium carrot, peeled and cut into thin 1-inch strips
6 green onions, cut diagonally into ½-inch pieces
2 teaspoons fresh ginger, minced
1 clove garlic, minced
1 pound sea scallops, rinsed, drained, and cut in half
¼ cup mushrooms, sliced
Garnish: 2 green onions, thinly sliced

In a small bowl, whisk together cornstarch and ¾ cup chicken broth until smooth. Whisk in sherry and soy sauce and set aside. In a wok or heavy skillet, heat remaining ¼ cup chicken broth over high heat. Add onion, celery, green beans, broccoli, carrot, green onions, ginger, and garlic. Cook 2 to 3 minutes, stirring frequently. Add scallops and mushrooms and stir-fry 1 minute. Add chicken broth mixture and bring to a boil. Cook 2 to 3 minutes, until scallops are tender. Remove from heat and serve immediately with steamed rice. Garnish with sliced green onions.

YIELD *4 servings*

SERVING 3 OZ.
SCALLOPS AND
½ C. VEGETABLES
Calories 134.0
Total fat 1.2 gm.
Cholesterol 37.0 mg.
Saturated fat 0.21 gm.
Protein 20.0 gm.
Carbohydrates 10.0 gm.
Sodium 300.0 mg.

SHRIMP AND PESTO OVER PASTA

4 tablespoons soubise (page 48)
½ cup chicken stock (page 41)
4 tablespoons Cilantro Pesto (page 66)
2 teaspoons olive oil
1 pound shrimp (16 to 20 per pound), shelled and deveined, tails
  intact
1 garlic clove, minced fine
½ cup white wine
1 pound pasta (such as fettuccine, linguini, angel hair), cooked
Garnish: cherry tomato halves; cilantro, finely chopped

Prepare the soubise and chicken stock ahead as directed. (See Basic
Stocks and Sauces, pages 48 and 41.) Prepare the Cilantro Pesto
ahead as directed.

Heat the oil in a large, heavy-bottomed sauté pan over medium heat.
Add the shrimp and garlic and sauté for 1 minute. Deglaze the pan
with white wine. Stir in the pesto, soubise, and chicken stock, and cook
until the mixture begins to bubble gently. Toss the pasta with the sauce
until thoroughly combined. Place in individual serving bowls. Add the
shrimp on top in a circle, tails facing down and outward. Garnish the
center with a cherry tomato half, sprinkled with chopped cilantro.

YIELD *4 servings*

Cilantro Pesto adds a novel dimension to the creamy garlic sauce used in this dish.

SERVING 5 SHRIMP
AND 1 C. PASTA
WITH ¼ C. SAUCE
Calories 327.0
Total fat 7.0 gm.
Cholesterol 138.0 mg.
Saturated fat 1.34 gm.
Protein 23.1 gm.
Carbohydrates 41.7 gm.
Sodium 195.0 mg.

RISOTTO WITH SEAFOOD

A specialty of northern Italy, risotto is known for the luscious, creamy texture the rice develops as the mixture slowly cooks. For this reason, we specify the use of arborio, an Italian rice traditionally used for the dish. Stirring the stock into the rice requires some attention, but the result is worth it.

SERVING ½ C. RICE
WITH 3 OZ. SEAFOOD

Calories 279.0

Total fat 3.3 gm.

Cholesterol 173.0 mg.

Saturated fat 0.68 gm.

Protein 36.1 gm.

Carbohydrates 28.5 gm.

Sodium 308.0 mg.

2 to 3 cups chicken stock (page 41)
¼ cup white wine
8 to 10 medium shrimp, peeled and deveined
8 ounces sea scallops, drained
2 teaspoons olive oil
½ small onion, finely chopped
1 clove garlic, finely chopped
1 cup arborio rice
½ tablespoon parsley, finely chopped
Black pepper, to taste
1 tablespoon Parmesan cheese
Garnish: thin lemon slices and whole leaves of Italian parsley

Prepare the chicken stock ahead as directed.

In a medium-size saucepan, bring 1 cup of the chicken stock with ¼ cup white wine to a boil. Add the shrimp and scallops and poach for 3 to 5 minutes. Remove the seafood and reserve the poaching liquid.

Heat the olive oil in a large, heavy-bottomed saucepan or Dutch oven. Add the onion and garlic and sauté for 2 to 3 minutes, until the onion clarifies. Add the rice and cook, stirring, until the rice appears translucent, 1 to 2 minutes. Then stir in 1 cup of the reserved poaching liquid and cook, stirring gently, but continually, until the liquid is absorbed. Continuing to stir, add additional liquid, ½ cup at a time, until it is absorbed and the rice is tender. This may take 20 to 30 minutes. When the rice is tender, add the poached seafood and heat thoroughly. Stir in the parsley and pepper to taste, and sprinkle with Parmesan cheese. Serve on warmed dinner plates, garnished with sliced lemons and whole parsley leaves.

VARIATION You may vary the recipe by substituting chicken breast or your favorite shellfish.

YIELD *6 cups*

GRILLED SHRIMP WITH BLACK BEAN AND GINGER SAUCE

24 large shrimp, peeled and deveined, tails removed
1 teaspoon sesame oil
1 cup Black Bean and Ginger Sauce (see below)
Garnish: 1 teaspoon sesame seeds and 1 teaspoon fresh cilantro, chopped

Brush shrimp with sesame oil. Grill shrimp 2 to 3 minutes on each side.

To serve, arrange 6 shrimp on each dinner plate. Nap with ¼ cup of sauce and sprinkle with toasted sesame seeds and chopped cilantro. Serve with steamed rice.

Y I E L D *4 servings*

BLACK BEAN AND GINGER SAUCE

½ cup low-sodium chicken broth
1 tablespoon dried red chilies, minced
2 tablespoons garlic, minced
2 tablespoons fresh ginger, minced
¼ cup black beans, cooked and drained
1 teaspoon sugar
¼ cup fresh orange juice
3 tablespoons tomato paste
3 tablespoons green onions, chopped

In a heavy saucepan, heat 2 tablespoons chicken broth. Add chilies, garlic, and ginger and cook 2 minutes over medium heat. Add beans and sugar and cook 1 minute. Stir in the remaining broth and the orange juice. Bring to a boil and whisk in the tomato paste. Cook 2 minutes and stir in the green onions, cooking for 30 seconds.

Y I E L D *1 cup*

SERVING 6 SHRIMP, ¼ C. SAUCE
Calories 149.0
Total fat 2.1 gm.
Cholesterol 172.0 mg.
Saturated fat 0.4 gm.
Protein 24.0 gm.
Carbohydrates 7.0 gm.
Sodium 176.0 mg.

SAUTÉED SHRIMP WITH CHAMPAGNE-SAFFRON SAUCE

Champagne, saffron, and truffles make this easy dish elegant enough for the most special occasion.

⅔ cup soubise (page 48)
⅓ cup champagne
1 tablespoon champagne vinegar
1 teaspoon shallots, minced
4 to 6 threads saffron
1 tablespoon tomato concassé (page 50)
1 teaspoon fresh tarragon, finely chopped
White pepper, to taste
1 tablespoon olive oil
1 pound shrimp (16 to 20 per pound), shelled and deveined, tails intact
Garnish: 1 teaspoon truffles, julienned

Prepare the soubise ahead as directed. (See Basic Stocks and Sauces, page 48.)

Add the champagne, champagne vinegar, shallots, saffron, tomato concassé, and tarragon to a medium-size, heavy-bottomed saucepan. Simmer over medium heat until the liquid is reduced to ½ its original volume. Stir in the soubise, heating until bubbles rise. Season with white pepper, then set aside and keep warm.

Heat the olive oil in a heavy-bottomed skillet or saucepan and sauté the shrimp until they turn opaque, approximately 3 minutes.

When ready to serve, nap each warm dinner plate with 2 tablespoons sauce and add the shrimp. Sprinkle with julienned truffles.

N O T E For the most concentrated flavor, use saffron threads. The powdered variety is sometimes mixed with other, less expensive ingredients. It also loses strength rapidly. You may vary the amount of saffron called for, according to taste.

Y I E L D *16 to 20 shrimp and 1 cup sauce*

SERVING 5 SHRIMP WITH 2 TBS. SAUCE

Calories 113.0

Total fat 4.1 gm.

Cholesterol 137.0 mg.

Saturated fat 0.67 gm.

Protein 15.3 gm.

Carbohydrates 2.8 gm.

Sodium 165.0 mg.

BLACKENED SHRIMP BALSAMICO

12 large shrimp, peeled and deveined, tails removed
½ teaspoon Spice Blend (page 55)
2 teaspoons olive oil
2 teaspoons shallots, minced
2 teaspoons garlic, minced
¼ cup white wine
¼ cup low-sodium chicken broth
1 tablespoon balsamic vinegar
½ teaspoon cracked black pepper
1 tablespoon fresh basil, julienned

Sprinkle shrimp with Spice Blend and set aside. Heat a heavy sauté pan or skillet until just below the smoking point and swirl in the olive oil. Heat the oil to smoking and add the shrimp, searing on each side for about 1 minute or until shrimp has blackened. Add shallots and garlic and sauté 30 seconds. Add white wine, broth, and balsamic vinegar. Cook until reduced to a glaze, about 1 to 2 minutes. Remove from heat and add cracked pepper and fresh basil. Serve immediately.

Y I E L D *4 servings*

*S*erve these shrimp as a delicious appetizer or as a dinner for two.

SERVING 3 SHRIMP, 2 TBS. SAUCE
Calories 118.0
Total fat 1.3 gm.
Cholesterol 221.0 mg.
Saturated fat 0.34 gm.
Protein 24.4 gm.
Carbohydrates 0.9 gm.
Sodium 255.0 mg.

FRESH LOBSTER AND PAPAYA WITH COLD CURRY SAUCE

The luxurious focal point of an elegant luncheon or light summer dinner.

6 cups Court Bouillon (page 44)
1¼-pound live lobster
½ cup Curry Sauce (opposite page)
2 papayas
2 tablespoons lemon juice
Garnish: leaves of red leaf or Boston lettuce; sprigs of parsley; lobster claw meat; 2 teaspoons parsley, finely chopped; lemon wedges

Prepare the Court Bouillon ahead as directed. (See Basic Stocks and Sauces, page 44.)

Drop the live lobster into the boiling Court Bouillon and cook for about 25 minutes, or until a small leg will pull off easily. Drain and chill. Meanwhile, prepare the Curry Sauce as directed.

Using a sharp knife, split the cooked lobster lengthwise. Remove the grit sac from behind the head and pull out the intestinal vein. Crack the claws and extract the meat carefully. Twist off the legs and remove the meat they contain. Remove the meat from the shell and cut into chunks. Place the meat from the shell and legs in a bowl, reserving claw meat for garnish.

Cut the papayas in half, remove the seeds, and scoop out ⅔ of the fruit with a spoon. (Do not peel.) Cut the fruit into small chunks and add to the lobster meat in the bowl.

Add the lemon juice and ½ cup Curry Sauce to the lobster-papaya mixture, tossing to combine. Refrigerate until thoroughly chilled.

When ready to serve, arrange the papaya shells on a bed of lettuce and fill them with the lobster mixture. Garnish each with sprigs of parsley and the meat from one claw. Sprinkle with chopped parsley and surround the papaya shell with lemon wedges.

YIELD *4 servings*

CURRY SAUCE

½ cup reduced-calorie mayonnaise
½ cup nonfat yogurt
2 teaspoons curry powder

Whisk all the ingredients together in a small bowl. Refrigerate until chilled.

Y I E L D   *1 cup sauce*

SERVING 3 OZ.
LOBSTER AND
¼ PAPAYA WITH
2 TBS. SAUCE
Calories 156.0
Total fat 3.0 gm.
Cholesterol 64.0 mg.
Saturated fat 0.50 gm.
Protein 18.6 gm.
Carbohydrates 13.3 gm.
Sodium 376.0 mg.

MEAT

....

ONE OF THE FEW INSTANTLY understandable dietary dicta pronounced by physicians during the past decade was the one urging us to restrict our consumption of red meat. So what are we doing with beef, lamb, veal, and pork in this book? Well, they're on our menu, too, because—as is true of so many other aspects of heart-healthy dining—the enjoyment of lean red meat is possible if consumed in moderate amounts, in balanced proportion to other parts of the meal and the day's eating plan.

There are, however, a few cautions that are worth remembering. First, you cannot substitute other cuts of meat willy-nilly for the ones called for in the following recipes. For instance, the medallion of lamb we refer to may be the nugget of a lamb chop, but that doesn't mean you can prepare the chop itself with our sauce and remain heart-healthy. Chops of all kinds are fatty, and, therefore, off limits.

We cut our medallions from the tenderloin, because—although certain other cuts may be somewhat leaner—this is the quickest cooking variety of low-fat meat. Some tenderloins, however, are leaner than others. Pork is one of these, despite its fatty reputation. In fact, the appropriate amount of trimmed pork tenderloin is lower in saturated fat than beef and lower in cholesterol than veal, while being roughly equivalent in other areas.

In the recipes that follow, you will notice the size of the suggested portions. We begin with 4 ounces of meat, by raw weight, and anticipate some shrinkage during cooking. The amount will depend on the length of time it is cooked. For purposes of nutritional analysis, we have used an average shrinkage of 1 ounce per portion, although rare beef, for example, may lose only ½ ounce. We recommend you enhance the appearance and flavor of the meat by slicing the medallions diagonally, so they form ovals instead of rounds.

....

Chez Eddy Chicken-Fried Steak

Whole Fillet of Beef with Brandy Reduction Sauce

Medallions of Beef Marchand de Vin

Grilled Medallions of Lamb with Chick-Pea Salsa

Broiled Lamb Medallions with Garlic Sauce

Medallions of Lamb with Rosemary–Port Wine Reduction Sauce

Medallions of Veal with Tarragon Sauce

Escallops of Veal with Apricot Coulis

Beef Brochette with Roasted Chile Sauce

Medallions of Pork with Cranberries and Hot-Pepper Jelly

Stir-Fried Beef with Sherry Sauce and Fresh Spinach

Roasted Pork Tenderloin with Cumberland Sauce

....

CHEZ EDDY CHICKEN-FRIED STEAK

Brown Gravy (next page)
4 beef tenderloin fillets, 4 ounces each
2 cups flour
1 teaspoon baking soda
1 teaspoon garlic powder
1 teaspoon onion powder
2 teaspoons ground black pepper
1 cup low-fat buttermilk
¼ cup egg substitute
1 egg
1 teaspoon corn oil

Prepare the Brown Gravy as directed. Keep warm.

Pound the meat to ¼-inch thickness.

In a large mixing bowl, sift together the dry ingredients. In a small bowl, whisk together the liquid ingredients, except for the corn oil. Make a well in the center of the dry ingredients and add the liquid ingredients. Stir until smooth. Let stand for 30 minutes.

Preheat the oven to 350°F. On the stove, heat the oil in a large, ovenproof, heavy-bottomed nonstick skillet. When the oil is heated to just below the smoking point, dip the steak into the batter and then sauté in the oil for 3 minutes on 1 side, or until well browned. Turn and sauté for 2 minutes on the other side. Place the skillet containing the meat into the oven for approximately 5 to 7 minutes. When the meat is done, remove and blot dry with paper towels.

Serve with Mashed Potatoes (page 290) and Brown Gravy.

N O T E In this dish we use a moist batter that absorbs less fat than the dry variety.

Y I E L D *4 servings*

We developed this recipe in response to a request from Larry L. Mathis, president and CEO of the Methodist Hospital System. We use very lean beef tenderloin, sautéed quickly in a minimal amount of very hot fat. It is not deep fried.

SERVING 3 OZ. MEAT
WITH 2 TBS. GRAVY
Calories 251.0
Total fat 12.9 gm.
Cholesterol 71.0 mg.
Saturated fat 3.78 gm.
Protein 25.7 gm.
Carbohydrates 6.6 gm.
Sodium 90.0 mg.

BROWN GRAVY

1 tablespoon soubise (page 48)
1 cup chicken stock (page 41)
1 teaspoon unsalted margarine, clarified (page 123)
1 teaspoon flour
Black pepper, to taste

Prepare the soubise and chicken stock ahead as directed. (See Basic Stocks and Sauces, pages 48 and 41.)

In a medium saucepan, simmer chicken stock until reduced by half. Add the unsalted margarine to a heated sauté pan or skillet. Sprinkle in the flour and cook until it is well browned, stirring constantly. Add the reduced chicken stock and soubise, and stir until it thickens to the consistency of gravy. Season with black pepper.

Y I E L D *½ cup*

SERVING 2 TBS.

Calories 13.0

Total fat 1.0 gm.

Cholesterol 0

Saturated fat 0.18 gm.

Protein 0.2 gm.

Carbohydrates 0.9 gm.

Sodium 1.0 mg.

WHOLE FILLET OF BEEF WITH BRANDY REDUCTION SAUCE

Brandy Reduction Sauce (see below)
1 teaspoon olive oil
1-pound piece of a whole beef tenderloin, trimmed of fat and
  silvery membrane
Garnish: bouquets of fresh watercress

Prepare the Brandy Reduction Sauce as directed.

Preheat the oven to 400°F. On the stove, heat the oil in a large, ovenproof, nonstick skillet over medium-high heat. Brown the tenderloin on all sides. Transfer to the oven and roast 7 to 10 minutes, for rare meat; 10 to 15 minutes for medium. When done, remove from the oven and let rest for 15 minutes before slicing.

When ready to serve, you may present the beef on a hot platter, napped with a ribbon of sauce and garnished with bouquets of watercress. Or place a 3-ounce portion on a warmed dinner plate, sauced and garnished similarly. In either case, our Tomatoes Provençal (page 274) make a good accompaniment.

Y I E L D   *12 ounces beef with 1 cup sauce*

BRANDY REDUCTION SAUCE

1½ cups demi-glace (pages 45–47)
2 tablespoons shallots, minced
2 teaspoons black peppercorns, cracked
2 ounces brandy or cognac

Prepare the demi-glace ahead as directed. (See Basic Stocks and Sauces, pages 45–47.)

In a small, heavy-bottomed saucepan, cook the shallots and the peppercorns in the brandy over low heat until the brandy is syrupy, stirring frequently, approximately 3 minutes. Add the demi-glace and simmer over medium heat until the sauce is reduced by ⅓ its original volume. It should coat the back of a spoon.

This luxurious dish, pungent with cracked peppercorns, is simple to prepare, yet suitable for the most formal dinner.

SERVING 3 OZ. BEEF
WITH 2 TBS. SAUCE

Calories 183.0
Total fat 9.0 gm.
Cholesterol 71.0 mg.
Saturated fat 3.24 gm.
Protein 24 gm.
Carbohydrates 0
Sodium 54.0 mg.

N O T E This sauce may be made a day or two in advance and refrigerated for 3 to 5 days. It may also be frozen for 2 to 3 months but the flavors may need to be freshened upon reheating.

V A R I A T I O N If you prefer to present this dish in the form of steaks, just cut the raw tenderloin into 3-ounce portions. Place them in a skillet containing 1 tablespoon of hot olive oil, and sear quickly on each side. Then place in a 400°F oven for 3 to 4 minutes for rare beef, or longer, if you prefer. Serve on warmed dinner plates, as above.

MEDALLIONS OF
BEEF MARCHAND DE VIN

Marchand de Vin Sauce (see below)
Nonstick spray
4 beef tenderloin fillets, 4 ounces each
Garnish: freshly chopped parsley

Prepare the Marchand de Vin Sauce as directed. Make a fire using your preferred materials. Let the fire burn down to hot coals. Prepare the grill by spraying with nonstick spray. When the fire is ready, place the fillets on the grill, and grill 2 to 3 minutes per side, or until done to taste. When ready to serve, arrange 1 fillet per serving on a warmed dinner plate, nap with 2 tablespoons of sauce, and garnish with chopped parsley.

VARIATION Add some horseradish to the sauce, for a little zing. As a visual variation, butterfly the meat after it is cooked, to give the appearance of rare, roasted beef. The meat also may be sautéed, or the tenderloin may be roasted whole (see page 239).

YIELD *12 ounces meat with ½ cup sauce*

MARCHAND DE VIN SAUCE

⅔ cup demi-glace (pages 45–47)
½ tablespoon olive oil
1 teaspoon shallots, finely chopped
1 teaspoon garlic, finely chopped
2 ounces red wine
Black pepper, to taste

Prepare the demi-glace ahead as directed. (See Basic Stocks and Sauces, pages 45–47.) Add olive oil to a hot, heavy-bottomed nonstick skillet and sauté the shallots and garlic lightly, without browning. Stir in the wine and demi-glace, and reduce to ½ its volume or until the sauce coats the back of a spoon. Season with black pepper.

We have adapted this dish from French and Creole cuisine to the requirements of heart-healthy dining. The heady reduction of red wine, shallots, and demi-glace more than holds its own against the smoky taste of grilled beef.

SERVING 3 OZ. MEAT
WITH 2 TBS. SAUCE
Calories 189.0
Total fat 9.6 gm.
Cholesterol 71.0 mg.
Saturated fat 3.32 gm.
Protein 24.0 gm.
Carbohydrates 0.1 gm.
Sodium 54.0 mg.

GRILLED MEDALLIONS OF LAMB WITH CHICK-PEA SALSA

SERVING 3 OZ. MEAT
WITH ⅓ C. SALSA

Calories 291.0

Total fat 9.3 gm.

Cholesterol 81.0 mg.

Saturated fat 3.0 gm.

Protein 30.0 gm.

Carbohydrates 20.0 gm.

Sodium 200.0 mg.

8 medallions of lamb, cut into 2-ounce portions
1 tablespoon balsamic vinegar
1 teaspoon Spice Blend (see page 55)
1 teaspoon fresh mint, chopped
1½ cups Chick-Pea Salsa (see below)
Garnish: fresh mint leaves

Sprinkle lamb medallions with balsamic vinegar, Spice Blend, and chopped mint. Grill or broil to desired degree of doneness. To serve, pool ⅓ cup salsa on each plate. Top with lamb medallions. Garnish with fresh mint leaves.

YIELD *4 servings*

CHICK-PEA SALSA

1 (15-ounce) can chick-peas, rinsed and drained
3 plum tomatoes, seeded and diced
½ small red onion, minced
½ small red bell pepper, minced
2 green onions, minced
1 jalapeño pepper, seeded and minced
1 teaspoon each garlic, fresh mint, fresh cilantro, minced
1 tablespoon rice wine vinegar

SERVING ⅓ C.

Calories 100.0

Total fat 1.0 gm.

Cholesterol 0

Saturated fat 0.1 gm.

Protein 4.45 gm.

Carbohydrates 20.0 gm.

Sodium 200.0 mg.

Place one third of the chick-peas in a medium bowl and mash with a fork until smooth. Stir in the remaining chick-peas. Add remaining ingredients. Refrigerate 2 hours before serving.

YIELD *1½ cups*

BROILED LAMB MEDALLIONS WITH GARLIC SAUCE

Garlic Sauce (next page)
Nonstick spray
1 pound boneless loin of lamb, cut into 8 medallions,
   2 ounces each
Garnish: 1 tablespoon chopped parsley

Prepare the Garlic Sauce as directed. Keep warm.

    Preheat the broiler. Spray the rack of the broiler pan with nonstick spray. Arrange the medallions of lamb on the rack 2 inches from heat and broil for approximately 2 to 3 minutes per side, depending on the desired degree of doneness.

    When ready to serve, place 2 medallions on each warmed dinner plate. Top with 2 tablespoons of Garlic Sauce and garnish with chopped parsley.

YIELD *12 ounces lamb*

Because it is baked, the garlic in this creamy sauce becomes surprisingly mild, a mellow complement to succulent broiled lamb.

SERVING 3 OZ. LAMB
WITH 2 TBS. SAUCE
Calories 173.0
Total fat 5.1 gm.
Cholesterol 88.0 mg.
Saturated fat 1.26 gm.
Protein 27.0 gm.
Carbohydrates 2.6 gm.
Sodium 68.0 mg.

GARLIC SAUCE

½ cup soubise (page 48)
1 cup chicken stock (page 41)
1 cup peeled garlic cloves
½ cup sliced onion
1 bay leaf
2 teaspoons sherry wine vinegar
White pepper, to taste

Prepare the soubise and chicken stock ahead as directed. (See Basic Stocks and Sauces, pages 48 and 41.)

Preheat the oven to 350°F. Place the garlic, onion, chicken stock, and the bay leaf in a deep ovenproof dish. Cover with foil and bake approximately 1 hour, or until the garlic is soft. Remove the foil for the last 15 to 20 minutes. Cool slightly and remove the bay leaf. Transfer to a blender or food processor. Add the soubise and vinegar, and process until smooth. Pour the mixture into a heavy-bottomed saucepan and cook over medium heat until bubbles begin to rise. Season with white pepper and keep warm until needed.

YIELD *1 cup*

SERVING 2 TBS.

Calories 13.0
Total fat 0
Cholesterol 0
Saturated fat 0.01 gm.
Protein 0.6 gm.
Carbohydrates 2.5 gm.
Sodium 5.0 mg.

MEDALLIONS OF LAMB WITH ROSEMARY–PORT WINE REDUCTION SAUCE

Rosemary–Port Wine Reduction Sauce (next page)
1 tablespoon unsalted margarine, clarified (page 123)
8 medallions of lamb, cut into 2-ounce portions
Garnish: rosemary branches, reserved from sauce

Prepare the Rosemary–Port Wine Reduction Sauce as directed. Keep warm until needed.

Preheat the oven to 400°F. In a hot, heavy-bottomed, ovenproof, nonstick sauté pan or skillet, heat the clarified margarine until just below the smoking point. Add the lamb to the hot skillet and sear quickly, about 1 minute on each side. Blot any excess oil that is visible on the surface of the skillet with paper towels, then place skillet in the oven for 3 to 4 minutes, or until done to your taste.

When ready to serve, arrange 2 medallions of lamb per serving on a warmed dinner plate. On top of each medallion, place 1 rosemary branch, which you have transferred from the sauce. Drizzle 2 tablespoons of sauce over the meat.

YIELD *12 ounces meat and ½ cup sauce*

This very intense sauce demonstrates memorably the special affinity of lamb for rosemary.

ROSEMARY–PORT WINE REDUCTION SAUCE

1 cup demi-glace (pages 45–47)
¼ cup port wine
2 tablespoons sherry wine vinegar
8 branches fresh rosemary, cut into 2-inch lengths
Chicken stock (page 41), if needed

Prepare the demi-glace ahead as directed. (See Basic Stocks and Sauces, pages 45–47.)

In a small saucepan, bring to a boil the port wine, demi-glace, sherry wine vinegar, and rosemary. Reduce the heat and simmer until reduced by ½ its original volume. The sauce should be of medium thickness and have a glazed, shiny appearance. Please note that this sauce thickens very suddenly. If it should become too thick, you may thin with a little water, chicken stock, or additional port wine.

SERVING 3 OZ. MEAT WITH 2 TBS. SAUCE

Calories 184.0

Total fat 8.0 gm.

Cholesterol 88.0 mg.

Saturated fat 1.79 gm.

Protein 26.4 gm.

Carbohydrates 0

Sodium 63.0 mg.

MEDALLIONS OF VEAL WITH TARRAGON SAUCE

Tarragon Sauce (next page)
Nonstick spray
1 pound veal medallions, 2 ounces each, cut from the ribeye
2 tablespoons cognac
Garnish: 4 sprigs fresh tarragon; bouquets of watercress

Prepare the Tarragon Sauce as directed. Keep warm.

Preheat the oven to 375°F. Spray a heavy-bottomed, nonstick skillet with nonstick spray. Heat until just below the smoking point. Add the veal and sear for 1 minute on each side. Remove the veal to a heated ovenproof dish and deglaze the skillet with cognac, simmering for 30 seconds to evaporate the alcohol. Pour the pan juices over the veal and place the veal in the oven for 3 to 4 minutes, or until done to your taste. (Keep a close watch. Veal overcooks easily.)

When ready to serve, arrange the veal medallions on a warmed dinner plate or platter. Remove the mushroom caps from the hot sauce and set aside briefly. Spoon 2 tablespoons of sauce over the veal and garnish each serving with a sprig of fresh tarragon, one of the reserved mushroom caps, and a small bouquet of fresh watercress.

Y I E L D *12 ounces meat with Tarragon Sauce*

Although veal is light in color, certain cuts may contain a higher percentage of fat than beef. Again, select lean cuts, such as this one, trimmed of all visible fat. Enjoy this dish with a generous portion of rice or pasta, so you can do justice to the delicious sauce.

SERVING 3 OZ. MEAT
WITH 2 TBS. SAUCE
Calories 173.0
Total fat 5.9 gm.
Cholesterol 128.0 mg.
Saturated fat 1.37 gm.
Protein 27.1 gm.
Carbohydrates 1.5 gm.
Sodium 82.0 mg.

TARRAGON SAUCE

1 cup demi-glace (pages 45–47)
1 tablespoon unsalted margarine, clarified (page 123)
¼ cup carrots, in ⅛-inch dice
¼ cup onion, in ⅛-inch dice
8 mushrooms, stems removed, in ⅛-inch dice
1 clove garlic, finely chopped
¼ cup red wine
2 teaspoons fresh thyme, finely chopped
1 teaspoon fresh chervil, finely chopped
2 teaspoons fresh tarragon, finely chopped
¼ cup tomato concassé (page 50)
4 fresh mushroom caps

Prepare the demi-glace ahead as directed. (See Basic Stocks and Sauces, pages 45–47.)

Heat the clarified margarine in a heavy-bottomed sauté pan or skillet. Add the carrot and sauté quickly, stirring constantly so it does not brown. Add the onion, diced mushrooms, and garlic, sautéing briefly; then add the demi-glace and wine. Simmer 10 minutes. Stir in the herbs and tomatoes and continue to simmer gently, stirring occasionally, until the mixture is reduced to the consistency of a sauce, about 15 to 20 minutes. The sauce should just coat the back of a spoon. Swirl in the mushroom caps, heat through, and set the sauce aside. Keep warm until needed.

Y I E L D *2¼ cups*

SERVING 2 TBS.
Calories 17.0
Total fat 1.2 gm.
Cholesterol 0
Saturated fat 0.22 gm.
Protein 0.4 gm.
Carbohydrates 1.5 gm.
Sodium 2.0 mg.

ESCALLOPS OF VEAL WITH APRICOT COULIS

1 cup demi-glace (pages 45–47)
Apricot Coulis (next page)
1 pound veal tenderloin, cut into 2-ounce medallions
Freshly ground white pepper, to taste
½ tablespoon unsalted margarine, clarified (page 123)
2 tablespoons red wine vinegar
1 tablespoon minced shallots

Prepare the demi-glace ahead as directed. (See Basic Stocks and Sauces, pages 45–47.)

Prepare the Apricot Coulis as directed. Set aside and keep warm.

Dry the veal with a towel and season lightly with freshly ground white pepper.

Heat the clarified margarine in a large, heavy-bottomed, nonstick skillet. Add the veal and sauté quickly for 2 minutes on each side. Remove the veal from the pan and keep warm on a plate, loosely covered with foil. Using paper towels, blot any excess oil in the pan, return to the heat, and add the vinegar and shallots. Scraping up any browned particles, add the demi-glace and any juices the resting veal may have released. Reduce the sauce over medium heat until it coats the back of a spoon.

When ready to serve, nap each warmed dinner plate with 2 tablespoons of Apricot Coulis. Rotate the plate to spread the coulis in a wide circle. Arrange 2 veal medallions along the curving edge of the coulis. Spoon 1 tablespoon of the vinegar reduction over the veal.

Y I E L D *12 ounces meat*

*F*resh apricot coulis, spiked with champagne, rounds out this robust vinegar- and demi-glace reduction.

SERVING 3 OZ. MEAT WITH 2 TBS. APRICOT COULIS

Calories 179.0
Total fat 5.8 gm.
Cholesterol 128.0 mg.
Saturated fat 1.31 gm.
Protein 30.0 gm.
Carbohydrates 3.5 gm.
Sodium 91.0 mg.

APRICOT COULIS

6 fresh apricots, pitted and halved
½ cup champagne
¼ cup champagne vinegar
2 tablespoons opal (red) basil, cut into julienne strips
  (see Note below)

Add the apricots, the champagne, and champagne vinegar to the container of a blender or food processor and process until smooth. Poor the purée into a saucepan and simmer over medium heat until reduced to the consistency of a sauce. Stir in the basil and remove the coulis from the heat.

Y I E L D *1 cup*

N O T E In this recipe we have specified opal basil, which is available in some vegetable markets, but if it is hard to find, you may substitute sweet basil.

SERVING 2 TBS.

Calories 14.0

Total fat 0.1 gm.

Cholesterol 0

Saturated fat 0.01 gm.

Protein 0.3 gm.

Carbohydrates 3.5 gm.

Sodium 0

BEEF BROCHETTE WITH ROASTED CHILE SAUCE

1 pound beef tenderloin, trimmed of fat and cut into 1-inch cubes
1 medium green bell pepper, blanched and cut into 1½-inch
  sections
1 medium red bell pepper, blanched and cut into 1½-inch
  sections
1 large red onion, cut into 1½-inch sections
Chef Palmer's Roasted Chile Sauce (see below)

Thread alternate pieces of beef cubes, peppers, and onions along four 10-inch stainless steel or bamboo skewers. Grill over hot coals or broil in the oven for approximately 5 to 7 minutes, or until desired doneness, basting liberally with the sauce.

Serve with Mexican rice (page 285), warm flour tortillas, and a small dish of remaining sauce.

Y I E L D *4 servings*

CHEF PALMER'S ROASTED CHILE SAUCE

½ medium onion, diced
1 medium tomato, halved
4 cloves garlic with skin
4 dried medium chilies, such as cascabel, ancho, or pasilla
1 teaspoon cumin seed
1 bay leaf
½ cup low-sodium chicken broth
1 tablespoon maple syrup or honey

Preheat oven to 350°F. Place onion, tomato, and garlic on a baking sheet and roast in the oven for 7 to 10 minutes or until soft. Place dried chilies in a preheated small skillet over medium heat. Turn chilies frequently until toasted. Cool slightly and remove seeds and stems (wear gloves).

SERVING 3 OZ. BEEF
AND 2 TBS. SAUCE
Calories 183
Total fat 8.0 gm.
Cholesterol 71.0 mg.
Saturated fat 3.0 gm.
Protein 24.4 gm.
Carbohydrates 1.7 gm.
Sodium 56.0 mg.

In a medium saucepan, combine toasted chilies, roasted vegetables, cumin, bay leaf, and chicken broth. Simmer, uncovered, 20 to 30 minutes. Cool the mixture and place in the container of a blender or food processor. Add maple syrup and process until smooth. Strain the mixture through a strainer or cheesecloth. Will keep refrigerated 3 to 5 days.

Y I E L D   *1 cup sauce*

MEDALLIONS OF PORK WITH CRANBERRIES AND HOT-PEPPER JELLY

Cranberries with Hot-Pepper Jelly (page 68)
Nonstick spray
1 pound pork tenderloin trimmed of visible fat, cut into 2-ounce
    medallions
Garnish: slices of fresh orange and fresh cilantro leaves

Prepare the Cranberries with Hot-Pepper Jelly as directed.

Preheat the oven to 375°F. Spray a heavy-bottomed, oven-proof, nonstick skillet with nonstick spray. Heat until just below the smoking point. Add the pork and sear for 1 minute on each side. Remove the pan containing the pork to the preheated oven and cook for 4 to 5 minutes, or until cooked through.

When ready to serve, arrange the pork medallions on a warmed dinner plate or platter. Mound 2 tablespoons of Cranberries with Hot-Pepper Jelly on the side and garnish with slices of fresh orange and cilantro leaves.

Y I E L D *12 ounces pork*

We use Cranberries with Hot-Pepper Jelly as a relish here in the old English manner of combining fruit compotes with meat. The old English, however, would find its jalapeño glow a considerable surprise.

SERVING 3 OZ. PORK
AND 2 TBS. OF
CRANBERRIES
Calories 161.0
Total fat 4.1 gm.
Cholesterol 9.0 mg.
Saturated fat 1.41 gm.
Protein 24.5 gm.
Carbohydrates 5.2 gm.
Sodium 58.0 mg.

STIR-FRIED BEEF WITH
SHERRY SAUCE AND FRESH SPINACH

3 tablespoons dry sherry or 3 tablespoons sherry vinegar plus
  1 teaspoon sugar
1½ tablespoons low-sodium soy sauce
1 teaspoon sugar
1 pound beef tenderloin, sliced into thin strips
¼ cup low-sodium chicken broth
1 teaspoon cornstarch
½ teaspoon sesame oil
2 tablespoons peeled and sliced fresh ginger
1 pound fresh spinach, washed and torn into large pieces, thick
  stems removed

In a medium bowl combine sherry, soy sauce, and sugar. Add beef strips and refrigerate for 2 hours. Drain beef and reserve marinade. Combine marinade with chicken broth and cornstarch. Stir to dissolve cornstarch.

   Heat a wok or heavy nonstick skillet over high heat. Swirl in sesame oil. Add beef and ginger, stirring until the meat loses its raw color, about 1 minute. Remove meat and ginger from pan. Add marinade to juices in the wok and cook 1 or 2 minutes. Add spinach and stir-fry until spinach is wilted. Return meat to the pan and stir for 1 minute. Serve immediately over steamed rice or noodles.

Y I E L D *4 servings*

SERVING 3 OZ. BEEF,
½ C. SPINACH, AND
2 TBS. SAUCE
Calories 215.0
Total fat 9.0 gm.
Cholesterol 71.0 mg.
Saturated fat 3.1 gm.
Protein 27.6 gm.
Carbohydrates 6.1 gm.
Sodium 325.0 mg.

ROASTED PORK TENDERLOIN WITH CUMBERLAND SAUCE

Cumberland Sauce, (page 69)
1 teaspoon olive oil
1 pound pork tenderloin, trimmed of visible fat
Garnish: watercress; fresh lemon and fresh orange slices, slit
  once, part of the way through

Prepare the Cumberland Sauce as directed. Cool to room temperature.

Preheat the oven to 325°F. In a large, nonstick skillet, heat the oil to just below the smoking point. Add the tenderloin, searing quickly on all sides. Set the pork on a rack in a shallow roasting pan. Insert a meat thermometer in the center of the thickest portion of the tenderloin (or check temperature periodically with an instant-read thermometer). Roast until the tenderloin reaches an internal temperature of 150°F. During the last 15 minutes of cooking, baste the roast with ¼ cup of the Cumberland Sauce.

When ready to serve, place the roast on a heated platter. Garnish with bouquets of watercress, in addition to partially slit fresh lemon and orange slices that have been twisted so they stand upright. Serve with room-temperature Cumberland Sauce.

YIELD *12 ounces pork*

The beautiful crimson sauce used in this recipe is even tastier if prepared a day or two in advance. It also goes well with game, particularly quail and wild boar.

SERVING 3 OZ. PORK
WITH 1 TB. SAUCE
Calories 161.0
Total fat 4.1 gm.
Cholesterol 79.0 mg.
Saturated fat 1.56 gm.
Protein 24.5 gm.
Carbohydrates 13.2 gm.
Sodium 60.0 mg.

GAME

A SIGNIFICANT DEVELOPMENT IN THE culinary revolution of the past two decades has been the increasing availability of "wild" game raised on farms. Prior to that time, many of us had to rely on the kindness of friends for our supply of venison and other varieties of wild meat. As a result, many people had no experience whatever with the cornucopia of game dishes familiar on our ancestors' tables.

Because it is lean and very flavorful, game is an excellent component of heart-healthy dining. Even when game is raised commercially, these outstanding qualities remain intact. In fact, people whose palates are more accustomed to beef and lamb may prefer the taste of farm-raised varieties, which lack the more assertive characteristics of "wildness." Nevertheless, should you come across any of the wild variety, don't hesitate to prepare it according to our recipes. In either case, you will be in for a memorable experience.

As you will note, we like a hint of sweetness with our game dishes, particularly with venison, boar, and pheasant. For this reason, Cumberland Sauce (page 69) and Cranberries with Hot-Pepper Jelly (page 68) are also good accompaniments, in place of the ones we've suggested.

....

Roasted Breast of Pheasant with Fresh Mushrooms and White Grapes

Sautéed Quail with Brandy-Pecan Sauce

Roasted Game Hens with Ancho Chile Seasoning

Southern-Style Braised Rabbit

Wild Boar with Plum Sauce

Venison with South Texas Game Sauce

Escallops of Venison with Red Wine and Fig Sauce

....

ROASTED BREAST OF PHEASANT WITH FRESH MUSHROOMS AND WHITE GRAPES

¾ cup demi-glace (pages 45–47)
2½ cups fully ripened white grapes
2 pheasant breasts, boned, skinned, and split into 4-ounce portions
2 teaspoons olive oil
¼ cup sherry wine
½ cup sliced fresh mushrooms
Garnish: grape leaves

Prepare the demi-glace ahead as directed. (See Basic Stocks and Sauces, pages 45–47.)

Preheat the oven to 400°F. Purée 2 cups of white grapes in the container of a blender or food processor. Strain and set aside the pulp, discarding the juice. Peel and halve the remaining grapes.

Sauté the pheasant breasts in a heated, oven-proof, nonstick skillet in the olive oil for 1 to 2 minutes on each side. Place the skillet containing the birds into the oven and cook until slightly resilient to the touch, approximately 7 to 10 minutes. Remove the pheasant to a heated platter and keep warm.

On top of the stove, over medium heat, deglaze the skillet with the sherry wine, stirring for 1 minute to incorporate coagulated juices. Add the demi-glace and mushrooms. If the pheasant has released any juices, stir them in as well. Cook until the liquid is the consistency of a thin sauce, adding grapes toward the end to heat through. Strain the sauce and keep warm, reserving the grapes and mushrooms.

When ready to serve, nap each heated dinner plate with 2 tablespoons of grape purée. Arrange a portion of pheasant on top of each and spoon the reserved mushrooms and grapes over it. Drizzle with 2 tablespoons of sauce and garnish with a grape leaf, arranged to one side of the grape purée.

YIELD *12 ounces pheasant, ½ cup puree, 1 cup mushroom sauce*

This unusual presentation reveals the full flavor of pheasant at its best.

SERVING 3 OZ. OF PHEASANT AND 2 TBS. GRAPE PURÉE WITH 2 TBS. SAUCE

Calories 244.0
Total fat 6.6 gm.
Cholesterol 70.0 mg.
Saturated fat 1.74 gm.
Protein 28.4 gm.
Carbohydrates 18.1 gm.
Sodium 40.0 mg.

SAUTÉED QUAIL WITH BRANDY-PECAN SAUCE

*T*he heady sauce used in this recipe greatly intensifies the flavor of farm-raised quail.

Brandy-Pecan Sauce (page 76)
1 tablespoon unsalted margarine, clarified (page 123)
8 whole quail, cleaned and boned
Garnish: rounds of grilled polenta (page 289) and
    Tomatoes Provençal (page 274)

Prepare the Brandy-Pecan Sauce as directed. Keep warm.

Heat the margarine in a heavy-bottomed, nonstick sauté pan or skillet. Sauté the quail until brown on all sides, approximately 3 to 4 minutes. Cover the pan, reduce the heat, and cook until tender, about 10 to 15 minutes. The juices where the leg joins the body should run clear when pierced with a fork.

Remove the quail to a heated platter. When ready to serve, arrange 2 grilled polenta rounds on a warmed dinner plate. Place 1 quail on each round and drizzle 2 tablespoons of Brandy-Pecan Sauce over them. Garnish with Tomatoes Provençal.

N O T E Partially boned quail is now available in many meat markets; that is, the body has been deboned, but the thighs are left intact. You may, however, prefer to bone the quail yourself. You do this by cutting along the backbone and carefully pulling away the breast and rib bones. Once deboned, the birds may be stuffed and reshaped.

Y I E L D *8 quail and sauce*

SERVING 2 QUAIL
WITH 2 TBS. SAUCE
Calories 195.0
Total fat 8.5 gm.
Cholesterol 0
Saturated fat 1.63 gm.
Protein 25.8 gm.
Carbohydrates 3.0 gm.
Sodium 98.0 mg.

ROASTED GAME HENS WITH ANCHO CHILE SEASONING

4 Cornish game hens, washed, giblets removed and discarded
1 fresh orange, cut into wedges
1 large onion, cut into wedges
1 bunch fresh cilantro
1¼ cups Ancho Chile Seasoning (see below)

Preheat oven to 325°F. Place 1 orange wedge, 1 onion wedge, and 2 or 3 sprigs of cilantro into the cavity of each hen. Truss or secure tightly with toothpicks. Place birds in a shallow pan, brush liberally with the seasoning, and roast for 30 to 35 minutes, brushing frequently with the seasoning. Remove trussing and discard stuffing before serving.

Y I E L D   *4 game hens*

ANCHO CHILE SEASONING

½ pound dried ancho chilies
½ teaspoon cumin seeds
6 whole allspice
1½ tablespoons achiote, soaked overnight in ½ cup water (see
    sidebar, page 201)
1 whole head of garlic, roasted (page 294) and peeled
1 tablespoon fresh oregano, minced
½ cup orange juice
¼ cup grapefruit juice

Heat a skillet until medium hot. Add chilies and toast, turning frequently, until evenly browned and puffed up. Remove from heat and let cool slightly. Remove stems and seeds. Place chilies and all other ingredients in a blender and purée until smooth.

Y I E L D   *1¼ cups*

SERVING 3 OZ.
GAME HEN
Calories 162.0
Total fat 6.0 gm.
Cholesterol 76.0 mg.
Saturated fat 1.7 gm.
Protein 25.0 gm.
Carbohydrates 0
Sodium 73.0 mg.

SOUTHERN-STYLE BRAISED RABBIT

Grilled Polenta (page 289) makes a fine accompaniment to this robust dish.

2 to 2½ cups demi-glace (pages 45–47)
1 tablespoon olive oil
2 rabbits, 3 pounds each, cut into 8 serving pieces
1 cup turnips, cut into ¼-inch dice
½ cup onion, cut into ¼-inch dice
1 cup carrots, peeled and cut into ¼-inch dice
½ cup leek, white part only, carefully washed and cut in slices
½ cup celery, thinly sliced
2 cloves garlic, finely chopped
1 sprig fresh thyme
1 sprig fresh rosemary
1 bay leaf
White pepper, to taste
2 cups white wine
2 tablespoons Dijon mustard

Prepare the demi-glace ahead as directed. (See Basic Stocks and Sauces, pages 45–47.)

Preheat the oven to 350°F.

Heat olive oil in a large, oven-proof, nonstick saucepan or Dutch oven. Add the rabbit pieces, searing quickly on both sides. Remove the rabbit from the pan and set aside.

Add the vegetables and garlic to the pan and sauté for 2 to 3 minutes. Stir in the thyme, rosemary, bay leaf, and pepper. Arrange the rabbit pieces on top of the vegetables. In a separate bowl, stir together 2 cups demi-glace, white wine, and mustard, and pour over the rabbit and vegetables. Cover with a tight-fitting lid and bake until the rabbit is tender, about 1 hour. Add extra demi-glace, if needed, to keep moist. Serve on individual warmed dinner plates with the sauce on top.

VARIATION Chicken prepared in this manner is equally good. Make sure it has been skinned and trimmed of all fat.

NOTE Whole rabbits can be found frozen in most grocery stores. If the rabbit is fresh, ask the butcher to cut it into pieces like chicken. Also request that it be trimmed of any visible fat. To section a whole rabbit yourself: First break away the front and hind legs from the body.

SERVING 3 OZ. RABBIT WITH ½ C. SAUCE

Calories 210.0
Total fat 9.05 gm.
Cholesterol 73.0 mg.
Saturated fat 23.8 gm.
Protein 26.5 gm.
Carbohydrates 4.1 gm.
Sodium 100.0 mg.

Cut them into two pieces with a sharp knife or poultry shears. Break the backbone by folding the ribcage backward until it snaps. Or you may chop it in two. Cut the pieces in half. Snip with cutting shears or remove with pliers any small bones that may have broken and protrude through the meat.

Y I E L D *8 serving pieces of rabbit with 2 cups sauce*

WILD BOAR WITH PLUM SAUCE

Pork's wild cousin is raised to new heights with this ambrosial sauce. Accompany the dish with wild rice and our succulent Red Cabbage and Apples (page 284).

Plum Sauce (opposite page)
For the marinade:
    ½ tablespoon garlic, finely chopped
    ½ tablespoon black pepper
    1 tablespoon Worcestershire sauce
    1½ tablespoons honey
    1 tablespoon fresh thyme, or 1 teaspoon dried thyme
    ½ cup olive oil
1 pound wild boar loin meat, trimmed of visible fat and the
    silvery membrane removed, cut into 2-ounce medallions
    (see Note below)
½ tablespoon garlic, finely chopped
1 tablespoon scallions, finely chopped
½ cup oyster mushrooms
1 teaspoon unsalted margarine, clarified (page 123)

Prepare the Plum Sauce as directed.

Whisk together the marinade ingredients in a nonreactive bowl. Pound the medallions to a thickness of ½ inch and add to the marinade. Cover and refrigerate overnight or at least 4 hours.

When ready to proceed with the recipe, sauté the garlic, scallions, and mushrooms in the margarine for 30 seconds. Keep warm until needed. Remove the wild boar from the marinade and wipe off any excess with paper towels. Heat a heavy-bottomed, cast-iron skillet or a nonstick pan and add the meat. Sauté rapidly on both sides, turning once, until well browned, about 2 minutes per side.

When ready to serve, nap each warmed dinner plate with 2 table-spoons of Plum Sauce. Arrange the boar attractively in the sauce, distributing the sautéed garlic, scallions, and mushrooms across the top.

N O T E Wild boar is quite versatile. It may be grilled, for example, or roasted. When you grill, however, remember to pound the medallions to an even thickness. The hindquarters may also be used for medallions. Just trim the meat well and cut across the grain.

Y I E L D *12 ounces meat*

SERVING 3 OZ.
WILD BOAR WITH
2 TBS. SAUCE
Calories 216.0
Total fat 4.8 gm.
Cholesterol 70.0 mg.
Saturated fat 1.3 gm.
Protein 24.9 gm.
Carbohydrates 20.1 gm.
Sodium 69.0 mg.

PLUM SAUCE

1 cup demi-glace (pages 45–47)
½ pound dried plums (or prunes), pitted
1 cup port wine
Dash Worcestershire sauce
White pepper, to taste

Prepare the demi-glace ahead as directed. (See Basic Stocks and Sauces, pages 45–47.)

In a medium-size saucepan, cook the dried plums in ¾ cup of the port wine until they are soft, 10 to 12 minutes. Cool. Place the plums and any cooking liquid into the container of a blender or food processor. Add the remaining ¼ cup of port wine, the demi-glace, and the Worcestershire sauce and process until smooth. Return the puréed mixture to the saucepan and heat until bubbly. Season with white pepper. Keep warm.

Y I E L D   *1 cup*

SERVING 2 TBS.

Calories 68.0

Total fat 0.1 gm.

Cholesterol 0

Saturated fat 0.01 gm.

Protein 0.7 gm.

Carbohydrates 17.8 gm.

Sodium 2.0 mg.

VENISON WITH SOUTH TEXAS GAME SAUCE

We imagine a particularly skilled camp cook preparing this delicious sauce over a fire in the Texas brush country. Here, we offer it with venison, which we suggest you serve rare to medium rare.

¾ cup South Texas Game Sauce (opposite page)
1 unpeeled apple (any tart red cooking apple)
1 teaspoon unsalted margarine, clarified (page 123)
½ cup chanterelles (or other wild mushroom)
½ tablespoon garlic, finely chopped
1 tablespoon scallions, finely sliced
2 teaspoons olive oil
1 pound tenderloin of venison (backstrap)
Garnish: 2 tablespoons nonfat yogurt

Prepare the Game Sauce as directed. Keep warm.

Preheat the oven to 400°F. Slice the apple into 8 very thin slices. heat ½ teaspoon of the margarine in a heavy-bottomed skillet, and sauté the apple slices until they are lightly browned on both sides. Drain on a clean paper towel. Place 2 apple slices on each serving plate and keep warm.

Add the remaining ½ teaspoon margarine, the chanterelles, garlic, and scallions to the pan and sauté for 1 to 2 minutes. Remove and set aside. Add the olive oil to the skillet and heat to just below the smoking point. Add venison tenderloin and brown quickly on all sides. Transfer to a roasting pan. Place in the oven for 6 to 8 minutes, or until cooked to taste. Remove the venison to a warmed platter.

When ready to serve, slice the venison on the bias into approximately 2-ounce portions. Arrange 2 slices per serving over the sliced apples and drizzle with 2 tablespoons of Game Sauce. Spoon ¼ of the sautéed chanterelle mixture across it and top with a spoonful of yogurt.

VARIATION You may cut the meat into 2-ounce medallions and sauté, if you prefer.

YIELD *12 ounces venison*

SERVING 3 OZ.
VENISON WITH
2 TBS. SAUCE

Calories 197.0
Total fat 6.1 gm.
Cholesterol 95.0 mg.
Saturated fat 0.52 gm.
Protein 26.6 gm.
Carbohydrates 8.1 gm.
Sodium 138.0 mg.

SOUTH TEXAS GAME SAUCE

1 cup demi-glace (pages 45–47)
1 tablespoon shallots, finely chopped
3 ounces cognac
3 tablespoons bottled chili sauce
Black pepper, to taste

Prepare the demi-glace ahead as directed. (See Basic Stocks and Sauces, pages 45–47.)

Add the shallots to the roasting pan and sauté over medium heat for 30 seconds. Add the cognac and deglaze, stirring, until the alcohol evaporates, 1 to 2 minutes. Stir in the chili sauce and demi-glace, and cook until the sauce has thickened so it coats the back of a spoon. Season with black pepper.

Y I E L D *¾ cup sauce*

SERVING 2 TBS.
Calories 8.0
Total fat 0
Cholesterol 0
Saturated fat 0.01 gm.
Protein 0.2 gm.
Carbohydrates 1.8 gm.
Sodium 86.0 mg.

ESCALLOPS OF VENISON WITH RED WINE AND FIG SAUCE

*R*ed meat eaters accustomed to beef or lamb will be surprised at the succulence of venison anointed with this aromatic sauce.

Red Wine and Fig Sauce (opposite page)
½ tablespoon unsalted margarine, clarified (page 123)
1 pound venison loin, cut into 8 escallops, 2 ounces each
Garnish: grated lemon zest and sprigs of thyme

Prepare the Red Wine and Fig Sauce as directed. Keep warm.

Preheat the oven to 400°F. Heat the margarine in a heavy-bottomed oven-proof skillet. Add the venison and sauté quickly on each side. Blot excess fat with paper towels and place the skillet containing the venison in the oven to cook until the meat reaches the desired degree of doneness, approximately 3 to 4 minutes.

When ready to serve, arrange the venison on heated dinner plates, nap with sauce, and garnish with a little grated lemon zest and sprigs of thyme.

VARIATION If you prefer the slightly juicier effect of roasted venison, you may follow these simple directions: Place whole venison tenderloin in a roasting pan in a 400°F oven and roast for 6 to 7 minutes. Then slice into medallion-size slices and present as directed above.

YIELD *12 ounces venison*

SERVING 3 OZ.
VENISON WITH
2 TBS. SAUCE
Calories 173.0
Total fat 4.5 gm.
Cholesterol 95.0 mg.
Saturated fat 1.06 gm.
Protein 26.0 gm.
Carbohydrates 6.2 gm.
Sodium 47.0 mg.

RED WINE AND FIG SAUCE

¾ cup demi-glace (pages 45–47)
1 cup red wine
1 strip orange zest, 4 inches long
1 strip lemon zest, 4 inches long
1 clove garlic, finely chopped
1 sprig thyme
4 ounces dried figs (¼ pound)
2 tablespoons cognac
Black pepper, to taste

Prepare the demi-glace ahead as directed. (See Basic Stocks and Sauces, pages 45–47.)

Bring the red wine and orange and lemon zests to a boil in a small saucepan. Reduce the heat and simmer for 2 minutes. Add the garlic, thyme, and figs, and simmer until the figs are soft, 10 to 12 minutes. Transfer the mixture to the container of a food processor. Add the demi-glace and cognac, and process until smooth. Return the puréed mixture to the pan and heat until bubbly, adding black pepper. Keep warm until needed.

Y I E L D *¾ cup*

SERVING 2 TBS.

Calories 24.0

Total fat 0.1 gm.

Cholesterol 0

Saturated fat 0.02 gm.

Protein 0.3 gm.

Carbohydrates 6.2 gm.

Sodium 1.0 mg.

VEGETABLES AND OTHER SIDE DISHES

....

AT CHEZ EDDY, WE ACCOMPANY the meat or seafood that forms the focus of the meal with a bouquet of steamed vegetables and a starch, perhaps mashed potatoes or grilled polenta. Because so many of our dishes are prepared *à la minute,* we look for vegetables that will complement a broad selection of our main courses. We think of them, also, as a visual element, adding color and variety to the plate.

At the same time, however, we recognize that occasionally more is needed. For example, our red cabbage is a delectable concoction that greatly contributes to the appeal of certain game dishes. Also, we understand that the home cook, faced with different challenges and different constraints, requires a variety of vegetables to stimulate the family's interest and ensure good nutrition. Fortunately, vegetables are ideally suited to heart-healthy preparation, as long as one omits the traditional pat of butter. It is the limitation on salt that renders the task more difficult.

In this chapter, therefore, we have included several of our favorite vegetable preparations that compensate for the absence of added salt by juxtaposing a variety of interesting flavors. In addition to these, we add numerous starchy side dishes that are very popular with our guests. You may draw from these suggestions more or less at will to accompany an entrée or to compose a delicious vegetarian meal.

....

Tomatoes Provençal

Mint-Glazed Carrots

Basic Steamed Vegetables

Grilled Vegetable Plate

Jicama Pancakes

Zucchini Boats

Sautéed Cherry Tomatoes and Mushrooms

Ratatouille

Sautéed Green Beans with Garlic and Mushrooms

Fettuccine with Sun-Dried Tomatoes and Garlic

....

Red Cabbage and Apples
Basic Rice
Spinach-Herbed Rice
Fettuccine with Chez Eddy Cream Sauce
Corn Cakes
Polenta
Mashed Potatoes
Lemon-Garlic Roasted Potatoes
Chez Eddy Scalloped Potatoes
Herbed-Bread Stuffing with Pumpkin Seeds
Roasted Garlic

TOMATOES PROVENÇAL

We like these tomatoes with less assertive or mono-chromatic dishes, where they add a little zip.

½ tablespoon olive oil
2 tablespoons onion, finely chopped
1 teaspoon garlic, minced
2 tablespoons breadcrumbs
2 tablespoons Parmesan cheese
½ teaspoon parsley, finely chopped
1 teaspoon fresh thyme, finely chopped
¼ teaspoon black pepper
2 medium tomatoes, peeled

Preheat the oven to 350°F. In a small, heavy-bottomed saucepan, over medium heat, heat the olive oil, add the onion and garlic, and sauté for 1 minute. Stir in the breadcrumbs, Parmesan cheese, parsley, thyme, and black pepper, mixing well, and set aside.

Slice the tomatoes in half. Remove the seeds by squeezing gently.

Place the tomato halves on a baking sheet and mound equal portions of the sautéed breadcrumb mixture over the top of each. Bake for approximately 10 minutes.

Y I E L D *4 tomato halves*

SERVING ½ TOMATO

Calories 54.0
Total fat 2.7 gm.
Cholesterol 2.0 mg.
Saturated fat 0.76 gm.
Protein 2.1 gm.
Carbohydrates 5.8 gm.
Sodium 75.0 mg.

MINT-GLAZED CARROTS

1 cup chicken stock (page 41)
½ tablespoon honey
2 cups carrots, peeled and cut in 1½-inch batons
1 teaspoon fresh mint, finely chopped
White pepper, to taste

Prepare the chicken stock ahead as directed.

Over medium heat in a medium-size, heavy-bottomed saucepan, simmer the chicken stock until it is reduced to ½ cup. Stir in the honey, then add the carrots, mint, and pepper. Cover and simmer until the carrots are tender but slightly resistant to the tooth, 10 to 12 minutes.

YIELD *2 cups*

To enhance the natural sweetness of carrots, we simmer them in a lightly honeyed chicken stock, perfumed with mint.

SERVING ½ C.

Calories 38.0

Total fat 0.1 gm.

Cholesterol 0

Saturated fat 0.02 gm.

Protein 0.7 gm.

Carbohydrates 9.1 gm.

Sodium 24.0 mg.

BASIC STEAMED VEGETABLES

This unadorned recipe, which may be used with most varieties of fresh vegetables, allows the natural flavors of the vegetables to be enjoyed without competition. It requires the use of a 2- to 3-quart saucepan with a tight-fitting lid and a stainless steel steamer rack.

1 pound fresh seasonal vegetables (carrots, cauliflower, broccoli, snap peas, asparagus, etc.), washed, skinned, and sliced
Cold water
Chicken stock (page 41), if needed

Add enough water to a 2- to 3-quart saucepan to measure 1 inch below the vegetables when they boil. Place a steamer rack in the pan. Bring water to a boil, then add the vegetables to the steamer rack. Steam for 3 to 4 minutes, or until al dente. They should be resistant to the tooth, but not have a raw taste. Serve immediately, if possible.

If not, remove the vegetables from the steamer and immerse quickly in ice water to stop the cooking. Remove from the water, drain, and chill. When ready to serve, reheat them by simmering for a minute in a small amount of chicken stock, which imparts flavor without adding fat.

Y I E L D *4 cups*

SERVING 1 C.

Calories 31.0

Total fat 0.2 gm.

Cholesterol 0

Saturated fat 0

Protein 2.0 gm.

Carbohydrates 6.8 gm.

Sodium 5.0 mg.

GRILLED VEGETABLE PLATE

1 medium zucchini, cut diagonally into ¼-inch slices
1 medium yellow squash, cut diagonally into ¼-inch slices
1 medium eggplant, cut crosswise into ¼-inch slices
1 medium red onion, cut into 8 wedges
1 medium sweet potato, cut into ¼-inch slices
4 plum tomatoes, halved lengthwise
8 green onions, whole
1 large red bell pepper, cut into 8 wedges
1 large green bell pepper, cut into 8 wedges
½ cup Balsamic Vinaigrette (page 148)
2 teaspoons Spice Blend (page 55)
Nonstick spray

Spread prepared vegetables in one layer on a tray or baking sheet. Sprinkle with ¼ cup Balsamic Vinaigrette and the Spice Blend. Refrigerate 2 hours before grilling.

Spray vegetables lightly with nonstick spray and grill, turning occasionally, until just tender. Since vegetables will vary in cooking time, test each with a fork and remove to a platter until all vegetables are ready. When ready to serve, alternate groups of vegetables on a dinner plate and drizzle each serving with 2 tablespoons of Balsamic Vinaigrette.

YIELD *4 servings*

*S*erve these vegetables chilled for a cool summertime luncheon.

SERVING 1¼ C.
VEGETABLES AND
2 TBS. VINAIGRETTE
Calories 86.0
Total fat 0.2 gm.
Cholesterol 0
Saturated fat 0
Protein 2.3 gm.
Carbohydrates 20.0 gm.
Sodium 9.0 mg.

JICAMA PANCAKES

This variation on the time-honored potato pancake makes an interesting companion to any strongly flavored main course. The pancakes are especially good with dishes whose sauces incorporate demi-glace.

1 pound jicama, peeled and shredded
½ pound white potatoes, peeled and shredded
1 egg, beaten
¼ cup egg substitute
Pinch fresh ground black pepper, to taste
1 teaspoon olive oil

In a bowl, mix together the jicama and potato. Squeeze out any excess moisture, so the mixture will be as dry as possible. Stir in the egg and egg substitute, and season to taste with pepper.

Heat a nonstick skillet or griddle. Add the olive oil, rotating the skillet so the oil covers the bottom. Pour off any excess. Spoon the batter onto the griddle to form 3-inch pancakes, and lightly brown each on both sides. Remove to a heated platter and keep warm, briefly, until ready to serve. They are best if served immediately.

YIELD *16 cakes, 3 inches each*

SERVING

4 PANCAKES

Calories 133.0

Total fat 3.2 gm.

Cholesterol 52.0 mg.

Saturated fat 0.77 gm.

Protein 6.1 gm.

Carbohydrates 20.4 gm.

Sodium 55.0 mg.

ZUCCHINI BOATS

4 medium zucchini, 1½ inches in diameter
1 large bulb fennel (about ¾ pound), trimmed and finely chopped
½ clove garlic, crushed
½ teaspoon dried thyme
½ onion, finely chopped
1 teaspoon lemon juice
Ground white pepper, to taste
1 teaspoon unsalted margarine
Nonstick spray
½ cup parsley, finely chopped

Halve the zucchini lengthwise, then halve them again, crosswise. Trim into 1½-inch-long cylinders. Scoop out the center with the small end of a melon-ball cutter and coarsely chop the pulp. Invert and drain the zucchini cylinders for 30 minutes on paper towels.

Preheat the oven to 350°F. Add all the other vegetables and seasonings to the container of a food processor or blender and process until finely chopped. Over medium heat, sauté the puréed mixture in the margarine until slightly crisp, about 10 minutes. Remove from the heat and let cool.

Fill the zucchini cylinders with the vegetable mixture and place on a baking sheet that you have sprayed with a nonstick vegetable coating. Sprinkle with parsley. Top with foil and bake for 30 minutes. (Zucchini should be al dente when done.)

YIELD *16 boats*

Zucchini Boats are a versatile garnish and may be filled with the colorful purée of your choice, or salsa. If fennel is unavailable for this recipe, you may substitute center stalks of celery, finely chopped.

SERVING 4 BOATS

Calories 38.0

Total fat 1.2 gm.

Cholesterol 0

Saturated fat 0.23 gm.

Protein 1.9 gm.

Carbohydrates 6.3 gm.

Sodium 33.0 mg.

SAUTÉED CHERRY TOMATOES
AND MUSHROOMS

A *quick and col-*
orful accompani-
ment to any meat
or fish.

2 teaspoons olive oil
¼ cup mushrooms, thinly sliced
1 cup cherry tomatoes, halved
½ teaspoon fresh parsley, finely chopped
½ teaspoon fresh basil, finely chopped
½ teaspoon fresh thyme, finely chopped
½ teaspoon fresh oregano, finely chopped
Black pepper, to taste

Heat a medium-size, nonstick skillet over medium heat. Add the oil and rotate the skillet to coat the bottom. Pour out the excess oil and return to the heat. Add the mushrooms and sauté for 1 minute. Add the tomato halves and sauté until the tomatoes are soft, about 2 minutes. Remove from the heat. Gently toss with the fresh herbs and sprinkle with pepper.

Y I E L D   *1¼ cups*

SERVING ¼ C.

Calories 34.0

Total fat 2.4 gm.

Cholesterol 0

Saturated fat 0.33 gm.

Protein 0.7 gm.

Carbohydrates 3.3 gm.

Sodium 6.0 mg.

RATATOUILLE

½ cup chicken stock (page 41)
1 tablespoon olive oil
1 cup onion, coarsely diced
1 clove garlic, chopped
½ cup red bell pepper, coarsely chopped
1 cup green bell pepper, coarsely chopped
½ cup yellow bell pepper, coarsely chopped
1 cup unpeeled zucchini, coarsely diced
½ cup unpeeled yellow squash, coarsely diced
½ cup eggplant, unpeeled and coarsely diced
1 bay leaf
2 dashes Worcestershire sauce
Pinch granulated sugar
1 tablespoon fresh basil, coarsely chopped
1 teaspoon fresh oregano, coarsely chopped
2 cups ripe tomatoes, peeled and coarsely chopped

Prepare the chicken stock ahead as directed.

In a large skillet over medium heat, add the olive oil and sauté the onion and garlic for 3 minutes. Add the peppers and sauté for another 3 to 4 minutes; then add the zucchini, yellow squash, eggplant, and bay leaf, sprinkling in the Worcestershire sauce and other seasonings. Cook, stirring, for 4 minutes. Add the tomatoes and stir for an additional 4 to 5 minutes; then pour in the chicken stock, and simmer, covered, over low heat for 15 to 20 minutes. Keep warm until ready to serve. Or refrigerate overnight and serve, warm or cold, the second day.

Y I E L D *4 cups*

This traditional Mediterranean dish may be served as a vegetable or as a topping for pasta when mixed with 2 cups of our Basic Tomato Sauce (page 49). Its sun-drenched flavors intensify if it is prepared a day in advance.

SERVING 1 C.

Calories 91.0

Total fat 4.1 gm.

Cholesterol 0

Saturated fat 0.57 gm.

Protein 2.6 gm.

Carbohydrates 13.4 gm.

Sodium 14.0 mg.

SAUTÉED GREEN BEANS WITH GARLIC AND MUSHROOMS

You may use any variety of green bean in this recipe, varying cooking time according to thickness. It is particularly good with haricots verts.

1 pound fresh green beans, washed and trimmed
1 shallot, finely chopped
1 teaspoon garlic, finely chopped
1 teaspoon olive oil
¼ cup sliced mushrooms

Steam the beans for 5 minutes, according to the directions given for Basic Steamed Vegetables (page 276). Immerse them in ice water to stop the cooking, drain, and set aside.

In a medium-size, heavy-bottomed skillet, sauté the shallot and garlic in the olive oil for 2 minutes over medium heat. Add the mushrooms and sauté for 1 additional minute. Stir in the steamed green beans and cook, stirring, until thoroughly heated. Serve immediately.

YIELD *2 cups*

SERVING ½ C.

Calories 46.0

Total fat 1.3 gm.

Cholesterol 0

Saturated fat 0.18 gm.

Protein 2.2 gm.

Carbohydrates 8.3 gm.

Sodium 7.0 mg.

FETTUCCINE WITH SUN-DRIED TOMATOES AND GARLIC

2 tablespoons garlic, minced
1 tablespoon green peppercorns
¼ cup sun-dried tomatoes, not packed in oil, rehydrated and julienned
1 tablespoon olive oil
½ cup low-sodium chicken broth
4 cups fettuccine, cooked al dente
½ cup frozen green peas, defrosted
¼ cup fresh basil, julienned
4 teaspoons Parmesan cheese, grated

In a medium-size heavy-bottomed saucepan over medium-low heat, sauté the garlic, peppercorns, and sun-dried tomatoes in the olive oil for 1 minute, being careful not to brown the mixture. Add the chicken broth and cook for 1 minute over medium-high heat. Add pasta, tossing well. Heat thoroughly and add the peas and half the basil. To serve, divide the mixture among four pasta bowls, garnish each with the remaining basil, and sprinkle with the Parmesan cheese.

YIELD *4 servings*

*T*his is a versatile pasta dish that can be used as a main course or side dish.

SERVING 1 C. PASTA
AND ¼ OF THE SAUCE
Calories 269.0
Total fat 5.1 gm.
Cholesterol 1.0 mg.
Saturated fat 0.9 gm.
Protein 9.4 gm.
Carbohydrates 46.4 gm.
Sodium 215.0 mg.

RED CABBAGE AND APPLES

This richly flavored red cabbage is wonderful with game and other meats, particularly when their sauce does not echo its predominant sweet-sour note. Preparing it a day in advance allows the flavors to meld. It keeps well in the refrigerator for 3 to 4 days.

½ medium-size head red cabbage, coarsely shredded
1 red cooking apple, cored and diced
½ onion, coarsely chopped
2½ tablespoons red currant jelly
2 tablespoons granulated sugar
3 tablespoons red wine vinegar
1 cup red wine
¼ teaspoon white pepper
2 bay leaves
Chicken stock (page 41), if needed to moisten

Combine all the ingredients in a large nonreactive container, mixing well. To assure that the vegetables remain submerged in the marinade, set an inverted dinner plate as a weight on top of them; then marinate, refrigerated, for 4 hours or overnight.

Drain the marinated vegetables, reserving the liquid. Place ¼ to ½ cup of the marinade, along with the cabbage mixture, in a Dutch oven or a large, heavy-bottomed saucepan. Cover and cook over medium heat until the marinade is absorbed and the cabbage is glazed, about 35 minutes, adding the reserved liquid in small amounts as necessary to keep from burning. If more liquid is needed, you may add the chicken stock in small amounts as well.

Y I E L D   *3 cups*

SERVING ½ C.
Calories 58.0
Total fat 0.3 gm.
Cholesterol 0
Saturated fat 0.04 gm.
Protein 1.1 gm.
Carbohydrates 14.1 gm.
Sodium 15.0 mg.

BASIC RICE

1 cup raw rice
2 cups water

Combine the rice with water in a medium-size saucepan. Cover and bring to a boil. Reduce heat and simmer 20 minutes, or until done.

Cumin Rice: Add ½ teaspoon ground cumin to the rice and water, and proceed as directed.

Pecan Rice with Red Bell Peppers: Sauté 2 tablespoons diced red bell peppers in 1 teaspoon of olive oil. Add the sautéed peppers and 2 tablespoons of chopped pecans to the rice and water, and proceed as directed.

Southwestern Rice: Sauté the following in 1 teaspoon oil for 2 to 3 minutes: ¼ cup each chopped onions, red bell pepper, yellow bell pepper, green bell pepper, and 1 finely chopped and seeded jalapeño. Add to the rice and water, and proceed as directed.

Mexican Rice: To the rice and water (or stock) listed above, add ¼ cup chopped tomato, 2 tablespoons chopped onion, 1 teaspoon finely chopped and seeded jalapeño, and 1 teaspoon fresh chopped cilantro, and proceed as directed.

Pineapple Rice: To the rice and water (or stock) listed above, add ¼ cup crushed or diced fresh pineapple, and proceed as directed.

Vegetarian Rice: To the rice and water (or stock) listed above, add ¼ cup each of diced fresh vegetables. Vegetables may include carrots, celery, onion, broccoli, or peas (may be frozen). Proceed as directed.

YIELD *2 cups cooked rice*

You may use packaged varieties of plain white or brown rice, or the bulk varieties that are widely available. In any case, the variations below make interesting side dishes with a number of our main courses. For more intense flavor, substitute chicken stock (page 41) for the water called for in the recipe.

SERVING ½ C.

Calories 103.0

Total fat 0.1 gm.

Cholesterol 0

Saturated fat 0.03 gm.

Protein 1.8 gm.

Carbohydrates 22.7 gm.

Sodium 1.0 mg.

SPINACH-HERBED RICE

In texture, this flavorful, colorful dish resembles a rice dressing. Accordingly, it may be used either as a vegetable or to stuff game birds such as quail and pheasant.

2 cups chicken stock (page 41)
1 teaspoon unsalted margarine
¼ cup onion, finely chopped
½ cup spinach, picked, cleaned, and cut into strips
½ teaspoon fresh thyme
½ teaspoon fresh oregano
½ teaspoon fresh sage
1 bay leaf
½ cup tomato concassé (page 50)
1 cup white rice

Prepare the chicken stock ahead as directed.

In a medium-size, heavy-bottomed saucepan, heat the margarine and sauté the onion until translucent. Add the spinach and herbs and stir for 1 minute. Add the concassé, rice, and chicken stock; cover and bring to a boil. Reduce the heat and simmer 20 minutes or until done. Remove bay leaf.

YIELD *4 cups*

SERVING ½ C.

Calories 97.0

Total fat 0.6 gm.

Cholesterol 0

Saturated fat 0.12 gm.

Protein 1.9 gm.

Carbohydrates 20.6 gm.

Sodium 5.0 mg.

FETTUCCINE WITH CHEZ EDDY CREAM SAUCE

⅓ cup soubise (page 48)
½ teaspoon shallots, finely chopped
¼ cup onion, finely chopped
½ teaspoon unsalted margarine, clarified (page 123)
¼ cup mushrooms, sliced
2 cups chicken stock (page 41)
2 tablespoons nonfat dry milk
Black pepper to taste
2 cups fettuccine, cooked al dente
2 tablespoons grated Parmesan cheese
Garnish: fresh parsley, finely chopped

Prepare the soubise and chicken stock ahead as directed. (See Basic Stocks and Sauces, pages 45 and 47.)

In a medium-size, heavy-bottomed saucepan over medium heat, sauté the shallots and onion in unsalted margarine until translucent. Add the mushrooms and sauté 1 additional minute. Add the chicken stock and simmer gently until the liquid is reduced by ½ its original volume. In a small bowl, stir the powdered milk into the soubise, combining thoroughly. Add to the chicken stock, stirring, and cook until heated through. Remove from the heat and season with pepper to taste.

When ready to serve, toss hot fettuccine with the sauce until thoroughly mixed. Sprinkle with Parmesan cheese. Garnish with chopped parsley.

Y I E L D *2 cups fettuccine with sauce.*

This heart-healthy substitute for voluptuous Fettuccine Alfredo may accompany any meat or game dish. With the addition of a little chopped fresh tomato on top, accompanied by a salad of radicchio, arugula, and fresh corn (page 113), it makes an attractive and delicious light lunch or supper.

SERVING ½ C.

Calories 142.0
Total fat 1.6 gm.
Cholesterol 3.0 mg.
Saturated fat 0.64 gm.
Protein 6.5 gm.
Carbohydrates 24.9 gm.
Sodium 75.0 mg.

CORN CAKES

The texture of fresh corn is necessary to the success of this recipe. Corn cakes are popular with game dishes or with any strongly flavored entrée.

1½ cups fresh corn, cut into whole kernels
½ cup flour
4 scallions, finely minced
1 teaspoon fresh garlic, finely minced
1 teaspoon olive oil
1 teaspoon white pepper, to taste
2 to 3 dashes Worcestershire sauce
1 cup egg substitute
Nonstick spray

Coarsely chop the corn in a blender or food processor. Transfer to a bowl and stir in the remaining ingredients, except for the nonstick spray.

Spray a heavy nonstick skillet or griddle with a nonstick coating and heat. Ladle 2 to 3 ounces of the corn mixture onto the griddle. When air bubbles appear, turn and cook 1 to 2 minutes more. Remove to a heated platter and keep warm.

Y I E L D *16 cakes*

SERVING 4 CAKES,
ABOUT 1 OZ. EACH

Calories 166.0
Total fat 4.0 gm.
Cholesterol 1.0 mg.
Saturated fat 0.70 gm.
Protein 11.0 gm.
Carbohydrates 22.7 gm.
Sodium 121.0 mg.

POLENTA

4 cups chicken stock (page 41)
1 bay leaf
1 cup ground cornmeal (see Note below)

Prepare the chicken stock ahead as directed.

Place chicken stock and bay leaf in a large heavy-bottomed sauce-pan. Bring to a boil over medium heat. Remove bay leaf and gradually add the cornmeal to the stock, stirring constantly. Reduce the heat and cook, continuing to stir constantly, about 20 minutes. The mixture will be heavy and thick.

V A R I A T I O N To grill polenta, first spread a ½-inch layer of the hot cornmeal in a pan you have sprayed with a nonstick coating. Cool. Refrigerate until firm. When ready to serve, cut the polenta into decorative shapes, such as squares, triangle, circles, or diamonds. Grill on a prepared grill until heated through. Serve hot.

N O T E We use a variety of yellow cornmeal, imported from Italy as *polenta*, but any cornmeal will do. The preference in Italy for finely ground versus the coarser stone-ground type varies according to region and personal taste.

Y I E L D *3 cups*

Polenta, a porridge made from cornmeal, is a specialty of northern Italy, where it is a staple of the diet, replacing pasta in many recipes. At Chez Eddy we use it grilled along with game dishes, such as Southern-Style Braised Rabbit (page 262). Grilling instructions are given as a variation at left.

SERVING ½ C.
Calories 64.0
Total fat 0.8 gm.
Cholesterol 0
Saturated fat 0.09 gm.
Protein 1.9 gm.
Carbohydrates 11.9 gm.
Sodium 0

MASHED POTATOES

4 cups chicken stock (page 41)
4 medium white potatoes
Skim milk, as needed
White pepper, to taste

Prepare the chicken stock ahead as directed.

Wash, peel, and quarter the potatoes. Bring the chicken stock to a boil. Add the potatoes and return the stock to a boil. Reduce the heat and allow to simmer, covered, for approximately 20 minutes, or until the potatoes are tender. Drain the potatoes, reserving the liquid for other uses. Mash the potatoes, adding the skim milk in small quantities, until you reach the consistency you desire. Season with pepper and serve hot.

YIELD *3 cups*

SERVING ½ C.

Calories 81.0

Total fat 0.1 gm.

Cholesterol 0

Saturated fat 0.04 gm.

Protein 1.9 gm.

Carbohydrates 18.5 gm.

Sodium 10.0 mg.

LEMON-GARLIC ROASTED POTATOES

1 to 2 pounds unpeeled new potatoes
Nonstick spray
½ tablespoon lemon juice
½ teaspoon garlic powder

Preheat the oven to 350°F. Bring 4 cups of water to a boil. While the water heats, wash the new potatoes, drain, and cut in half. Add them to the boiling water and return water to a boil. Reduce the heat and cook 3 to 4 minutes, then drain. Place the potatoes in a pan sprayed with nonstick coating. Sprinkle the potatoes with lemon juice and garlic powder and roast until tender and well browned (about 10 to 20 minutes).

Y I E L D *2 cups*

These delicious potatoes are one of our most popular side dishes.

SERVING ½ C.

Calories 68.0

Total fat 0.1 gm.

Cholesterol 0

Saturated fat 0.02 gm.

Protein 1.3 gm.

Carbohydrates 15.8 gm.

Sodium 4.0 mg.

CHEZ EDDY SCALLOPED POTATOES

Enjoy this traditional favorite with our red meat dishes or with duck.

⅛ cup soubise (page 48)
1 cup chicken stock (page 41)
4 medium potatoes, peeled and thinly sliced
1 medium onion, diced
1 teaspoon olive oil
Nonstick spray
2 tablespoons nonfat dry milk
1 bay leaf
½ teaspoon nutmeg
White pepper, to taste
Garnish: chopped parsley

Prepare the soubise and chicken stock ahead as directed. (See Basic Stocks and Sauces, pages 48 and 41.)

Preheat the oven to 350°F. Blanch the potatoes by adding them to 5 cups of boiling water. Cook for 2 minutes and drain. Sauté the onion in the olive oil until translucent. Layer the potatoes with the onion in a casserole dish sprayed with a nonstick coating. Whisk together the soubise, chicken stock, and nonfat dry milk. Add the bay leaf and season with nutmeg. Pour the sauce over the potatoes and onion.

Bake until the potatoes are tender. Remove bay leaf. Season potatoes with white pepper and sprinkle with chopped parsley. Serve piping hot.

YIELD *3 cups*

SERVING ½ C.

Calories 109.0

Total fat 0.9 gm.

Cholesterol 1.0 mg.

Saturated fat 0.15 gm.

Protein 3.1 gm.

Carbohydrates 22.5 gm.

Sodium 23.0 mg.

HERBED-BREAD STUFFING WITH PUMPKIN SEEDS

1 cup warm chicken stock (page 41)
2 cups celery, in thin diagonal slices
1 cup white onion, chopped
2 cloves garlic, finely chopped
4 bay leaves
2 teaspoons olive oil
1 cup skim milk
13 ounces stale bread, torn into small cubes
½ cup scallions, finely sliced
¼ cup fresh parsley, finely chopped
2 tablespoons fresh sage, finely chopped
1 tablespoon fresh thyme, finely chopped
1 cup pumpkin seeds, toasted
1 cup egg substitute
Nonstick spray

Prepare the chicken stock ahead as directed.

Preheat oven to 350°F. In a medium skillet over medium-low heat, sauté the celery, onion, garlic, and bay leaves in the olive oil until the celery is soft. Add the milk and chicken stock to the bread in a large bowl and soak for 2 to 3 minutes. Stir in the sautéed vegetables, together with the scallions, parsley, sage, thyme, pumpkin seeds, and egg substitute. Mix thoroughly.

Pour into a deep 2-quart casserole that has been sprayed with nonstick spray. Bake until the center is resilient to the touch, 30 to 35 minutes.

Y I E L D   *2 quarts*

This delicious stuffing may be enjoyed with roasted birds of all kinds, or in place of potatoes or rice with other recipes. For variations on the traditional holiday turkey, try it with pheasant, quail, or chicken. If you wish a southern-style dish, cornbread may be substituted for the bread, but remember to prepare the cornbread without salt.

SERVING ½ C.
Calories 126.0
Total fat 5.5 gm.
Cholesterol 1.0 mg.
Saturated fat 1.02 gm.
Protein 6.3 gm.
Carbohydrates 14.8 gm.
Sodium 158.0 mg.

ROASTED GARLIC

*D*elicious as an
appetizer spread
on low-sodium
crackers or toast,
this is also a per-
fect side dish for
grilled or sautéed
meats.

1 whole head of garlic
½ teaspoon olive oil

Preheat oven to 325°F. Slice the top off the head of garlic and trim the
roots even with the base of the bulb without cutting into garlic cloves.
Remove some of the papery skin from the outside of the head but do
not separate cloves. Place the garlic head in a small baking dish, drizzle with ½ teaspoon of olive oil, and cover with foil. Bake 10 to 15 minutes or until garlic begins to soften. Cool briefly and peel or squeeze
garlic from each clove. The garlic will keep refrigerated 5 to 7 days.

Y I E L D   *1 head garlic*

SERVING 4 CLOVES

Calories 18.0

Total fat 0.1 gm.

Cholesterol 0

Saturated fat 0.01 gm.

Protein 0.8 gm.

Carbohydrates 4.0 gm.

Sodium 2 mg.

DESSERTS

....

AT CHEZ EDDY, YOU MAY indulge the longing we all have for a cool and creamy finish to the meal without the guilt that often comes with it. Our low-fat desserts run the gamut from the lightest sorbet, no more than a melting essence of chilled fruit, to more formal pleasures based on a frozen yogurt so good you'll forget the seductions of ice cream. You may even enjoy an ethereal cheesecake—in fact, three cheesecakes.

This chapter catalogues such delights, among others. There are recipes for brownies, too, as well as flan, and even fruit cobbler, all to be devoured with a guilt-free conscience. The reason has become a refrain by now: We've removed the fat, not the flavor. We haven't even removed the sugar. That's because sugar contains only 16 calories per teaspoon. Even so, in some of our recipes, we've gone a step further and substituted fructose, sugar derived from fruit, which packs almost twice the sweetness into the same calorie load.

As with some of our other recipes, you'll find that our techniques may be used to adapt your family's favorite desserts to heart-healthy requirements. In fact, that's how we went about developing these recipes. We hope you will enjoy preparing, serving, and devouring the delicious desserts as much as we do!

....

Chez Eddy Homemade Vanilla Frozen Yogurt

Cinnamon-Raisin Frozen Yogurt

Dutch Cocoa Frozen Yogurt with Toasted Almonds

Rhubarb Frozen Yogurt

Coupe Chez Eddy

Orange Glacée

Melon Sorbet

Strawberry Sorbet

Pumpkin Flan

Semolina Cake Infused with Orange Syrup

Poached Pears in Orange Sauce

Orange Custard

....

....

Chez Eddy Cheesecake

Chez Eddy Ricotta Cheesecake

Chocolate Crepes with Macerated Berries

Pineapple Cheesecake

Angelfood Cake with Raspberry Sauce

Blueberry Cobbler

Lemon Crepes

Apple Brownies

Chocolate Sauce

Vanilla Sauce

Mrs. Fisher's Chocolate Brownies

....

CHEZ EDDY HOMEMADE VANILLA FROZEN YOGURT

An all-purpose, infinitely adaptable dessert.

1 pint nonfat vanilla yogurt
2 tablespoons liquid fructose
¼ teaspoon pure vanilla extract

In a large bowl, whisk together the yogurt, fructose, and vanilla extract until well blended. Freeze in an ice cream maker according to the manufacturer's directions.

VARIATION You may add any variety of puréed fruit to this yogurt. Because frozen yogurt freezes at a lower temperature than ice cream, however, remember to make sure the purée is fine, rather than chunky, so the fruit won't turn into chunks of ice.

YIELD *2 cups*

SERVING ½ C.

Calories 64.0

Total fat 0.2 gm.

Cholesterol 2.0 mg.

Saturated fat 0.13 gm.

Protein 6.5 gm.

Carbohydrates 8.7 gm.

Sodium 86.0 mg.

CINNAMON-RAISIN FROZEN YOGURT

¼ cup raisins
¼ cup water
1 pint Chez Eddy Homemade Vanilla Frozen Yogurt
  (opposite page)
1 teaspoon cinnamon

Prepare the frozen yogurt ahead as directed.

Simmer the raisins in the water until they are plump, then drain and cool. Fold them into the yogurt, and stir in the cinnamon until well mixed. Serve immediately.

Y I E L D *2 cups*

We serve this yogurt with our Apple Brownies, but it is also delicious on its own or with cobbler.

SERVING ½ C.

Calories 91.0

Total fat 0.2 gm.

Cholesterol 2.0 mg.

Saturated fat 0.14 gm.

Protein 6.8 gm.

Carbohydrates 15.9 gm.

Sodium 87.0 mg.

DUTCH COCOA FROZEN YOGURT WITH TOASTED ALMONDS

Intense chocolate flavor, without the guilt!

⅔ cup cocoa
¾ cup sugar
½ cup water
2 cups Chez Eddy Homemade Vanilla Frozen Yogurt (page 298)
Garnish: ¼ cup almonds, toasted (page 150)

Prepare the frozen yogurt ahead as directed.

In a small or medium saucepan, stir together the cocoa and sugar until well combined. Add the water and stir until thoroughly mixed. Over low to medium heat, cook for about 3 minutes, or until the sugar has completely dissolved and the mixture is syrupy. Let cool and refrigerate until thoroughly chilled.

When ready to serve, stir into the yogurt and decorate with toasted almonds.

YIELD *2 cups*

SERVING ½ C.

Calories 85

Total fat 1.7 gm.

Cholesterol 2.0 mg.

Saturated fat 0.28 gm.

Protein 7.1 gm.

Carbohydrates 15.6 gm.

Sodium 87.0 mg.

RHUBARB FROZEN YOGURT

1 pint nonfat vanilla yogurt
¼ teaspoon pure vanilla extract
¾ cup rhubarb purée (see below)
Garnish: sprigs of fresh mint

Mix all the ingredients together thoroughly, then freeze in an ice cream maker according to the manufacturer's directions.

RHUBARB PURÉE

1½ cups young rhubarb, chopped
¾ cup liquid fructose
2 tablespoons sweet dessert wine
¼ cup cold water

Place all the ingredients in a small saucepan. Bring to a simmer, cover, and simmer, covered, for 20 to 30 minutes until the rhubarb is soft. Strain and reserve the liquid. Purée the rhubarb, adding the liquid as necessary to achieve the proper consistency. Cool completely.

N O T E   In all frozen fruit yogurts, the puréed fruit must be blended together thoroughly. Also, the finer the texture of the purée, the better.

Y I E L D   *2 cups*

The mellow sweetness of vanilla yogurt balances the tartness of rhubarb in a nonfat dish reminiscent of rhubarb fool.

SERVING ½ C.

Calories 82.0

Total fat 0.3 gm.

Cholesterol 2.0 mg.

Saturated fat 0.15 gm.

Protein 6.9 gm.

Carbohydrates 11.1 gm.

Sodium 89.0 mg.

COUPE CHEZ EDDY

This elegant layered dessert is both delicious and beautiful to look at.

SERVING ½ C.
YOGURT WITH
FRUIT AND PURÉE

Calories 100.0

Total fat 0.6 gm.

Cholesterol 2.0 mg.

Saturated fat 0.17 gm.

Protein 7.3 gm.

Carbohydrates 16.8 gm.

Sodium 87.0 mg.

2 cups Chez Eddy Homemade Vanilla Frozen Yogurt (page 298)
½ cup strawberry purée (see below)
4 twelve-ounce stemmed glasses, chilled
4 tablespoons fresh strawberries, sliced
4 tablespoons kiwi, sliced
4 sprigs fresh mint

Prepare the frozen yogurt and strawberry purée ahead as directed.

For each serving, place 1 tablespoon of strawberry purée in a chilled 12-ounce stemmed glass. Rotate the glass to spread purée decoratively around the base of the glass, to a level of approximately 1 inch. Add ¼ cup of frozen vanilla yogurt to the glass. Slip alternating strawberry and kiwi slices vertically down the sides of the glass so they form a band within the yogurt layer that is visible from the exterior. Add another ¼ cup of yogurt. Top with 1 tablespoon of strawberry purée and garnish with sprigs of mint.

Y I E L D   *2 cups yogurt, plus fruit and purée*

STRAWBERRY PURÉE

2 cups fresh strawberries

Wash, drain, and hull the strawberries. Add to the container of a blender or food processor, and process until smooth. Strain the purée through a fine mesh strainer or colander lined with dampened cheesecloth.

Y I E L D   *½ cup purée*

SERVING 2 TBS.

Calories 22.0

Total fat 0.28 gm.

Cholesterol 0.50 mg.

Saturated fat 0.04 gm.

Protein 0.45 gm.

Carbohydrates 5.23 gm.

Sodium 21.0 mg.

ORANGE GLACÉE

3 cups Chez Eddy Homemade Vanilla Frozen Yogurt (page 298)
4 medium navel oranges, prepared as directed below and frozen
  overnight
4 teaspoons Grand Marnier
Garnish: mint sprigs (optional)

Prepare the frozen yogurt ahead as directed.

From the stem end of each orange, cut off a thin slice, no more than ⅛ inch thick. (This makes a flat base for the orange cup.) From the bud end, remove a thick slice, approximately ½ inch thick; this will be the "cap." Lift off the cap and place it, rind down, on cutting board. With a small spoon scrap out all the flesh inside the cap and then inside the orange. Reserve the orange flesh in a bowl, taking care to remove any remaining pith. Cut out the inside stem remaining in the orange cup with a small knife. Freeze the orange shells and caps overnight. Stir Grand Marnier into the orange pulp and refrigerate overnight.

When ready to proceed with the recipe, purée the chilled, marinated fruit pulp and liquid in a blender or food processor for 2 minutes, or until smooth in texture. In a bowl, very rapidly whisk together the puréed fruit and frozen yogurt. Remove the frozen shells and caps from the freezer. Fill the shells completely with the yogurt mixture and place the orange caps on top. Immediately return the filled orange shells to the freezer and let sit for 5 minutes.

Garnish with mint sprigs.

N O T E You may prepare and fill shells a day in advance and freeze overnight.

Y I E L D *4 oranges*

The sophisticated accent of Grand Marnier transforms vanilla yogurt into a voluptuary's delight. This elegant presentation is suitable for a formal dinner.

SERVING 1 ORANGE

Calories 106.0

Total fat 0.2 gm.

Cholesterol 1.0 mg.

Saturated fat 0.07 gm.

Protein 3.7 gm.

Carbohydrates 21.0 gm.

Sodium 33.0 mg.

MELON SORBET

This lightest of desserts also makes a tantalizing respite between courses of a formal dinner.

4 cups very ripe cantaloupe or honeydew melon purée, chilled
1 cup cold water
¼ to ½ cup granulated sugar, depending upon sweetness of the melon
2 egg whites
Garnish: sprigs of mint

Add peeled and seeded chunks of melon to the container of a blender or food processor, and purée. Strain the purée through a fine mesh strainer or colander lined with dampened cheesecloth, and chill.

In a small saucepan, boil the water and the sugar together for a few minutes without stirring, then cool. Mix with the chilled purée. In a bowl, beat the egg whites until they form stiff peaks, then gently fold in the purée. Freeze in an ice cream maker, following the manufacturer's instructions. Garnish each serving with a sprig of mint.

YIELD *1¾ quarts*

SERVING ½ C.

Calories 91.0

Total fat 0.3 gm.

Cholesterol 0

Saturated fat 0.14 gm.

Protein 1.7 gm.

Carbohydrates 22.0 gm.

Sodium 22.0 mg.

STRAWBERRY SORBET

2 pounds fresh strawberries, to make 3 cups of strained purée
Juice of 1 lemon
¼ cup liquid fructose
1 cup water

Wash, drain, and hull the strawberries. Add to the container of a blender or food processor, and process until smooth. Strain the purée through a fine mesh strainer or colander lined with dampened cheese-cloth, then transfer to a bowl.

Stir in the lemon juice, fructose, and water. Freeze in an ice cream maker according to manufacturer's directions.

V A R I A T I O N This sorbet may be adapted to use any variety of fruit purée in the proportions given above, unless it is quite thick.

Y I E L D   *4 cups*

SERVING ½ C.
Calories 34.0
Total fat 0.4 gm.
Cholesterol 0
Saturated fat 0.02 gm.
Protein 0.7 gm.
Carbohydrates 8.0 gm.
Sodium 1.0 mg.

PUMPKIN FLAN

Our lightened version of the delicate Mexican egg custard—embellished here with pumpkin and spices—is quite good in place of pie at holiday time.

Nonstick spray
1 cup canned pumpkin purée
½ cup egg substitute
1 egg
¼ cup sugar
1½ teaspoons pure vanilla extract
½ teaspoon cinnamon
¼ teaspoon grated nutmeg
2 cups evaporated skim milk
Garnish: orange-zest strips

Spray an 8-inch round baking dish with vegetable spray. Whisk together the pumpkin purée, egg substitute, egg, sugar, vanilla, and spices in a large bowl until blended. Gradually whisk in the evaporated milk and pour the mixture into the prepared dish. Set the dish in a larger baking pan and place in the oven. Pour hot water into the pan so that it reaches halfway up the side of the dish. Bake about 35 minutes, or until a knife inserted halfway between the edge and center comes out clean. Place the baking dish on a wire rack and let cool. Cover with plastic wrap and refrigerate until cold, at least 2 hours. Cut into wedges and garnish with zest.

N O T E Use as a filling for our Basic Cobbler Crust (page 319).

Y I E L D *1 flan*

SERVING ½ C.
Calories 107.0
Total fat 1.4 gm.
Cholesterol 29.0 mg.
Saturated fat 0.44 gm.
Protein 7.9 gm.
Carbohydrates 16.1 gm.
Sodium 111.0 mg.

SEMOLINA CAKE INFUSED WITH ORANGE SYRUP

1½ cups sugar
1½ cups nonfat yogurt
3 cups semolina, finely ground
1 teaspoon baking soda
¼ teaspoon cinnamon
⅛ teaspoon vanilla extract
1 teaspoon rosewater or orange water (optional)
¼ cup pine nuts
¼ cup Orange Syrup (see below)

Preheat oven to 325°F. Combine sugar, yogurt, semolina, baking soda, cinnamon, vanilla, and flavored waters in a large mixing bowl. Stir well until all ingredients are combined. Pour mixture into an ungreased 8 x 10-inch baking dish and bake for 20 minutes. Sprinkle top with pine nuts and bake another 10 to 12 minutes or until nuts are lightly browned. Remove from oven and brush with Orange Syrup.

YIELD *20 servings*

ORANGE SYRUP

½ cup sugar
¼ cup water
Zest from 1 orange

Combine ingredients in a heavy saucepan over low heat, stirring until the sugar dissolves. Increase the heat and bring the mixture to a rolling boil without stirring. Cook until the mixture becomes a thin syrup and has a golden color. Cool slightly and brush over cake.

YIELD *¼ cup*

Semolina is a pale ivory-colored grain with a nutty flavor. Because semolina dough is firm and elastic, it is used most often for pastas. This cake has a firmer texture than most.

SERVING 1 SLICE
Calories 170.0
Total fat 1.2 gm.
Cholesterol 0
Saturated fat 0.2 gm.
Protein 3.6 gm.
Carbohydrates 37.0 gm.
Sodium 17.0 mg.

POACHED PEARS IN ORANGE SAUCE

A very beautiful, uncluttered fruit dessert.

2 tablespoons fresh lemon juice
4 large, ripe, firm pears, such as Bosc or Bartlett
4 cups fresh orange juice
¼ cup liquid fructose
1 cinnamon stick
1 teaspoon pure vanilla extract
¾ cup orange liqueur, Cointreau or Grand Marnier
½ cup cognac or brandy
Zest of 1 orange, cut into julienne strips
Garnish: fresh mint leaves

Stir the lemon juice into a large bowl filled with cold water. Peel the pears and drop into the bowl of water to prevent discoloration.

In a large saucepan, combine the orange juice, fructose, cinnamon stick, vanilla, ½ cup of the orange liqueur, and the brandy.

Bring to a simmer over moderately low heat.

Drain the pears and add them to the saucepan, simmering until the pears are tender when pierced with a sharp knife, approximately 25 minutes to 1 hour, depending on the type of pear and degree of ripeness. Remove the pears with a slotted spoon, cover loosely, and let cool.

Boil the poaching liquid until reduced to about 1½ cups of syrup.

In a small, heavy-bottomed saucepan, bring the remaining ¼ cup liqueur to a boil. Add the orange zest and reduce the heat to a moderately low level. Cover and simmer until the zest is soft, about 15 minutes. Add to the reduced syrup.

When ready to serve, spoon 4 tablespoons of syrup over each pear and garnish with a fresh mint leaf, placed at the stem end of the pear.

YIELD *4 pears*

SERVING 1 PEAR
WITH 4 TBS. SAUCE

Calories 209.0

Total fat 0.8 gm.

Cholesterol 0

Saturated fat 0.05 gm.

Protein 2.3 gm.

Carbohydrates 51.7 gm.

Sodium 2.0 mg.

ORANGE CUSTARD

1 navel orange
1 whole egg
½ cup egg substitute
1 tablespoon liquid fructose
2 cups evaporated skim milk
¼ teaspoon pure orange extract
1 teaspoon corn or canola oil
Garnish: fresh mint sprigs; 2½ teaspoons maple syrup

Preheat the oven to 300°F. Lightly oil five ½-cup custard molds and set aside on a baking sheet. With a fine grater, remove the zest from the orange and reserve the orange.

Pour the egg and egg substitute through a fine mesh sieve into a medium bowl. Whisk in the fructose, evaporated milk, orange extract, and canola oil. Add the grated orange zest. Divide this mixture among the prepared molds and cover with aluminum foil. Bake for 25 to 30 minutes, until about ⅔ of the custard is set; the center will continue to set as it cools. Let the custard cool to room temperature, then refrigerate at least 1 hour, until thoroughly chilled.

With a sharp paring knife, remove the white pith and membrane from the reserved orange and divide the fruit into sections. Unmold the custards onto small plates. Garnish with the orange sections and mint sprigs. Drizzle ½ teaspoon of maple syrup over each custard.

YIELD *5 custards*

Another version of flan, perfumed with orange.

SERVING ½ C.
CUSTARD WITH
½ TSP. MAPLE SYRUP
Calories 136.0
Total fat 2.1 gm.
Cholesterol 46.0 mg.
Saturated fat 0.64 gm.
Protein 12.3 gm.
Carbohydrates 17.1 gm.
Sodium 176.0 mg.

CHEZ EDDY CHEESECAKE

Heart-healthy cheesecake has been one of Chez Eddy's most celebrated innovations. To slice the cake smoothly, use a sharp knife you have dipped into hot water. Wipe after each slice.

1 cup Strawberry Purée (page 302)
1 teaspoon corn oil margarine
4 tablespoons flour (to prepare pan)
3 cups part-skim ricotta cheese
8 ounces reduced-calorie cream cheese, or Neufchâtel cheese
16 ounces nonfat yogurt
Zest of 1 lemon, grated
Zest of 1 orange, grated
3 whole eggs
½ cup egg substitute
1 cup honey
2 teaspoons pure vanilla extract
¼ cup flour, sifted with arrowroot
¼ cup arrowroot
Garnish: sliced strawberries

Prepare the purée as directed. Preheat the oven to 350°F. Prepare a 10- x 3-inch springform pan by lightly rubbing with margarine and dusting with flour. Place the pan on a large sheet of heavy-duty aluminum foil. Wrap the pan tightly to prevent the water from the water bath (see below) from seeping into the pan.

With an electric mixer, cream the ricotta, cream cheese, and yogurt together in a large mixing bowl. Stir in the lemon and orange zests. With the motor running, add the eggs, egg substitute, honey, and vanilla, beating until smooth. Gradually add the flour and arrowroot mixture and beat until fully incorporated. Pour the batter into the prepared pan.

Place the pan in a bath of cold water that reaches halfway to the top of the pan. Bake for 1 to 1½ hours or until a toothpick inserted in the center comes out clean. Transfer to a rack and cool. Refrigerate 3 to 4 hours or overnight before serving. Serve napped with Strawberry Purée and garnished with sliced strawberries.

Y I E L D *1 cheesecake (16 slices)*

SERVING 1 SLICE
WITH 2 TBS. PURÉE

Calories 211.0

Total fat 8.2 gm.

Cholesterol 64.0 mg.

Saturated fat 4.75 gm.

Protein 10.0 gm.

Carbohydrates 25.5 gm.

Sodium 136.0 mg.

CHEZ EDDY RICOTTA CHEESECAKE

1 cup granulated sugar
4 tablespoons water
3 tablespoons pine nuts
5 tablespoons golden raisins
2 tablespoons Galliano liqueur
1 tablespoon Tuaca liqueur
3¼ cups flour
1 tablespoon baking powder
½ cup firmly packed light-brown sugar
½ cup ground toasted almonds
3 tablespoons unsalted margarine, chilled
½ cup egg substitute
1 teaspoon vanilla extract
1½ pounds part-skim ricotta cheese
1 tablespoon grated lemon zest

This Italian-style cheesecake is somewhat drier in texture than our other varieties, but equally delicious.

Heat ¼ cup of the sugar and the water in a medium-size saucepan over high heat. When the mixture boils and the sugar dissolves, add the pine nuts. Continue cooking, stirring occasionally, until the sugar turns light brown. Do not let it scorch.

Turn the mixture onto an oiled baking sheet and let cool. Break up into small chunks of brittle. Combine the raisins, Galliano, and Tuaca in a small bowl. Set aside to soak for 1 hour.

Place the flour, baking powder, brown sugar, and almonds in the container of a food processor or blender and process for 5 seconds. Add the margarine and process until the mixture resembles coarse meal, about 10 seconds. Whisk together ¼ cup of the egg substitute and the vanilla extract and add this to the processor, with the motor running. Process until the dough just barely holds together. Turn the dough out onto a board, gather into a ball, and wrap in plastic. Refrigerate for 1 hour.

In a large bowl combine the ricotta, remaining sugar, remaining egg substitute, lemon zest, raisins, Galliano, and Tuaca. Add the pine nut brittle, mixing well.

Preheat the oven to 350°F. Line the outside, bottom, and sides of a 10- x 3-inch springform pan with aluminum foil. Place a little more than ½ the pastry dough on the bottom of the pan, patting it into place

SERVING 1 SLICE

Calories 291.0

Total fat 9.3 gm.

Cholesterol 13.0 mg.

Saturated fat 2.91 gm.

Protein 9.7 gm.

Carbohydrates 41.7 gm.

Sodium 151.0 mg.

and pushing it up the sides. Spoon in the ricotta filling. Roll out the remaining pastry into a 10-inch round and lay over the top of the filling. Bake until the top is slightly brown, 50 to 55 minutes.

Transfer to a rack and cool in the pan. Release the sides of the springform pan and gently peel back the foil. Lift the bottom of the cake gently with a spatula and pull away the foil. Serve barely warm or at room temperature.

Y I E L D *1 cheesecake (16 slices)*

CHOCOLATE CREPES WITH MACERATED BERRIES

½ cup flour
2 tablespoons cocoa powder
¼ cup sugar
½ cup egg substitute
1 cup skim milk
1 teaspoon vanilla extract
Nonstick spray
1 cup Macerated Berries (next page)
Garnish: 4 sprigs fresh mint

Combine the flour, cocoa powder, and sugar in a medium bowl. Add egg substitute, skim milk, and vanilla. Whisk together until smooth. Strain mixture through a fine sieve to remove any lumps. Lightly coat a 6-inch crepe pan with nonstick spray and heat until just below the smoking point. Pour a thin coating of the mixture into the pan. Cook the crepe until set, about 45 seconds, or until the edges are dry and crispy brown. Turn and cook the other side. Transfer to a sheet of wax paper or parchment, layering wax paper between the crepes. To serve, fold 3 crepes into triangles and place on a dessert plate. Spoon ¼ cup macerated berries on top. Garnish with a sprig of fresh mint. Crepes may be refrigerated up to 5 days or frozen for up to 2 months.

Y I E L D *18 to 20 crepes*

Fold ½ teaspoon cinnamon into 1 cup nonfat frozen yogurt and serve with these crepes. Crepes are also delicious drizzled with Chocolate Sauce (page 323) or Vanilla Sauce (page 324).

SERVING 3 CREPES
AND ¼ C. BERRIES
Calories 51.0
Total fat 0
Cholesterol 1.0 mg.
Saturated fat 0
Protein 3.0 gm.
Carbohydrates 7.3 gm.
Sodium 34.0 mg.

Macerating is the same process as marinating, a term most often applied to meats, fish, poultry, or vegetables. Macerating is usually associated with fruits soaked in spirits.

MACERATED BERRIES

2 cups fresh berries such as raspberries, blackberries, dewberries, or strawberries
½ cup orange liqueur or sweet Muscat wine

Combine berries and liqueur or wine in a medium bowl. Refrigerate 1 to 4 hours before serving. The berries will keep refrigerated for up to 3 days.

YIELD *2 cups*

PINEAPPLE CHEESECAKE

4 cups nonfat vanilla yogurt (see Note below)
1 teaspoon unsalted margarine
2½ cups fresh pineapple, diced
½ cup granulated sugar
2 tablespoons cornstarch
1 tablespoon calvados or applejack liqueur
¼ cup egg substitute

Another scrumptious cheesecake with a different texture and method of preparation.

Drain the yogurt overnight to make the yogurt curd or "cheese." Preheat the oven to 325°F. Very lightly grease a 7-inch springform pan with margarine.

Combine the pineapple and ¼ cup of the sugar in a small saucepan. Simmer for 35 minutes. Drain the pineapple in a fine sieve or colander lined with dampened cheesecloth. Press out as much liquid as possible from the pineapple.

Combine the yogurt "cheese," the remaining sugar, cornstarch, liqueur, and pineapple in a bowl, mixing gently. Stir in the egg substitute. Pour mixture into a prepared pan and bake until a toothpick inserted in the center comes out clean.

N O T E This recipe requires the use of a nonfat vanilla yogurt prepared without gelatin. Check the label before purchasing. To extract the yogurt curd, spoon yogurt onto a piece of cheesecloth large enough to hold it and tie the edges so that it forms a bag. Let it drain overnight suspended above the kitchen sink. (You can loop the end of the cheesecloth bag over the faucet to facilitate draining, if you wish.) Approximately ½ the yogurt will be left as curd while the other half is released as whey. Keep the curd in the refrigerator in a covered container until ready to use. It may continue to release whey, so pour off any accumulated liquid before proceeding with the recipe.

Y I E L D *1 cheesecake (10 slices)*

SERVING 1 SLICE
Calories 114.0
Total fat 0.5 gm.
Cholesterol 2.0 mg.
Saturated fat 0.16 gm.
Protein 6.1 gm.
Carbohydrates 21.7 gm.
Sodium 81.0 mg.

ANGELFOOD CAKE WITH RASPBERRY SAUCE

*H*omemade angelfood cake may be used in many satisfying low-fat desserts.

1½ cups sifted cake flour
1¾ cups granulated sugar
14 egg whites
1 teaspoon cream of tartar
2 teaspoons vanilla extract
½ teaspoon almond extract
1 teaspoon lemon juice
Raspberry Sauce (opposite page)
Garnish: fresh raspberries and mint leaves; nonfat vanilla yogurt

Preheat the oven to 300°F. Sift the flour into a mixing bowl. Sift the sugar into a separate bowl. Set aside.

Beat the egg whites until they are foamy; add the cream of tartar and continue to beat until they form soft peaks. Gently fold in the sugar. Fold in the flour a little at a time. Add the vanilla, almond extract, and lemon juice. Pour the batter into a 10-inch tube pan and bake until the cake is light brown, about 1 hour. The top should spring back when gently touched. Cool upside down in the pan.

When ready to serve, run a knife between the sides of the cake and the surface of the pan and gently remove the cake. Decorate with fresh raspberries and mint and serve with Raspberry Sauce. To serve the cake, nap each plate with a thin film of sauce; place 3 dots of vanilla yogurt equidistant from each other on the sauce. Gently draw the blade of a knife through each dot so it makes a decorative line. Center a slice of cake between the decorative lines and decorate with raspberries and mint.

Y I E L D *1 cake (12 slices)*

SERVING 1 SLICE
WITH 2 TBS. SAUCE

Calories 223.0

Total fat 0.04 gm.

Cholesterol 0

Saturated fat 0.03 gm.

Protein 5.1 gm.

Carbohydrates 51.1 gm.

Sodium 57.0 mg.

RASPBERRY SAUCE

10 ounces fresh raspberries
2 teaspoons fresh lemon juice
⅓ cup confectioner's sugar

Add the raspberries to the container of a blender and purée. Stir in the lemon juice and sugar. Pass through a strainer, discarding the solids.

Y I E L D *¾ cup*

SERVING 2 TBS.

Calories 49.0

Total fat 0.3 gm.

Cholesterol 0

Saturated fat 0.01 gm.

Protein 0.4 gm.

Carbohydrates 12.1 gm.

Sodium 0

BLUEBERRY COBBLER

Our low-fat cobbler and pie crust open up a new world of old favorites.

1 Basic Cobbler Crust (opposite page)
Nonstick spray
Filling:
    6 cups fresh blueberries
    1 cup water
    2 teaspoons arrowroot
    ½ cup sugar
    2 teaspoons orange zest
    2 pinches of cinnamon
    ½ teaspoon pure vanilla extract

Prepare the cobbler crust ahead as directed.

Spray an 8-inch square baking dish or 10 individual tart molds with nonstick spray.

Combine the filling ingredients in a medium saucepan and bring to a boil. Reduce the heat and simmer for 1 minute until slightly thickened. Pour into prepared baking dish or tart molds and top with the crust. Bake at 425°F for 15 to 20 minutes, until the filling is bubbly and the crust is golden.

Y I E L D   *1 cobbler or 10 individual tarts*

SERVING ½ C.

Calories 212.0

Total fat 6.2 gm.

Cholesterol 0

Saturated fat 0.99 gm.

Protein 2.3 gm.

Carbohydrates 38.8 gm.

Sodium 73.0 mg.

BASIC COBBLER CRUST

1 cup all-purpose flour
Pinch of nutmeg
¼ cup margarine, cut into small pieces and chilled
3 tablespoons plus 1 teaspoon ice water

Combine the flour and nutmeg in a bowl; cut in the margarine with a pastry blender until the mixture resembles coarse meal. Sprinkle the surface with ice water, 1 tablespoon at a time; toss with a fork until the dry ingredients are moistened. Shape into a ball; wrap in wax paper and chill for 15 minutes.

Roll the dough into a rectangle approximately ⅛ inch thick.

The pastry can be cut into circles for individual tarts or cut into ½-inch lattice strips.

Y I E L D *1 top crust for an 8-inch square baking dish or enough for 10 individual tarts*

SERVING 1 SLICE OR
1 TART
Calories 103.0
Total fat 5.8 gm.
Cholesterol 0
Saturated fat 0.96 gm.
Protein 1.6 gm.
Carbohydrates 11.0 gm.
Sodium 6.7 mg.

LEMON CREPES

An elegant finish to the most formal meal, or a delectable option for brunch.

1 cup all-purpose flour
½ cup egg substitute
1½ cups skim milk
½ tablespoon corn oil
Zest of 1 lemon, grated
Lemon Sauce (opposite page)
Garnish: confectioners' sugar; ¼ cup unsalted pistachio nuts, finely chopped

Add the flour, egg substitute, milk, and oil to the container of a blender and process until smooth. Stir in the grated lemon zest. Cover and refrigerate the batter for at least 1 hour.

When ready to proceed, whisk the batter so it is thoroughly blended. Pour a thin coating of the batter into a 6-inch nonstick crepe pan that you have heated until just below the smoking point. (Test by flicking water onto the pan; the drops will dance frantically across it before vaporizing.) Cook the crepe until set, about 1 minute. (The edges will begin to look dry.) Then turn and cook the other side about 45 seconds. Transfer to a sheet of wax paper or parchment, layering wax paper between the crepes as you proceed. Wrapped in foil, they may be refrigerated for 3 to 5 days or frozen for up to 2 months.

Make the sauce as directed.

When ready to serve, fold each crepe in half once, then again to make a small triangle. Arrange three of these triangles on a warmed dessert plate so they overlap one another. Pour ¼ cup of the Lemon Sauce over the crepes, dust with powdered sugar, and sprinkle with 1 teaspoon of finely chopped pistachio nuts. Repeat with the remaining crepes.

YIELD *16 crepes with sauce*

LEMON SAUCE

2 cups granulated sugar
2 tablespoons cognac
¼ cup fresh lemon juice

Stir the sugar in a hot saucepan, over medium heat, until it is lightly browned. Add the cognac and stir for about 15 seconds, until the sugar dissolves. Add the lemon juice and continue to stir to make a thin sauce, the consistency of light syrup, about 2 minutes.

Y I E L D *2 cups*

SERVING 2 CREPES
WITH ¼ C. SAUCE
Calories 60.0
Total fat 0.6 gm.
Cholesterol 0
Saturated fat 0.12 gm.
Protein 2.1 gm.
Carbohydrates 11.6 gm.
Sodium 21.0 mg.

APPLE BROWNIES

This toothsome brownie is one of our most popular desserts. It is also a splendid example of how moderate restriction of the fat content in a favorite food can produce a variation that's as tasty as it is heart-healthy. We serve Apple Brownies with our Cinnamon-Raisin Frozen Yogurt (page 299).

Nonstick spray
1½ cups flour
2 teaspoons baking powder
⅓ cup unsalted margarine
1 cup brown sugar
½ cup granulated sugar
½ cup egg substitute
1 teaspoon pure vanilla extract
1 cup apples, peeled, cored, and chopped
⅓ cup applesauce
½ cup walnuts or pecans, shelled and chopped

Preheat the oven to 350°F. Prepare an 8-inch square pan by spraying with nonstick spray. In a medium-size bowl, combine the flour and baking powder and set aside. Cream the margarine with a small mixer until fluffy. Gradually add the brown and granulated sugars, beating well after each addition. Still gradually, beat in the egg substitute and the dry ingredients. Stir in the vanilla, apples, applesauce, and nuts.

Spread the mixture in the prepared pan and bake for 30 to 35 minutes, or until a toothpick inserted into the center comes out clean. Let cool in the pan 10 minutes. Cut into squares. Store tightly covered.

Y I E L D   *16 brownies*

SERVING 1 BROWNIE
Calories 158.0
Total fat 5.5 gm.
Cholesterol 0
Saturated fat 0.81 gm.
Protein 2.3 gm.
Carbohydrates 25.3 gm.
Sodium 99.0 mg.

CHOCOLATE SAUCE

2 cups skim milk
2 tablespoons cornstarch
¼ cup cocoa powder
¼ cup sugar
½ teaspoon cinnamon
Orange liqueur to taste

In a small bowl, stir 3 tablespoons milk with the cornstarch until smooth. In a medium saucepan whisk together cocoa powder, sugar, and cinnamon. Add remaining milk and bring to a boil over medium heat, stirring constantly. Add cornstarch mixture and cook 1 minute, stirring so mixture does not scorch. Remove from heat and add orange liqueur. Cool slightly before serving. The sauce will keep refrigerated for up to 7 days.

YIELD *2½ cups*

*C*hoose fine-quality cocoa powder for rich chocolate flavor. Serve with angelfood cake and nonfat frozen yogurt.

SERVING 2 TBS.
Calories 40.0
Total fat 4 gm.
Cholesterol 1.0 mg.
Saturated fat 0.25 gm.
Protein 1.7 gm.
Carbohydrates 8.3 gm.
Sodium 22.0 mg.

VANILLA SAUCE

1 cup skim milk
1 tablespoon cornstarch
½ cup egg substitute
1 tablespoon margarine
¼ cup sugar
1 teaspoon vanilla extract
1 teaspoon orange liqueur

In a small bowl, whisk 3 tablespoons milk with the cornstarch until smooth. Add egg substitute and stir until well blended. Place the remaining milk, the margarine, and the sugar in a medium saucepan. Bring to a boil over medium heat. Whisk in the cornstarch mixture and cook until mixture returns to a boil. Remove from the heat, add vanilla and orange liqueur. Strain if necessary to remove any lumps. Cool slightly before serving. The sauce will keep refrigerated for up to 5 days.

Y I E L D *1½ cups*

SERVING 2 TBS.
Calories 35.0
Total fat 0.4 gm.
Cholesterol 1.0 mg.
Saturated fat 0
Protein 2.0 gm.
Carbohydrates 5.8 gm.
Sodium 29.0 mg.

MRS. FISHER'S CHOCOLATE BROWNIES

Nonstick spray
¾ cup all-purpose flour
½ cup cocoa
2 teaspoons baking powder
¼ cup corn-oil margarine
1¼ cups granulated sugar
¾ cup egg substitute
2 teaspoons pure vanilla extract
½ cup chopped nuts, walnuts, or pecans

Preheat the oven to 325°F. Prepare an 8-inch pan by spraying with nonstick vegetable spray. Sift together the flour, cocoa, and baking powder and set aside. With a mixer, cream the margarine and the sugar in a medium-size bowl. Add the egg substitute, beating well. Stir in the vanilla extract, then, gradually, the flour mixture until thoroughly combined. Fold in the nuts.

Add the mixture to a prepared pan and spread evenly. Bake for 25 to 30 minutes or until a toothpick inserted at the edge comes out clean. (The center may remain somewhat soft.) Cool on a wire rack. Cut into squares and store tightly covered.

YIELD *16 brownies*

*Y*es, chocolate brownies—and they're wonderful, too.

SERVING 1 BROWNIE
Calories 118.0
Total fat 4.2 gm.
Cholesterol 0
Saturated fat 0.81 gm.
Protein 2.7 gm.
Carbohydrates 20.3 gm.
Sodium 84.0 mg.

SPECIAL-OCCASION MENUS

....

WHEN HEART-HEALTHY CUISINE BECOMES a part of your lifestyle, you'll find that entertaining takes on a fresh appeal. No longer do you need to worry about putting your health and that of your friends at risk. Even holiday dinners can be enjoyed without guilt when the stuffing for your turkey and the components of the gravy and dessert are low in fat and calories, but so full of flavor that your guests will be delighted.

In this chapter we offer seven menus for special occasions. All utilize recipes drawn from other sections. In addition to the Thanksgiving Holiday Dinner, we've outlined suggestions for a cocktail buffet (Southwestern Pool Party), a traditional South Texas Game Dinner, a Chez Eddy Italian Dinner, and an intimate Candlelight Dinner for Two, suitable for Valentine's or any other special evening. To illustrate the breadth of entertaining you can undertake with recipes from this book, we have also composed menus for a Spring Luncheon with Friends, a Super Bowl Buffet, and an elegant Summer Picnic on the Beach.

We hope these choices demonstrate that even friends who remain oblivious to the advantages of heart-healthy dining—a category that includes many of our sons and daughters—can be as pleased as anyone with celebrations that feature our recipes.

....

South Texas Game Dinner

Southwestern Pool Party

Chez Eddy Italian Dinner

Candlelight Dinner for Two

Thanksgiving Holiday Dinner

Super Bowl Buffet

Summer Picnic on the Beach

Spring Luncheon with Friends

....

SOUTH TEXAS GAME DINNER

This hearty menu would be excellent in the fall or early winter.

Salmon Bisque (page 133)
Sautéed Quail with Brandy-Pecan Sauce (page 260)
Spinach and Mushroom Salad with Zesty Buttermilk Dressing (page 116)
Venison with South Texas Game Sauce (page 266)
Pecan Rice with Red Bell Peppers (page 285)
Red Cabbage and Apples (page 284)
Pumpkin Flan (page 306)

SOUTHWESTERN POOL PARTY

A sumptuous cocktail buffet composed of luxurious-tasting, heart-healthy treats.

Beggars' Pursers with Ancho Chili Sauce (page 91)
Campechana de Marisco (page 97)
Crudités with Three Dips (page 102)
Crabmeat Enchiladas with Green Chili Sauce (page 220)
Sesame Chicken Fingers LeBlanc with Two Dipping Sauces (page 98)
Salsa Tray: Black Bean Salsa (page 86), Pico de Gallo (page 84),
Spicy Corn Relish (page 67)
Cold Boiled Shrimp on Ice with Horseradish-Gazpacho Sauce (page 70)
Salmon Crabcakes with Dill Sauce (page 104)
Pineapple Cheesecake (page 315)
Coupe Chez Eddy (page 302)
Apple Brownies (page 322)
Mrs. Fisher's Chocolate Brownies (page 325)
Tray of Fresh Seasonal Fruit

CHEZ EDDY ITALIAN DINNER

Vitello Tonnato (page 100)
Angel-Hair Pasta with Crabmeat and Tomatoes (page 225)
Radicchio, Arugula, and Fresh Corn Salad (page 113)
Southern-Style Braised Rabbit (page 262)
Steamed Green Beans (page 276*)
Grilled Polenta (page 289)
Chez Eddy Ricotta Cheesecake (pages 311)

CANDLELIGHT DINNER FOR TWO

The distinct, bright flavors of this elegant dinner will sharpen all the senses.

Cream of Chicken and Watercress Soup (page 134)
Lettuce, Jicama, and Orange Salad with Lime Dressing (page 110)
Medallions of Lamb with Rosemary–Port Wine Reduction Sauce (page 245)
Lemon-Garlic Roasted Potatoes (page 291)
Sautéed Cherry Tomatoes and Mushrooms (page 280)
Steamed Haricots Verts (page 276*)
Dutch Cocoa Frozen Yogurt with Toasted Almonds (page 300)

*Basic Steamed Vegetable

THANKSGIVING HOLIDAY DINNER

Cream of Pumpkin Soup (page 135)
Waldorf-Squash Salad (page 108)
Roasted Turkey Breast with Thyme Sauce (page 171)
Herbed-Bread Stuffing with Pumpkin Seeds (page 293)
Cranberries with Hot-Pepper Jelly (page 68)
Tomatoes Provençal (page 274)
Sautéed Green Beans with Garlic and Mushrooms (page 282)
Blueberry Cobbler (page 318)
Chez Eddy Homemade Frozen Vanilla Yogurt (page 298)

SUPER BOWL BUFFET

This robust spread would be delicious for any winter event.

Vegetables Marinated in Picante Vinaigrette (page 82)
Southern Black Bean Soup (page 127)
Crab- and Wild-Rice-Stuffed Tomatoes with Vincent Sauce (page 94)
Whole Fillet of Beef with Brandy Reduction Sauce (page 239)
and Whole Grain Rolls
Lemon-Garlic Roasted Potatoes (page 291)
Watercress, Fennel, and Roasted Red Pepper Salad (page 109)
Poached Pears in Orange Sauce (page 308)
Mrs. Fisher's Chocolate Brownies (page 325)
Mini-Wedges of Chez Eddy Ricotta Cheesecake (page 311)

SUMMER PICNIC AT THE BEACH

Cooling seasonal foods of surprising elegance.

Tomato Bisque with Avocado Sorbet (page 120)
Fresh Lobster and Papaya with Cold Curry Sauce (page 232)
Grilled Thai Chicken Salad (page 143)
Country Garden Pasta Salad (page 152)
Platter of Crudités
Basket of Bread
Platter of Fresh Fruit
Blueberry or Peach Cobbler (page 318)
with Chez Eddy Homemade Vanilla Frozen Yogurt (page 298)

SPRING LUNCHEON WITH FRIENDS

Welcoming the change of seasons for charity, or just for fun.

Mimosas or Fresh Orange Juice Cocktails
Crudités with Three Dips (page 102)
Curried Zucchini Soup (page 119)
Stuffed Chicken Breast with Green Peppercorn Sauce (page 107)
Chez Eddy House Salad with Almond-Herb Dressing (page 111)
Orange Glacée (page 303)
Apple Brownie Fingers (pages 322)

APPENDICES

....

APPENDIX 1: UNSATURATED FATTY ACID CONTENT OF SELECTED FOODS

(Listed in Order of Saturation)

1 Tablespoon	Polyunsaturated Fatty Acid (Grams)	Saturated Fatty Acid (Grams)	Monounsaturated Fatty Acid (Grams)
POLYUNSATURATED OILS			
Safflower Oil	10.1	1.2	1.6
Sunflower Oil	8.9	1.4	2.7
Corn Oil	8.0	1.7	3.3
Soybean Oil	7.9	2.0	3.2
MONOUNSATURATED OILS			
Canola Oil	4.5	0.8	8.7
Peanut Oil	4.3	2.3	6.2
Olive Oil	1.1	1.8	9.9
MARGARINES			
Safflower Oil Margarine (tub)	6.3	1.2	3.3
Corn Oil Margarine (tub)	4.5	2.1	4.5
Corn Oil Margarine (stick)	3.3	2.1	5.4
Soybean Oil Margarine (tub)	3.9	1.8	5.1
Soybean Oil Margarine (stick)	3.6	1.8	5.4
NUTS			
Walnuts, Black	2.9	0.3	1.0
Brazil Nuts	2.1	1.4	2.0
Peanuts	1.4	0.6	2.2
Pecans	1.1	0.4	2.8
Almonds	1.0	0.4	3.0
Cashews	0.7	0.8	2.3
Pistachios	0.6	0.5	2.6
Macadamias	0.1	0.9	4.9
SEEDS			
Sunflower	2.9	0.5	0.9
Sesame	2.0	0.6	1.7
Pumpkin/Squash	1.8	0.7	1.2
SHORTENINGS			
Soybean and Cottonseed	3.3	3.2	5.7

*per 1 tablespoon

APPENDIX 2: NUTRITIONAL ANALYSIS

(Listed in Order of Saturation)

Item	Calories	Protein	Fat	Carbohydrates	Cholesterol	Sodium	Saturated Fat
GAME: *3 ounces cooked, lean and roasted*							
Antelope	127	25.03	2.27	0	107	46	.83
Beefalo	160	26.06	5.37	0	49	70	2.28
Wild Boar	136	24.05	3.72	0	*	*	1.10
Water Buffalo	111	22.8	1.53	0	52	48	.51
Caribou	142	25.3	3.76	0	93	51	1.40
Deer	134	25.6	2.71	0	95	46	1.06
Elk	124	25.6	1.62	0	62	52	.60
Rabbit	131	19.37	5.36	0	55	31	1.60
MEAT AND POULTRY							
Veal, Sirloin	143	22.3	5.29	0	89	72	2.04
Beef, Tenderloin	208	22.97	12.17	0	72	52	4.68
Lamb	183	25.5	8.2	0	80	71	2.9
Chicken, Breast	147	26.1	3.8	0	72	65	1.07
Duck	141	18.3	7.03	0	75	63.4	4.7
FISH: *3 ounces*							
†Bass, Striped	82	15.07	1.98	0	68	59	.43
†Bluefish	105	17.03	3.60	0	50	51	.79
†Catfish, Channel	92	14.36	3.37	0	46	50	.77
Cod, Atlantic (Cooked, Dry Heat)	89	19.41	.73	0	47	66	.14
Flounder, Sole	99	20.53	1.3	0	58	89	.31
Grouper	100	21.12	1.11	0	40	45	.25
Haddock	95	20.61	.79	0	63	74	.14
Halibut	119	22.68	2.49	0	59	35	.35
Mackerel, Atlantic	223	20.27	15.14	0	64	71	3.55
Mahi Mahi	73	15.73	.60	0	62	74	.16
Perch, Atlantic; Ocean (Redfish)	60	11.94	1.05	0	27	48	.16
Pike, Northern	79	16.27	1.03	0	73	43	.21
†Roughy, Orange	107	12.50	5.95	0	17	54	.111
†Salmon, Atlantic	121	16.87	5.39	0	47	37	.834
Salmon, Coho	157	23.26	6.40	0	42	50	1.19

*per 1 tablespoon
†Raw.

APPENDIX 2: NUTRITIONAL ANALYSIS (CONT'D)

(Listed in Order of Saturation)

Item	Calories	Protein	Fat	Carbohydrates	Cholesterol	Sodium	Saturated Fat
Snapper	109	22.35	1.46	0	40	48	.31
Swordfish	132	21.58	4.37	0	43	98	1.195
Trout, Rainbow	94	16.33	2.67	0	45	21	.52
Tuna, Fresh; Bluefin	157	25.42	5.34	0	42	43	1.4
SHELLFISH							
Mussels	147	20.23	3.81	6.28	48	313	.72
Oysters	58	5.93	2.08	3.29	46	94	.53
Clams	126	21.71	1.65	4.36	57	95	.16
Shrimp	84	17.77	.92	0	166	190	.246
Lobster	83	17.43	.50	1.09	61	323	.09
Crab, Blue	87	17.17	1.51	0	85	237	.19

Game reference: "Composition of Foods: Lamb, Veal, and Game Products," Agricultural Handbook 8–17, USDA, April 1989.
Fish reference: "Composition of Foods: Finfish and Shellfish Products," Agricultural Handbook USDA (in press).

INDEX

....